NOI

D0201431

E

MINISTRY by the PEOPLE

Theological Education by Extension

Edited by
F. ROSS KINSLER

WCC PUBLICATIONS
1211 Geneva 20, Switzerland

ORBIS BOOKS
Maryknoll, New York 10545

Published for the Programme on Theological
Education of the World Council of
Churches by WCC Publications, Geneva,
in collaboration with Orbis Books, Maryknoll, NY 10545, USA
ISBN No. 2-8254-0742-9 (WCC)
ISBN No. 0-88344-334-1 (Orbis)

Cover: David Walker, IKON
Cover photo: Mike Abrahams/Network
© 1983 World Council of Churches, 150, route de Ferney,
1211 Geneva 20, Switzerland
Printed in Switzerland

Contents

Foreword   *Emilio Castro*   ix

Preface   *F. Ross Kinsler*   xiii

Theological education by extension: Equipping God's people
for ministry   *F. Ross Kinsler*   1

LATIN AMERICA AND THE CARIBBEAN

Presbyterian Seminary of Guatemala: A modest experiment
becomes a model for change   *Kenneth B. Mulholland* and
Nelly de Jacobs   33

Study by Extension for All Nations: Passing on the faith
Michael Crowley   42

Extension Bible Institute (Northern Honduras): Theological
education and evangelism by extension   *George Patterson* ..   52

Theological Community of Chile: Extension training for indigenous church leaders   *Agustín* and *Rosario Batlle*   61

Latin American Biblical Seminary: Distance education in a
revolutionary situation   *Irene Westling Foulkes* and *Rubén
Lores*   68

Bible Study Centre for People's Pastoral Action (Brazil): The
use of the Bible among the common people   *Carlos Mesters*   78

Guyana Extension Seminary: A response to local needs for
lay training   *Dale A. Bisnauth*   93

AFRICA

TEXT-Africa: Programming for ministry through theological education by extension *Fred Holland* 103

Fambidzano (Zimbabwe): African Independent churches adopt theological education by extension *Peter M. Makamba* 116

Lutheran synod and Roman Catholic diocese of Arusha: Training village ministries in Tanzania *Bumija Mshana* and *Dean Peterson* 127

Botswana Theological Training Programme: Grassroots theology in Botswana *Richard Sales* and *Jacob Liphoko* ... 135

Diocese of Mt Kenya East (Anglican): Meeting community needs through theological education by extension *Keith B. Anderson* and *N. Kiranga Gatimu* 148

Centre for Applied Religion and Education: Theological education and human development *Adeolu Adegbola* 161

Organization of African Independent Churches: Spiritual revival Bible school *Agustín* and *Rosario Batlle* 169

NORTH AMERICA

Southern Baptist Seminary Extension: Increasing accessibility through inter-seminary cooperation *Raymond M. Rigdon* and *Lee Hollaway* 179

San Francisco Theological Seminary: We heard the church— towards a many-celled seminary *John S. Hadsell* 185

New York Theological Seminary: Seeking the shalom of the city *George W. Webber* 192

Hartford Seminary: A doctor of ministry approach to continuing education—pastor and laity learning and growing together *Douglass Lewis* 204

Cook Christian Training School: New directions for Native American theological education *Cecil Corbett* and *Gary Kush* 214

School of Theology, University of the South: Theological reflection—a necessary skill in lay ministry   *David P. Killen*   225

ASIA AND AUSTRALIA

The Association for Theological Education by Extension: An Indian approach to training for ministry   *Vinay Samuel* and *Chris Sugden*   239

TEE in North Sumatra: Building theological education networks among the Batak churches   *Warner W. Luoma*   247

Union Seminary: Alternative education for church workers in the Philippines   *José Gamboa, Jr.*   256

Nanking Union Theological Seminary: Theological education in New China   *K. H. Ting* and *Raymond Fung*   264

New England TEE: A rural Australian experiment in training church leaders   *Patricia J. Harrison*   274

EUROPE

International Correspondence Institute: From all nations to all nations   *John F. Carter*   287

Northern Ordination Course (UK): Alternative training for Anglican ministries   *M. A. H. Melinsky*   298

International Institute of Theology at a Distance: Continuing theological formation for priests, religious and laity   *Agustín García-Gasco y Vicente*   304

Ecumenical Theology Workshop of Geneva: An experiment in adult theological education   *Henry Mottu*   309

Resources   319

Foreword

It would be very difficult to find anyone better qualified than Ross Kinsler to bring together this extraordinary collection of reports under the title *Ministry by the People*. Dr Kinsler served for thirteen years on the faculty of the Presbyterian Seminary of Guatemala, where he was involved in the development of the theological education by extension programme which has served as a prototype for the extension movement. Now as a staff member of the World Council of Churches in the Programme on Theological Education, he is in touch with developments in theological education around the world.

If the mandate for theological education is, as Dr Kinsler writes, to "motivate, equip, and enable the people of God to develop their gifts and give their lives in meaningful service", we immediately see the centrality of theological education to the mission of the church. We must ask ourselves what *kind* of theological education will best fulfill this mandate?

It is easy to detect problems with our traditional theological training. There is, first of all, the matter of professionalism. A selective system of education conditions the students to aspirations of success and motivates them to climb the promotional ladder provided by the church hierarchy. Pastors, in some places, are considered successful according to the level of salary they receive, the degrees they accumulate, the titles they hold. Educational systems or philosophies that equip people for the competitiveness of society could be defended in their own terms, but they cannot be tolerated inside the Christian community, where we are called to serve and to train others to serve — not to strive for honours and monetary reward.

A related problem we are obliged to face is that this Western model of ministry has been exported to the rest of the world. The missionaries went from their homelands to devote themselves full-time to the religious task, supported by the love and gifts of the sending churches in the richest parts of the world. In general they developed a style of life which, though lower than that in their home country, was higher than that of the people they were serving. The natural inclination of the coming generations of national pastors is to imitate the life-style patterns and behaviour of the foreign missionary. This has created a tremendous burden on the resources of the churches and is a handicap to the real mission of the church, because so much of the resources of the total Christian community must go for the support of a professional class.

Another difficulty with the traditional theological educational process is that it takes young people out of a given cultural milieu and makes them totally unsuitable to come back to that milieu. The attraction of the big city operates in most countries and in every discipline; this is an understandable human temptation. But it must be resisted in a Christian perspective. If the calling to the ministry is a calling to equip the people of God for their mission, Christian leaders should be involved in the realities of the daily life of the people they want to serve. If our educational system raises barriers between theological graduates and the rest of the people, the educational system must go.

It is not only the difficulties that impel us to seek alternatives; it is also the possibilities and challenges. The growth of the churches in third world countries demands a growing number of ministers to serve newly-founded congregations. Traditional systems of theological training simply take too much time and train too few persons to cope with the needs and the possibilities.

There is also the growing conviction among Christians that the theological task of the church belongs to the whole people of God. Theology is made by and in the interplay with people of the congregation. Such participation in the theological task by members of congregations demands theological training beyond the "professional" level. Systems of theological education that do not develop the gifts of the local leaders of the Christian congregations do not meet the needs of today nor profit from the tremendous explosion of theological, missiological reflection taking place in the churches. There is a role to be played by the expert in the total orchestra of gifts provided by the Christian community. One is better equipped to play that role — to help the people in the fulfilment of their daily mission — if one is close to the realities of life and to the ongoing dialogue among Christians.

Finally, the real challenge is to recapture for theological education the missionary passion and missionary vision it never should have lost. Doctrinal discussions cannot be held in a vacuum. They are not simply repetitions of the past history of the church; they are interpretations of that history to illuminate and to inspire the actual mission of the churches today. The drafting of doctrinal or theological statements is not to make the students happy or to satisfy the teachers, but an attempt to express the significance of our Christian convictions for the vital issues of today. The teaching of evangelism or Christian education or pastoral care cannot be done as a science unrelated to the struggles of congregations and the dreams of the total population. Theological education should be passionately concerned with the development of a church that cares for the world and proclaims the gospel to every creature. That means being passionately concerned with equipping the church to be the church of Jesus Christ.

This volume focuses specifically on theological education by extension as one approach to developing all the potential of the Christian community so that the mission of the church can be best served. The pages that follow suggest that this approach is indeed enabling the people of God to participate actively in proclaiming the good news and in meeting the needs of their societies. Evangelism in many parts of the world is coming from a new base of people's participation. The local networks of cooperation that are being developed across church traditions have profound significance for the ecumenical vision.

There is also a warning to be heeded. Most of the people writing in this book and those who are active in theological education by extension have been trained in traditional ways and have profited by their time in seminaries in the West. We might be seen to be saying: "This has been good for me, but it is not good for you." The decision concerning the best methodologies should belong to the Christian community as a whole and not to the experts who strategize in terms of general categories or general priorities. We need to develop new alternatives to the traditional teaching methodology, but in such a way that we never cut off further possibilities for the people involved. We have learned in the area of development, particularly in the transfer of technology, that help is not sufficient if it doesn't transmit to people the capacity to develop their own scientific knowledge, to do their own research. We would not, therefore, *a priori* cut off the development of scientific theological training in countries of the third world. We must avoid the pretension that the scientific knowledge of the history of the peoples of the Middle East, the original languages and the history of the church, are the territories of people in the North Atlantic world, while the rest of the Christian community benefits from their publications and the results of their work.

In theology, as in many other areas of human knowledge, there are no neutral thoughts. Our ideologies enter into our exegetical work. It is necessary for people in the third world to have the scientific equipment to work with the original texts and to provide the fruits of their reflections to the local churches and to the church universal, coming from entirely different ideological and cultural presuppositions than those of the North Atlantic world. We are not blind to the "brain-drain"; the best people trained in the third world for the teaching of theology are being coopted by universities in Europe or in North America. The "brain-drain" must be fought; the solution is not, however, to eliminate the possibility of higher knowledge to Christians living in the third world.

The reports that Dr Kinsler has gathered point in exciting ways to a process of theological education that is motivating, equipping and enabling the people of God in every part of our world to carry out the mission of the church.

EMILIO CASTRO
Director, WCC Commission
on World Mission and Evangelism

Preface

All God's people are called to minister, and all theological education is ultimately dedicated to the equipping of God's people for
ministry. During the last twenty years we have observed the birth and
remarkable growth of Theological Education by Extension (TEE), a
movement and a model that take up old challenges and offer new
possibilities for ministerial formation among the people of God.
Because it is both a dynamic movement and a pragmatic model, TEE
merits the attention of all who are concerned with the reform of
theological education and the renewal of the church.

The purposes of this book are to make available detailed reports of
what is happening in theological education by extension in the
various church traditions and geographical regions, to explore the
educational designs and their theological and missiological underpin-
nings, to examine the problems and issues that these programmes are
dealing with, and to widen our horizons of what really can be done to
respond to unmet needs in our diverse cultural contexts. It provides
both exciting raw material and, especially through the opening article, a critical framework by which the churches and their institutions can re-examine their vision of theological education and renew
their efforts to equip all God's people for ministry.

Theological education by extension is not simply an extension or
adaptation of what is done in the classrooms of theological
seminaries and Bible schools. Some TEE programmes are not even
linked to established institutions. Nor does the concept used here embrace all kinds of non-traditional or non-residential theological
study. Rather, TEE is that model of theological education which pro-

vides systematic, independent study plus regular, supervised seminars in the context of people's varied life and work and ministry. From one perspective it opens up a wide range of degree and non-degree theological education options to the whole people of God, whatever their age, educational level, family situation, social position, language, race, sex or occupation. From another perspective it opens up theological education itself to the experiences and perceptions and gifts of God's people. TEE establishes new relationships between theological education and the church, teachers and students, theory and practice, theology and context, clergy and laity.

In many cases TEE is, of course, an extension of the vision and practice of theological schools that are committed to the ministry of all God's people. TEE has been perceived by some as a threat to more centralized institutions and the values that they represent. There has been sharp debate, mutual criticism, and challenge between the advocates of both types of education. It is now generally accepted, however, that extension programmes are dependent on the established theological centres for the basic tools of theological research and teaching, while centralized institutions need extension networks to gain access to the wider dimensions of the churches' leadership and the dynamic realities of the churches' life and mission. Thus the future effectiveness of both lies in building close partnerships and combinations for the equipping of God's people.

One of the extraordinary dimensions of the extension movement evidenced in this book is its ecumenical spectrum and depth. It is interesting to note that, although TEE is a very recent development, it has already been adopted by Anglicans, Baptists, Congregationals, Roman Catholics, Presbyterians, Lutherans, Nazarenes, Methodists, Pentecostals, Orthodox, Independents, united churches, and many others. In some places, such as Guyana, Switzerland and South Africa, Protestants and Roman Catholics are working together in ecumenical extension programmes. An extension programme among the African Independent churches is developing rapidly in Kenya through initiatives taken by an Orthodox bishop and a Presbyterian consultant with the assistance of the National Council of Churches and the Association of Theological Schools. Programmes reporting from Brazil, Costa Rica, Nigeria, the USA and the Philippines demonstrate serious engagement in such current ecumenical issues as people's participation, healing and wholeness, struggles for justice, and witness in a divided world. The decisive importance of all these initiatives is that they are being taken at the grassroots level, affecting many congregations and communities, integrating theory and practice naturally and immediately, in all the regions of the world.

The title *Ministry by the People* underlines the theological, missiological and practical significance of theological education by extension. Most ecclesiastical traditions and their theological institutions affirm that the basic call to ministry is given to all the members of the church by their incorporation into Christ's body. It is increasingly evident that ministry must be undertaken by God's people if it is to serve the needs of the whole church and the needs of the wider human community. Theological education by extension brings these truths to fruition not only by equipping many more people for ministry but also by engaging those whose gifts and service most qualify them for leadership among the people of God.

The reader is invited to use this anthology critically and selectively. The long initial chapter provides an overview of the recent development of theological education by extension and poses important questions and issues to which this movement relates. With this framework in mind one can turn to significant extension experiments within the different traditions, in the various regions, with varied goals, constituencies and educational designs. The reports portray the rich diversity and wide range of possibilities now being pursued; they also reveal a remarkable convergence of imaginative new approaches to ministerial formation.

During the last five years the Programme on Theological Education of the World Council of Churches has been in touch with these and many other programmes of alternative theological education. In order to promote the widest possible dialogue and cooperation, we agreed to publish nine of these reports in the April 1982 issue of the *International Review of Mission;* others have appeared in *The Ecumenical Review* and *Ministerial Formation;* requests from other journals have already been received and approved. Our hope is that those who are involved in these programmes and those who read about their experiences will challenge each other through critical evaluation of intentions, practice and results and through continuing, creative response to gospel and context. TEE is, after all, only a small phenomenon on the map of theological education, but it seems to manifest the mystique and the momentum — and the pitfalls — of a movement.

At a time of rising costs and shrinking resources, the churches and their theological schools can be expected to cut back on marginal and innovative programmes. The evidence presented in this book is that many have chosen rather to expand their vision and extend their resources in response to unmet needs and new challenges. The reports from their experience will inspire many more churches and institutions to join in these efforts to equip God's people for ministry and mission.

F. Ross Kinsler
Assistant Director
WCC Programme on Theological Education

Theological education by extension: Equipping God's people for ministry

F. ROSS KINSLER

In recent decades the churches have increasingly affirmed that theological education is central to their life and witness. It is assumed that theological education, in whatever ways it is conceived and practised, is necessary for the training of those who in turn are called to mobilize and equip the people of God for ministry and mission. Though theologies and structures of ministry vary widely between and within the various ecclesiastical traditions and cultural contexts, there is a significant move from what might be called "ministry to the people" to "ministry by the people of God".

In 1972 the Theological Education Fund enumerated several types or forms of alternative theological education: study centres, lay training centres, centres for urban mission and training, theological education by extension, other decentralized programmes, clinical pastoral education, community-based theological learning, cell groups for study and mutual care and team ministry, theological reflection in liberation movements, and ad hoc educational events (workshops, conferences, short courses, etc.). On the one hand many elements and insights from these alternatives have now been integrated into the ongoing work of residential or full-time theological schools. On the other hand there has been a remarkable expansion and escalation of theological education by extension, which not only complements residential training but offers an alternative way of approaching the whole range of theological education tasks.

Theological education by extension is for a growing number of people both a vision and a movement, a philosophy of theological education and an instrument for change, a new conceptualization and a new methodology of ministerial formation. The purpose of this book is to gather together reports on the experiences of major extension programmes in order to enable people engaged in mission, ministry, and theological education to read first-hand about this vision, to examine for themselves the educational and theological components of these programmes, to explore the early results, and to foresee possibilities for more effective use of this approach in meeting needs in their churches and societies. It is altogether evident that the whole people of God are called by the gospel and by the massive human needs that surround them to enter fully into Jesus' ministry. Theological education by extension is one way to respond to that challenge.

Basic shifts in the Christian movement

The significance and potential of theological education by extension lie not primarily in the movement itself but in the spiritual and social dynamics to which it relates. Our first consideration will therefore be a brief resumé of important developments in the Christian movement that provide perspectives from which the present experience and future potential of TEE should be viewed.

The world church

Years ago William Temple spoke eloquently of "the great new fact of our time", the fact that by the early decades of this century Christian churches had been firmly planted in all corners of the globe. The striking fact of the last two decades of the twentieth century is that the whole base of the Christian movement is shifting from North to South, that is, from the so-called first world and second world to the third world. In sheer numbers, there will be more Christians in Africa, Asia, and Latin America than in Europe and North America by the year 2000. In terms of active, meaningful participation, a large majority are already third world Christians. In terms of missionary engagement in evangelism and discipleship, in the struggle for human rights and liberation, in bringing good news to the poor, it is especially in the third world that we see signs of hope and the movement of God's Spirit today.

The second shift, which accompanies the first, is from hierarchies and institutions to the basic, grassroots church of the people. This is most notable among the Pentecostal churches of Latin America, whose dynamic life and witness have been generated almost without

formal theological education; among the African Independent churches, which have incorporated African traditional values and leadership patterns; and among indigenous churches in other third world
regions. Historic Protestant churches in these regions have experienced dynamic growth partly through their theologically trained
leaders, but probably far more through the leadership of untrained,
local leaders and the witness of ordinary members who have taken
full responsibility for the ministries of their congregations. Similarly
the Roman Catholic Church has been facing an enormous shortage
of priests in much of the third world, and it is experiencing an un-
precedented flourishing of basic ecclesial communities, small local
groups that meet for biblical reflection, share common concerns, and
work together to build a more human society.

These two shifts in the world church suggest that theological
educators and church authorities may need to re-evaluate their
assumptions and redirect their efforts. The institutions and structures that have evolved in Europe and North America can no longer
presume to hold the keys to theological understanding, prophetic insight, or spiritual vitality. Genuine spiritual, prophetic, and
theological life emerges from the basic church as "ordinary" Christians engage in their daily vocation. The task of theological education is to release, not bypass or supplant, that source of life and
power. Theological education by extension has a unique opportunity
to recognize and strengthen local congregations and their leaders as
the primary agents of mission, unity, and renewal.

Mission priorities

The old debate about evangelism and social action has perhaps
been necessary; it has served to focus attention on two dimensions of
sin and salvation. But it has always been in danger of polarization
and distortion; these are inseparable aspects of the same reality. Today there is a growing recognition among Christians of all kinds that
the human predicament and the gospel must be understood in a
holistic way. The mission which Jesus himself incarnated is the mission of God's redemptive kingdom, which transforms human life in
all its relationships. This is becoming increasingly clear to rural
Christians in Africa as they discuss the causes of underdevelopment,
to urban Christians in Asia who are engaged in struggles for human
rights, to Christians involved in popular liberation movements in
Latin America, and to Christians in North America and Europe who

are challenging the unjust structures of political and economic power that continue to exploit the world's human and material resources. The message we proclaim and live by must be prophetic and pastoral, social and personal, global and local.

Another important development is the growing commitment to "a church of the poor". It is now becoming evident in a new way that the kingdom of God must not only be proclaimed as good news to the poor but that God's church must be a church of the poor. From the first century until now the poor have always responded to the gospel, but the churches' structures and leadership patterns have usually reflected the elitism of their societies. A recent survey of the lay representatives in the Church of England's General Synod indicated that only one per cent are from the working classes, while the clergy are all highly educated. In Africa, Asia, and Latin America there is an increasing tendency for Christian leaders to move up the schooling ladder into successive levels of social and economic privilege. One of the most serious and difficult questions we all face is how to be a church that not only serves the poor but remains a church of the poor.

Both of these mission priorities have fundamental implications for theological education, and theological education by extension is peculiarly equipped to take up these challenges. As long as theological education is preoccupied with the full-time training of a few candidates for ordained ministry, it is destined to be narrow and elitist. In contrast, the growing extension networks are able to include all kinds of people, whether they hope to be ordained or not, whatever their social, ethnic, racial, and educational background. More specifically, it is now possible to develop effective resources for theological reflection and education among the poor themselves.

Understanding of human development

In spite of the vast resources that governments, churches, and other agencies have invested in programmes for development during the last twenty years, the plight of the poor around the world is becoming more and more desperate. Much of the blame for this failure is placed on the top-down or trickle-down approach. The process of development has generally been tied to the dominant patterns of modernization and economic growth which retain initiative, know-how, and decision-making in the hands of a few. The poor remain powerless and continue to be exploited and marginalized. The primary lesson from this tragic experience is that the poor must be the primary agents of their own development.

One sector of human need that is now being faced through a remarkable new approach is health care. No field of service has become more specialized and expensive and thus inaccessible to the majority of the world's population. As scientific medicine was exported to the third world, it discredited and even outlawed traditional remedies and practitioners that were available to all and replaced them with professional physicians, drugs and hospitals which only the rich could afford. As alternatives were considered, it became evident that scientific medicine is in any case ill equipped to meet the basic health needs of the poor — or even of the rich. The only effective road to health is for local communities to identify their own needs and take responsibility for meeting those needs — through sanitation and clean water supply, agricultural development and improved nutrition, land reform and community organization, and community-based, public health care programmes. The empirically trained village health promoter who lives among his or her peers at their level may in fact be a more effective agent for health and development than the typical M.D.

The churches need to learn these same lessons concerning their own development, particularly with regard to theological education. In the past it was assumed that the churches' "health" and "development" depended upon professional clergy trained at the highest academic levels possible. It is now evident that the vast majority of congregations in Africa, Asia and Latin America will not be able to hire seminar graduates for a long time to come. Moreover, dependence upon professional clergy, particularly as it has developed in Western Christianity, alienates the people from their own ministries and from their own spiritual health. Theological education by extension encourages and enables all kinds of congregations — poor and rich, Western and non-Western — to develop their own ministries among their own members. It may also become a channel for the transformation of those ministries to embrace the concerns of the kingdom, holistic evangelism, and community health.

The focus of theological education

When the Theological Education Fund came to a close in July 1977, Dr Shoki Coe, the Director, summarized the TEF's twenty years' work in the regions of the third world. He characterized that period as a progressive search for quality, authenticity, and creativity. The first step was to build up strong institutions for academic excellence, largely following the assumptions and patterns of Europe and North America. The second was to examine critically the relevance of these institutions for the various socio-cultural and ecclesial contexts of the third world. The third was to encourage new methods and approaches that would respond more flexibly, more widely, and more effectively to the ecumenical demands and global needs of our time.

It was also in July 1977 that the Programme on Theological Education was created to carry on the work of the TEF within a wider, six-continent perspective. The PTE chose to focus its mandate upon "ministerial formation", which was interpreted in the broadest sense to include all the people of God and in the particular sense to be concerned with "enabling the enablers". By choosing this focus the PTE affirmed clearly that theological education is not an end in itself, that it is not simply an academic or professional enterprise, that it is not even bound to institutions. Ministerial formation is as concerned with personal growth and maturity as it is with theological knowledge, with spiritual gifts and commitment for service as well as pastoral skills. These qualities and aspects of leadership can perhaps best be identified and fostered within the practice of ministry in congregations and communities. They are as important for ministry in Europe and North America as they are in other regions.

The principal model for ministerial formation is Jesus himself, who continues to call his followers into his ministry and mission, and the classic text is Mark 10:42-45, which speaks of service and self-giving. One of the enigmas we face is that theological education, along with all other kinds of education, leads to privilege and power, whereas ministerial formation is fundamentally concerned with servanthood.

Once again it appears that theological education by extension is a significant alternative response to the spiritual and social dynamics at work in the churches and in the world. By placing the academic as well as the practical aspects of training in the normal context of life and ministry, it may be possible to integrate them more effectively in relation to real human problems. By taking theological education to those who are already serving in their congregations, supporting themselves and their families, and making their contributions in society, it may be able to avoid the professionalization and elitization of the ministry. The challenge to the extension movement, which is the mandate of all theological education, is to motivate, equip, and enable the people of God to develop their gifts and give their lives in meaningful service for others.

Regional developments

Following is an overview of what is happening in theological education by extension in the various regions. By reviewing these developments we can consider the extent to which TEE is being accepted as an alternative or as complementary to residential, institutional training and begin to evaluate its potential as a vehicle for ministerial formation and for the renewal of the churches for mission. The issues and questions raised in the subsequent sections of this paper take on importance in relation to the people and institutions now engaged in the movement.

Latin America and the Caribbean

As an identifiable model of theological education TEE began at a small, denominational institution in Central America in 1963. The first international workshop on extension was held in Armenia, Colombia, in 1967. By 1977 Wayne Weld reported 133 known programmes with 19,384 students in Latin America and the Caribbean. Recent evidence demonstrates that these programmes are growing, some of them very rapidly, and that new programmes are being added each year.

In 1968 an association of extension programmes (AETTE) was formed in Brazil, and in 1973 a similar association (ALISTE) developed for the Spanish-speaking countries, in addition to the associations established previously by the residential schools (ASTE, ASIT, and ALET). In May 1980 representatives of ALISTE and ALET met to form a common association for theological education in the northern region of Latin America (ALIET) because the differences that separated them were no longer valid. The major residential institutions in Latin America now have their own extension programmes, and they are playing an important role in the preparation of leaders and materials for the extension movement. The Latin American Biblical Seminary, for example, has initiated a continent-wide extension network (PRODIADIS) of university-level studies comparable to its residential programmes; the residential programme of this institution includes a specialization in TEE; and several staff members are active in promoting, consulting, and writing for TEE.

Three of the four institutions that make up the Theological Community of Mexico have or work closely with extension programmes. The Theological Community of Chile runs an enormous extension programme with up to 4,000 students, mostly Pentecostal, up and down that 4,000-kilometre-long country. ISEDET in Buenos Aires, the dean of the Protestant theological institutions in Latin America, is now developing extension courses, and the Association of Seminaries and Theological Institutes (ASIT), which serves Argentina, Bolivia, Chile, Paraguay, and Uruguay, is running a series of intensive workshops for writers of extension textbooks. The International Baptist Theological Seminary of Buenos Aires initiated an extension programme for Argentina in 1968; it now has 13 centres with 600 students.

In Brazil there are still separate associations for residential schools and extension programmes, but several institutions belong to both. When AETTE celebrated its tenth anniversary in 1978, there were 44 extension programmes with about 5,000 students in Brazil. The numerous Pentecostals of Brazil have now begun to develop their own TEE programmes, and apparently they already have 2,000-3,000 students.

In the Caribbean region there are several extension programmes, mostly among conservative Protestant groups. The most important ecumenical effort is the Guyana Extension Seminary, which was launched by the Guyana Council of Churches in 1976 and now has several hundred students representing 15 denominations, including Roman Catholics.

There are at least a dozen creative centres which provide resources, training and new directions for the extension movement in Latin America. The Guatemalan Centre for Studies in Theological Education and Ministry continues to edit the *Extension Seminary* quarterly newsletter (Spanish and English versions), organize workshops on various aspects of TEE, publish extension course materials, and consult with the many extension programmes in Central America. The Anglican Extension Seminary (SEAN), formerly based in northern Argentina but now in Chile, has formed an international team of writers and produced a rigorously tested and widely accepted series of integrated extension study materials, which are now used in various languages not only in many Latin American countries but also in parts of Africa, Asia, Europe, and North America. The Association for Theological Training by Extension (AETTE) in Brazil has developed a plan by which cooperating institutions set aside staff members for training seminars and writing of extension texts; some forty or fifty texts have been produced, and those writers who complete all the requirements receive a Master's degree.

Africa

The second region to experience rapid growth of theological education by extension is Africa. A first workshop on TEE was held in Kenya in 1969; others followed in 1970, 1971, and 1972 in various parts of Africa. In 1977 Wayne Weld's survey indicated that there were 57 extension programmes in Africa and Madagascar with a total of 6,869 students. The incompleteness of his data is indicated by a January 1978 report from Nigeria showing 10 programmes and 5,923 students in that one country.

As in Latin America the rapid growth of TEE in Africa is due above all to the inability of traditional residential schools to meet the needs of rapidly growing churches. The Christian population in Africa is increasing so fast that it is expected to reach 350 million — 50 per cent of the total population — by the year 2000. Both Roman Catholics and Protestants commonly face situations in which there is one trained clergy for 5 to 25 congregations.

The five major associations of theological schools in the sub-regions of Africa (ATIEA, WAATI, ASTHEOL, ASATI, ATTM) have all considered the problems and possibilities of TEE. The association of Southern Africa held a major consultation with church leaders in 1975, which mobilized interest and resources and led to the launching of a major ecumenical effort, the TEE College, which is now in its fifth year and has an enrolment of more than 1,200 students, one third of them Roman Catholics. In 1980 this pro-gramme had a budget of $200,000, a full-time staff of 16, including several course writers, a large printing operation, and a network of 85 centres and 124 local tutors throughout South Africa plus Lesotho, Swaziland, Namibia, Malawi, and Zimbabwe. Students at the "highest" level sit the same examinations for the joint diploma as those who attend the residential colleges, and early reports indicate that they are doing comparable work. Materials for the "lower" level are now being translated, adapted, and published in five of the seven major South African languages.

The association of theological schools for francophone Africa (ASTHEOL) discussed TEE at its 1975 meeting and has attempted to set up another consultation with the extension programmes. A 1977 report indicated that there were at that time 11 extension programmes with 2,661 students in Zaire. Other extension programmes have been reported in Rwanda, Burundi, Congo, Cameroun, Ivory Coast, Togo, and Central African Republic.

The association for Eastern Africa (ATIEA) held a consultation at Limuru, Kenya, in December 1979. It was reported that there are 12 extension programmes in Kenya alone. There are additional programmes in Tanzania, Ethiopia and Sudan. The Sudan Council of Churches held a consultation in January 1980 to take steps towards cooperation among Protestants, Catholics and Orthodox in TEE.

The West African association of theological schools (WAATI) has a working group on alternative patterns of ministry and ministerial formation, and its 1980 conference focused on this theme, especially in relation to TEE developments in that sub-region. The association for Madagascar (ATTM) is beginning to explore the possibilities of extension training for the independent churches as well as the historic denominations. At its first general meeting in Swaziland (March 1980) the Conference of African Theological Institutions, which brings together the five sub-regional associations, set up a provisional plan for coordinating extension efforts and sharing information throughout the region.

The oldest and most extensive scheme for the production of extension study materials was initiated by Fred Holland in the early 1970s and is now sponsored by the Association of Evangelicals in Africa and Madagascar. Teams of African and expatriate writers have been trained through workshops held periodically in various parts of Africa; they are working on a commonly agreed series of 40 basic texts for local church leaders with limited formal education. Evangel Publishing House reported recently that it has printed nearly a quarter of a million of these texts in English and Swahili; in addition 196 translations have been made in 43 languages, mostly in Africa but also in parts of Asia and Latin America.

North America

Among all the regions probably the US and Canada are experiencing the fastest growth of theological education by extension at the present time. In 1968 the first workshops on TEE, held at

Philadelphia and Wheaton, were primarily for mission personnel interested in overseas possibilities. Since then more and more church leaders and theological educators have come to see that TEE can respond to urgent needs in North America.

In January 1979 several bodies sponsored a consultation at Tempe, Arizona, on "New Approaches to Leadership Development in North America". Eight case studies described extension-type programmes among native American, Hispanic, and black minority churches and among the majority white "mainline" churches. During the last five years TEE programmes have been initiated among Indian peoples across the US, including Alaska, and in parts of Canada. New York Theological Seminary has gone through radical institutional change in order to serve the charismatic leadership of hundreds of minority congregations in the metropolitan area. Fuller Theological Seminary in California, which has an enormous residential enrolment, now has five different extension programmes for various constituencies, both majority and minority. The University of the South (Episcopal) runs a rapidly growing TEE programme (last report 4,850 enrolled) mainly for lay people who want to take a full basic course in theology for their Christian vocation in the world. The oldest (1950) and largest extension programme in the world is the Southern Baptist Seminary Extension Department, which in 1981 reported a total of 11,000 students and 400 centres in all 50 states and 18 foreign countries.

Extension was first seen as relevant for minority churches because their leadership patterns are based on maturity, gifts and experience more than schooling. Also, minority candidates are at a serious disadvantage in the dominant school-college-seminary pattern. Extension is now being considered as a response to a double crisis among the smaller congregations of the major denominations. On the one hand the seminaries are producing larger numbers of candidates for professional ministry; on the other hand increasing numbers of congregations cannot afford to hire a full-time minister. During the past decade 76 seminaries have developed D.Min. programmes, which are field-based continuing education for pastors. This extension model is now accepted by the Association of Theological Schools in the US and Canada and should open the door to seminaries that may want to offer the full range of theological education by extension methods.

Of particular interest now is the development of resource centres and networks which will carry on and coordinate the concerns of alternative theological education and relate to similar efforts in other regions. A number of important studies which have just been completed or are being undertaken at the present time are likely to provoke increasing interest in alternative theological education in the coming years: the Auburn History of the American Protestant Seminary, the Hartford study on supply and demand of the clergy, the Readiness for Ministry study of the Association of Theological Schools, the Lilly Endowment survey of congregation-based theological education, and John Fletcher's study on the future of theological education. The ATS is now in the process of drawing up criteria for evaluation and accreditation of "extension satellite degree programmes". Several theological institutions in the US and Canada have in recent years chosen to close their full-time residential programmes and to dedicate all their resources to alternatives.

Asia, Australia-New Zealand, the Pacific

There is neither space nor sufficient data for a survey of theological education by extension in these regions, but certain trends and examples may be useful. The more industrial countries, such as Australia, New Zealand, Japan, and Korea, have been slower to develop alternatives, but extension programmes are being initiated there. TEE seems to be multiplying most in India, the Philippines, Hong Kong, and Taiwan. There are also TEE programmes in Pakistan, Bangladesh, Sri Lanka, Burma, Malaysia, Indonesia, Singapore, Thailand, Papua New Guinea and other parts of the Pacific.

No one country could be considered typical, but recent developments in India portray some of the ways in which basic change is taking place. A 1970 workshop on TEE brought together conservative-evangelical missionaries and church leaders and led to the founding of the Association for Theological Education by Extension (TAFTEE). A small central office and staff was set up in Bangalore to provide basic services, programmed study materials, examinations, and orientation for the centres. By 1980 there were 51 centres with 483 students, all studying at the B.Th. level in English. A certificate level programme is now being introduced for persons with five to eight years of schooling, utilizing vernacular adaptations of the widely-endorsed SEAN materials from South America. This new programme has the potential of reaching the tens of thousands of village leaders who have long been exempted from serious theological education and disenfranchized from the ministry; in one year the enrolment in Maharastra State grew to 1,000.

The historic Protestant churches and their institutions have also been deeply engaged in the search for alternatives and the development of TEE. In 1974 the Board of Theological Education of the National Council of Churches of India held a major consultation on "Theological Training of the Whole Church and New Patterns of Training", which recommended that local leaders should involve their teachers and students in extension programmes, and that extension efforts should be coordinated at the national level. In 1975 four major seminaries (Andhra Christian Theological College, Kerala United Theological Seminary, Tamilnadu Theological Seminary, and the United Theological College at Bangalore) initiated the Teach Yourself Programme of Theological Education (TYPTE), which provides some extension services for external students preparing to take the B.D. examinations of Serampore University. Present enrolment is over 400. In addition two of these seminaries require their regular students to spend at least a year off-campus in order to learn how to do theology in context, "making it relevant to the needs of the church and the world today". They offer additional extension and external degree programmes for people in business, government, industry and the professions. During 1979 each of the four seminaries held a sub-regional consultation on TEE; a national consultation was held in September 1980.

These developments demonstrate that, at least in India, alternative, contextual theological education is of major importance for the theological education establishment as well as for marginal groups, for ordinands as well as lay people, for historic churches as well as conservative-evangelicals, for theological as well as pragmatic reasons. It is being pursued because it is a new way of integrating theology and life, of incorporating the people of God in the ministry, of equipping the church for its mission in the world.

Eastern and Western Europe

Probably much less is happening in alternative theological education in Europe than in other parts of the world, but several important programmes can be mentioned. In Russia both Orthodox and Baptist clergy are trained by correspondence or independent study. The Moscow Academy (Orthodox) enrolls about 800 external students all over the country. They study at home, go to Zagorsk twice a year to attend lectures, present papers, and write examinations, and work towards the same degrees as the residential students (Candidate, M.Th., Th.D.). In November 1978 a workshop on TEE held in Yugoslavia brought together Protestant, Orthodox and Roman Catholic theological educators. The new Protestant Faculty at Zagreb and the Orthodox Faculty at Belgrade have more external than residential students; the Roman Catholic Faculty at Zagreb has 900 correspondence students; and the Baptists and Pentecostals have initiated extension programmes. There are correspondence programmes in other countries of Eastern Europe, and there is interest in exploring the possibilities of TEE due to the limitations placed on theological institutions in socialist countries and the growing shortage of clergy.

Western Europe is noted for its lay academies, study centres of various kinds, and adult education programmes. The International Institute of Theology at a Distance (Roman Catholic) reported in 1981 an enrolment (mostly in Spain and Latin America) of 6,700 priests, religious, and lay persons in a full range of correspondence courses in Bible, church history, theology, practical theology, and sociology of religion. The Assemblies of God (Pentecostal) International Correspondence Institute, based at Brussels, now has a total enrolment close to two million students in 113 countries, most of them at a very simple academic and theological level, and about 2,000 taking a complete college course in Bible, theology, religious education, or church administration. There are many more localized training programmes, conferences, evening classes, and groups for reflection and action among clergy and laity in different parts of Western Europe.

In the UK there is now considerable reform of theological education and widespread experimentation with alternative patterns — due both to vocational and economic crises and to a new understanding of ministerial formation. Over the past five years the cost of training ordinands of the Church of England has increased 200 per cent; 11 theological colleges have been closed or combined; there has been a marked decline in the number of clergy; and many parishes are becoming non-viable. On the other hand there are now 14 alternative, non-residential training schemes, some for laity or non-stipendiary clergy and others for regular clergy. In 1977 the House of Bishops recommended the formation of ten sub-regional institutes which would coordinate all theological education resources and offer extension options throughout the country. In April 1979 a consultation on "Alternative Theological Education", held at Sheffield, brought together theological educators of several ecclesiastical traditions and reflected on historic and current models for training, in an attempt to establish spiritual, theological, and sociological criteria as well as pragmatic solutions for the current crises. The different approaches to theological education in the UK have focused on various important emphases: academic scholarship (universities), spiritual formation in community (theological colleges), experience in the secular world (adult education), action and reflection in context (the Urban Theology Unit), indigenous leadership of congregations (TEE), and congregation-based pastoral training (Alternative Pattern of Training). The present ferment and experimentation, drawing from all these alternatives, will bring new insights and possibilities in the coming years.

The importance of these developments should not be underestimated. In other parts of Western Europe theological education and the clergy are largely dependent on direct or indirect taxation. They continue to flourish even though the churches are empty. This raises serious questions about their relevance and also about their capacity to survive if state support is cut off. It may be that lessons now being learned in the UK and Eastern Europe will have some application in these other countries. Furthermore critical reappraisal and redirection of theological education in Europe could have implications for other regions that have built their patterns of ministry on this heritage. It is important to see that traditional patterns are no longer adequate in Europe, that new approaches there closely parallel new patterns in the younger churches, and that the third world experience has much to contribute to the older churches in this respect.

Summary
The numerical and geographical expansion of the extension movement — from a handful of experiments in Latin America at the end of the 1960s to 300 or 400 programmes with perhaps 100,000 students around the world at the end of the 1970s — has been extraordinary. During this decade the initiative of the extension movement has passed from small, marginal, ill-equipped schemes led by expatriate missionaries to large, well-endowed efforts run by major theological institutions and promoted by associations of theological schools.

For a time it was commonly assumed that TEE was only acceptable for low-level training, for non-industrialized countries, or for lay people, and that extension training must be of lesser quality. In third world countries it is still true that most extension programmes operate at "low" academic levels, because that is the overwhelming need of the churches, but extension programmes in all regions now prepare students for the same examinations and qualifications as the parallel residential programmes, and these students are beginning to prove themselves not only by their academic achievements but by their leadership in ministry in their churches and communities. The cumulative effect of all these developments is difficult to evaluate at this stage, but present indications are that escalation will continue at least through the 1980s.

Major questions, issues, needs

Many questions and issues about alternative theological education have emerged in recent years. This section gathers major issues and needs into four areas that must be dealt with by all who are concerned about the renewal of the church for ministry and mission.

Theological education by extension is a new movement, which explains in part both its vitality and its shortcomings. But the tremendous growth noted above suggests that it has come of age and that these shortcomings can no longer be overlooked. TEE must submit to the same rigorous critique that has been applied to other forms of theological education. Furthermore, insofar as theological education by extension is, as we have suggested, in a favourable position vis-à-vis the social and spiritual dynamics at work in the churches and in the world, it must fall under greater condemnation if it does not carry out faithfully its mandate.

Ministerial formation

1. *We must ask, first, for more adequate definition or conceptualization of TEE as an alternative form of ministerial formation.* What are the essential ingredients or processes whereby men and women are motivated and equipped for witness and service? How does TEE incorporate or provide these ingredients? Many of the reports to which we have referred simply record the numbers and levels of students and describe the mechanics of these programmes without any analysis of the various dimensions of the learning process. It almost seems as if many TEE programmes are engaged only

in the simplification, packaging, and diffusion of elementary theological knowledge and pastoral skills.

2. *We must question the educational philosophy underlying these extension programmes.* There has been considerable talk of conscientization and contextualization but little demonstration of what these concepts mean in practice. Many extension programmes appear to combine the worst of traditional schooling (memorization of a predetermined body of information) with new programming techniques. Extension students are generally more capable of meaningful participation in the learning process because of their maturity and involvement in congregations and communities, but some TEE programmes may in fact be manipulative and domesticating, imposing irrelevant information, legalistic doctrinal formulae, and narrow pastoral stereotypes.

3. *We must consider the methods, materials, and personnel that are being utilized.* There is talk of action and reflection, of materials that pose open questions for discussion, and of teachers that are tutors and co-learners, but what takes place in the thousands of extension groups that are now meeting weekly or bi-weekly? Are the students in fact the subjects rather than the objects or receptacles of TEE? Do the extension tutors actually go through the necessary "pedagogical conversion" in order to become co-learners? Is real communication and critical analysis taking place?

4. *Who are the students? How are they selected? What is their motivation?* These questions are as important as the goals and content of any programme. Some extension promoters seem to be excited simply by the growing numbers of students, but others have noted the danger that this phenomenon may simply reflect the widespread social pressure for certification. In some cases TEE is perceived as a back door into the ordained ministry, a cheap way to provide or to obtain theological studies.

5. *These points indicate that there is a very basic need for guidelines and procedures for evaluation.* It may well be that traditional criteria are not appropriate for alternative programmes; in that case new approaches to evaluation must be adopted. Some extension programmes are in fact preparing students to take established examinations for certificates of various kinds; others have developed their own systems but tend to focus exclusively on cognitive learning.

6. *TEE is merely an instrument,* like other approaches to theological education, and it can be used to pursue very diverse

goals. *The content and purpose of these programmes should be determined by raising further questions about ministry, the church, and mission.*

Ministry

1. It is certainly true that TEE is now reaching grassroots leaders of all kinds and in many cases is qualifying them for ordination, but it is still not clear how this affects the structures, style and dynamics of ministry. Do the newly ordained pastors easily assume the prerogatives and perquisites of other seminary graduates, or are they reshaping the ministry to make it less hierarchical and more community-based, less professional and more indigenous?

2. TEE brings new possibilities not only for training indigenous pastors but also for the theological education of the "laity" for Christian vocation in society. How is this task perceived and pursued? Are these lay leaders simply becoming clergy assistants or clergy substitutes oriented primarily to the churches' inward focus, or are they discovering meaningful ways to minister within the social structures, to challenge those structures prophetically, and to turn the church's vision outward?

3. Ultimately, the effectiveness of all programmes of theological education must be evaluated in terms of the graduates' ability to motivate and equip their congregations for witness and service. Are the new extension graduates, those who become pastors and those who minister in other ways, motivating and equipping others for their ministries? Are they building up a sense of and commitment to ministering communities that value and support the various gifts and talents among all the members?

The church

1. Probably most extension programmes have been initiated in order to meet evident needs of established churches. As theological education and the ministry engage more and more people at the local, congregational level, it becomes possible not only to fill gaps but to explore new visions or even, as some Latin Americans are saying, to recreate the church. As extension teachers and students begin to permeate their churches, they must ask themselves whether their task is to carry on existing patterns of church life or to transform them, to shore up the old structures of leadership and ministry or to

change them, to promote the accepted understanding of the churches' life and mission or to challenge it.

2. Since extension students are fully involved in their local communities, are employed and hold responsible positions in society, and share all the vicissitudes of their fellow citizens, they are ideally situated to develop new understandings of the gospel, of the church, and of theology in terms of human realities and human transformation. Is this in fact happening, or are they simply falling back into the age-old traps of theoretical theology, institutionalized religion, and pious jargon? Are students and teachers being challenged to reinterpret their own daily, ecclesial, and theological vocation as they grapple seriously with both the living, biblical text and the living, contemporary context?

3. Because extension students do not leave their local contexts, the question is often raised whether they therefore remain provincial and parochial in outlook. Do they perpetuate the prejudices and narrowness of their own people, or do they gain new perspectives and attitudes which enable them to lead their people into an ecumenical, global understanding of reality and of the church? Do they take up for themselves and encourage among their congregations new paths of discipleship and life-style, new approaches to witness and service?

4. The involvement of many local leaders in critical theological reflection, in rethinking the nature and mission of the church, and in relevant discipleship should in turn generate new spiritual dynamics in their congregations. As more and more members participate in this process, the vitality of their ministry should be felt not only in their congregations but also in their homes and in their communities.

Mission

1. If genuine progress is being made in the ways suggested above, then theological education by extension should be a significant instrument for mobilizing the people of God for mission in the perspective of the kingdom. But we must ask whether in fact these programmes enable the participants to perceive and pursue the mission of the church in terms of the whole range of human needs, to which they bring a wealth of experience, perspectives, talents and gifts. This challenge is for those who are at the bottom of society and for those who are at the top, for those who live in Europe and North America and for those who live in third world countries.

2. Civilization has changed enormously since the first century, especially in our own generation; the human predicament has become tremendously complex; recent developments in geo-politics, the economic crises, science and technology, and militarism have seemingly got totally beyond solution. Yet Christians cannot abandon hope or renounce their responsibility as agents of peace, reconciliation, justice, and human development. In this context theological education cannot be confined to the preparation of clergy, nor can it be considered a minor avocation for lay people. It must challenge the churches' total human and spiritual resources to face the tragic needs all around us, to struggle against every form of evil, to work for a more human society, and to give our lives for the salvation of many. Is TEE doing this?

3. Ultimately we face an ideological problem — not in terms of particular political ideologies but in terms of commitment to people and to human development. In the past Christians have been naive about social structures, and even those with the best intentions have inadvertantly supported interests alien to the people they serve. Therefore it is essential to include social-historical analysis as an essential component of theological education. We must ask what is the ideological content, commitment, and effect of theological education by extension. Do TEE students engage in critical social and theological analysis of their own churches, communities, and societies? Are they concerned about and involved in the struggle for human rights locally and globally? Are they challenging sexism, racism, economic exploitation, superstition, and corruption where they live and work? Are their local congregations becoming healing communities and signs of liberation?

Priorities for the eighties

An enormous amount of work is now going into theological education by extension all over the world. The questions raised here suggest, however, that there is a certain lack of direction in all this activity. It is still unclear whether the extension movement will in fact respond to the major challenges set forth at the beginning of this article concerning basic shifts in the world church, mission priorities, understanding of human development, and ministerial formation. This final section will therefore propose priorities for the content and purpose of extension programmes for the current decade by means of a series of vignettes from extension programmes in different parts of the world.

Kingdom-oriented curricula

1. In 1963 the Presbyterian Seminary of Guatemala made simple structural changes that opened up new relationships between the institution and the church, teachers and students, theory and experience, theology and context. It was soon evident that the new model, which gave currency to the name theological education by extension, had great potential for the pursuit of the commonly accepted goal of preparing leaders for evangelism and church growth. The rapid increase in enrolment and the enormous task of providing study materials and weekly tutorials for an expanding extension network left little time or energy for serious questioning or broadening of that goal. There has been a growing consciousness among staff and students that the calling of God's people is not only to build the church but to proclaim the coming of God's kingdom of justice and peace. But in Guatemala violence and repression have reached such a level that those who speak out against oppression are now threatened and exiled or tortured and killed, particularly religious leaders, journalists, educators, and all political opponents of the military-dominated government. Priests and pastors have been assassinated; informants attend worship services; whole families have been murdered and congregations machine-gunned; the Seminary itself has been under surveillance for long periods and was occupied briefly by soldiers. It almost seems as if it is too late for this extension programme to become an effective instrument for training God's people for kingdom service and witness. If it does not, however, it leaves that church in grave danger of being an acquiescent or willing partner of the forces of death.

2. Having served for many years as Principal of Immanuel Theological College and as Director of the Institute for Church and Society in Ibadan, Nigeria, Adeolu Adegbola initiated in 1979 a Centre for Applied Religion and Education. His underlying assumptions are that life must be seen whole, that the needs of communities must be dealt with holistically, and that ministerial formation must prepare people for a wide range of tasks, including evangelism and political education, agricultural cooperatives and industrial missions, pastoral care and health care, church growth and urban renewal. A consultation of church workers at Bukuru in 1978 analyzed the causes of injustice and called on theological institutions to provide "more appropriate preparation of ministers for the proclamation of the Christian gospel to the whole man [sic] in northern Nigeria".

Adegbola affirms that this kind of training has to be done in context, through decentralized networks, as long-term, continuing education for people in all walks of life, including pastors and evangelists. The Centre is now making available resources, models and training for various levels and kinds of extension education. It is mobilizing church leaders, educators and professionals and other institutions for the mammoth tasks of ministry in Africa today.

3. In his report on the extension programme of the School of Theology, University of the South (USA), David Killen emphasizes the necessity of equipping the laity for serious theological reflection because the mission of the church is to pray and work for God's coming kingdom. "A world less and less conscious of the gospel of Jesus and its crucial impact is far more the habitat of the laity than it is of the clergy." Lay people must therefore develop the essential theological skills to discern, own and implement the processes by which the kingdom is being manifested in their lives and in their world. The pursuit of this agenda covers four years of rigorous study, 24 specially prepared texts, and weekly seminars where the interpretation of experience and the tradition is tested and the formation of beliefs and values is affirmed. The expansion of this programme is far greater than the School of Theology ever imagined. Its impact on the parishes and communities of North America (and elsewhere) is still to be assessed.

Contextual models for theological learning

1. The Pentecostals of Latin America have written an extraordinary chapter in contemporary church history. Some groups trace their roots back to the early part of this century, but most are very young, and already they make up 70-80 per cent of the Protestant population. There has been an anti-intellectual tendency, but they have developed a remarkable system of non-formal or informal leadership formation which is far more effective — in terms of leadership — than any theological training offered by the other churches. All the members are expected to be active participants in the evangelistic witness and frequent worship of their congregations; leaders are selected not on the basis of academic credentials but gradually on the basis of their dedication, maturity, gifts, and service; ministry thus involves and represents the life of the people. In Mexico, Central America, Chile, Argentina, and Brazil, where they are most numerous, the Pentecostals have begun to adopt theological

education by extension, because it builds on this dynamic process of leadership selection and formation. The extension programme of the Theological Community in Chile, for example, has adopted adult education philosophy which recognizes and values the fact that each person brings the knowledge of experience that permits him or her to be a learner and an educator simultaneously. Thousands of independent Pentecostal church leaders, whose religious experience has been very real but whose schooling opportunities have been extremely limited, have found this to be a liberating experience, learning through dialogue, adding new information to experience and testing new insights through practice, and forming criteria for critical reflection on the mission of the church and the realities of their social context.

2. A similar story can be told of the African Independent churches, which are said to number 7,000 groups with a rapidly growing constituency of perhaps 30 million. There have been many large and small breakaways from the mission-established churches, large and small indigenous prophetist movements, further divisions and new groupings. In most cases leadership is formed and selected empirically and charismatically, that is, through the demonstration of spiritual power and leadership gifts in the life of the church. Few African Independent churches have Bible schools or seminaries. Some have tried sending promising young leaders to institutions run by the mission-established churches, but generally they do not return to serve their own churches because their theological formation, pastoral style, and personal expectations are no longer suitable. In 1980 the Organization of African Independent Churches, under the leadership of Bishop Antonious Markos, initiated a pilot extension programme in Kenya. Agustin and Rosario Batlle, who had developed and directed the extension programme in Chile, were invited to serve as consultants. Within a year they had visited many church leaders, held workshops to identify needs and discuss possibilities for programmes, initiated training for local coordinators and course writers, prepared the first lesson materials for several courses, distributed a promotional brochure, and received 1,114 applications. The hunger for training among Independent church leaders is overwhelming; extension education provides a channel through which their needs can be met. "What gives meaning to this TEE work in Kenya is that one feels in tune with the aspirations of so many people."

3. During the last decade one of the most notable changes in theological education in North America has been the rapid expansion of D.Min. programmes of continuing education for clergy, most of which utilize a contextual or extension model. Hartford Seminary, which in 1974 dropped its regular M.Div. and Ph.D. programmes in order to become a centre for continuing education of clergy and laity, parish development, and research on ministry, decided to focus its D.Min. programme on the quality of life and ministry of the congregation. Pastors and their congregations are enrolled together; the congregation, not the pastor, is the primary focus; the general goal is growth and change in parish life, which includes the pastor; the four principal partners in the programme are the seminary faculty, the pastor, the laity, and the congregation as an organizational entity. The programme itself is a model of mutual ministry and experiential education that should carry on indefinitely after formal course work is completed. The first stage of learning is for pastor and parish to assess where they are, what changes are needed, and how they can grow. The second is for these partners, not the seminary, to set goals in terms of growth in ministry. Third, they must identify appropriate resources for learning and growth in terms of teaching, consulting, library, curriculum materials, and educational design. Fourth, pastors and lay leaders need support groups and accountability that will sustain and critique them in the process. Finally growth and change require evaluation and feedback, not just between faculty and students but also between pastors and congregations, mutually. This model was not easy to develop; the new and unfamiliar roles have caused understandable tensions for all the partners, including the seminary faculty.

Grassroots theology

1. In their report of the Botswana Theological Training Programme Richard Sales and Jacob Liphoko emphasize that their extension programme is not simply offering a new kind of ministerial training and reaching out to many who could not enter traditional theological schools; it is creating "grassroots African theology" among local congregational leaders. As the tutors visit the small extension groups around that large, sparsely populated country, as Christians engage themselves fully with the gospel, as they relate the Bible and tradition to their own experience and environment, something dynamic is happening. New insights are coming forth that

no one had foreseen. Extraordinary leadership is emerging in remote places. For the first time women are enrolling in theological studies, opening up new relationships between women and men, bringing their gifts and understanding of the gospel to the churches' ministry. "A slow but very significant revolution is in the making today."

2. Cook Christian Training School turned to TEE after research about Native American congregations revealed that there was a very serious leadership crisis. In 1974 only 68 ordained Native clergy could be identified in the 499 Native churches and chapels among the seven participating denominations, and only four Native theological students were found among the 28,000 students attending the 202 accredited seminaries in the US and Canada. Since then, Cook has worked with a network of seminaries, colleges, training programmes, and denominations in the design and development of various extension training programmes for native peoples throughout the region. These programmes not only recognize and build on Native realities and leadership patterns; they are opening up new possibilities for widespread, grassroots pursuit of Native theologies. From the beginning, courses have been prepared not only in the areas of Bible, theology and ministry, but also on such matters as "Federal and church Indian policies", "The Indian Bill of Rights", "Native American church history", and "Current Indian issues". Even more basic is research and discussion about Native creation stories and the Genesis narratives, the Native spiritual heritage and the Christian life, and other fundamental theological themes that are for the first time being given full attention not only among Natives themselves but also among participating white seminaries and churches.

3. "The experience of poverty, dependence, and exploitation that prevails in Latin America imposes on theological institutions a new agenda and a new way of doing theology which takes as its point of departure that kind of experience and the struggles it generates." The Latin American Biblical Seminary of San José, Costa Rica, has in recent years taken an increasingly prophetic stance in this regard. While maintaining its highly regarded, university-level residential programme, the Seminary launched in 1976 an extension programme for individuals and groups all over Latin America that wish to pursue bachelor and licenciate degrees without necessarily going to Costa Rica. Although this programme utilizes the personnel and other resources of the residential programme, it is an open curriculum that recognizes and validates each candidate's experience and prior for-

mal and non-formal education, provides general background studies and basic tools needed for doing theology, offers a wide range of modules for guided study in dialogue (by correspondence) with a professor of the Seminary, and allows maximum freedom both as to entry point and area of concentration. Extension students are required to design and carry out action/reflection projects based on analyses of particular needs in their own churches and communities. They can include a wide variety of activities to meet these needs, as long as they describe and document these activities fully and set up and report on the means of evaluating their effectiveness. This work is finalized through reflection papers that integrate theological, ideological, and strategic insights gained by the experience.

Primary ministries

1. One of the essential goals of theological education by extension must be to let the church be the church, or more specifically, to let the people of God become the primary agents of ministry. This is actually happening today in many parts of the world, but nowhere more dramatically than in Brazil, where the sleeping giant Roman Catholic Church has awakened through the spontaneous creation of 80,000 basic ecclesial communities. No longer is pastoral action the exclusive prerogative of professional, highly qualified priests, carried out in isolation from social realities. It is now regarded as the work of the entire Christian community, inspired by pastoral agents, who can be bishops, pastors, catechists, workers, peasants, men or women. The contribution of the Bible Study Centre for People's Pastoral Action, a small ecumenical agency, is to provide biblical training and materials for these pastoral agents so that they can strengthen the basic communities as they read the Bible from the perspective of the life issues of the people, relate their hopes to the promises of the gospel, and engage in concrete joint action with the wider human community. The Centre organizes periodic Bible courses according to the capabilities and conditions of the various groups of pastoral agents within the limitations of its own small, part-time staff. This programme is strikingly different from most theological institutions, but that in itself is an important lesson which some theological institutions may be willing to learn, particularly as they face growing doubts about the viability of their present structures and about the adequacy of their present programmes.

2. Another central goal of theological education by extension must be to enable the church to understand and carry out holistic ministry. The biblical concept of salvation clearly includes physical, emotional, and social as well as spiritual health or wholeness. Christian congregations are called to be caring, healing communities. New approaches to primary health care, which are of great importance to people in all parts of the world, require a base of support such as these congregations can provide and local health promoters who understand and are accepted by their people. On the basis of wide experience of primary health care systems and exposure to theological education by extension, Ronald and Edith Seaton have proposed a comprehensive strategy for the mobilization of the world's health resources in the book *Here's How: Health Education by Extension* (1976). They are now engaged in training local pastors and congregational leaders in India for holistic ministry, and a course on community health has been added to the curriculum of the Association for Theological Education by Extension (TAFTEE), which now has thousands of students scattered around that sub-continent. The potential of this development, if it were taken up by TEE programmes around the world, is difficult to imagine — both for the health of millions of people and for the health of the churches themselves.

3. A third major goal of theological education by extension during this decade must be to equip the church for the ministry of liberation, justice and development in each local and national context. Union Seminary in the Philippines initiated its extension programme in 1975 with this very goal: to provide theological education for the many church workers, including the majority of the pastors, who had not received seminary training; to prepare them "for leadership in the ministry of liberation, justice, and development in the context of Philippine society". The basic components are the self-directed study module, which enables students to carry out autonomous individual study, and the self-propelled study group module, which serves as a laboratory for group learning and as a source of mutual support for the individual study programme. Both components are built on the assumption that people can educate themselves and have the right to develop according to their convictions as God has called them to serve in the world. Church workers must go through this process of liberation, experiencing the gifts of their humanity in God's creation, in order to lead the church in its ministry of liberation. The first curriculum area, called "The contemporary world", provides tools of

research and social analysis to study the world in microcosm (the local community) and in macrocosm (the nation and the world). The second area, "The Christian tradition", makes use of the Bible, doctrine, the social creeds of the church, and lessons from history in order to reflect on the conditions of people in their local and national contexts, to understand the will of God, and to consider what the Christian community can do in bringing about God's will. The third area of the curriculum, "The Christian vocation", provides learning experiences for church workers to gain skills and deeper commitment to Christian service as they go into action in the world. The 701 extension students scattered around the great Philippine archipelago are beginning to discover with their congregations and communities deeper and wider dimensions of the gospel as they struggle for a just and sustainable society in the midst of widespread poverty, exploitation, and oppression.

Conclusion

The reports that follow in this book provide some of the flesh and blood of the extension movement as it is now developing in all the regions, among most of the church families, within many different cultural contexts. Any assessment of its significance must attempt to weigh these initial efforts, most of them less than ten years old, over against the gospel mandates and global realities, and also to project the goals and experience of these programmes into the future.

It is difficult to imagine what the extension movement will look like even ten years from now. In China, for example, it is reported that 32,290 Christians, most of them members and leaders of house churches, are now enrolled in correspondence programmes and training seminars. The basic ecclesial communities, which have already provided a deeply Christian conscience and a popular base for revolutionary movements in Central America, may play a similar role in other parts of Latin America. The African Independent churches and the mission-founded churches in Africa have only begun to adopt extension training methods for their own needs and to share their dynamism with the wider church. The churches of Europe and North America are beginning to recognize the non-viability of inherited patterns of ministry, church life, and theological education and to experiment with alternatives. In all the regions it must be said that the churches and their theological institutions have just begun to explore the possibilities of theological education by extension and to direct some of their vast but all too narrowly conceived theological and educational resources in this direction.

To say that theological education by extension has come of age is not only to recognize the rapid growth and acceptance it has experienced in recent years, but also to place upon it heavy responsibilities for the years to come. These responsibilities must be defined in terms not only of the church but of the kingdom of God. The challenge of the extension movement is to take up the mission that Jesus pursued and that the world of the 1980s requires — *to prepare all God's people for the work of Christian service* (Eph. 4:12).

Latin America and the Caribbean

Presbyterian Seminary of Guatemala

A modest experiment
becomes a model for change

KENNETH B. MULHOLLAND (and Nelly de Jacobs)

Theological education by extension began in 1963 at the Evangelical Presbyterian Seminary of Guatemala as a modest experiment. It did not result from the implementation of a carefully predesigned theoretical model with a fully developed theology of ministry or philosophy of education, but rather in response to the needs of a church faithfully engaged in mission in an obscure corner of a small Central American republic.

It is the contention of both this writer and of the late Prof. Nelly de Jacobs that theological education by extension is truest to its original intent when it is seen as a renewal movement aimed at the integral growth of the church through ministry by the whole people of God. As such, theological education by extension is a change agent capable of promoting the positive transformation of both church and society. This is not to deny the distinction between clergy and laity, nor the need to "equip the equippers". It is simply to affirm the essential oneness of God's people in their common calling.

• Kenneth B. Mulholland, currently Professor of Missions and Pastoral Studies at Columbia Graduate School of Bible and Missions, was previously Rector of the Theological Institute of the Evangelical and Reformed Church in Honduras and Dean of extension ministries at the Latin American Biblical Seminary in Costa Rica. During 1977 he was Visiting Professor at the Presbyterian Seminary in Guatemala. Nelly de Jacobs was Secretary and Professor at the PSG, Editor of the quarterly newsletter *Extension Seminary,* and Director of the Guatemala Centre for Studies in Theological Education and Ministry, when she was tragically killed in a road accident on 18 September 1981. She was planning to write this article on the basis of her unfinished thesis, which was being supervised by Prof. Mulholland for presentation at the LABS. The address of the Seminary is Apartado 3, San Felipe Reu., Guatemala.

The Presbyterian Church of Guatemala was founded in 1882 by missionaries who entered the country in response to an invitation extended by president Justo Rufino Barrios. Throughout most of the succeeding century work was confined to a 100 × 300 mile rectangle in the southwestern quadrant of that nation. In this zone, which includes both steaming tropical plains and cold, windswept highlands, one finds the entire spectrum of Guatemalan society: urban professionals, the rising middle-class, rural Latins, both progressive and isolated Indian tribes.

Steps in the process of change

Theological education by extension took shape in the Presbyterian Seminary as a series of responses to a series of problems encountered in the task of ministerial formation among the sectors of society represented in the Presbyterian Church.

Problem: The numerical growth of the church led to the need for trained national leadership.

Solution: In 1938, a seminary was founded in Guatemala City, the nation's capital, to train leadership for the entire denomination.

Problem: Most of the graduates trained by the Seminary either never entered the specific ministry for which they were trained or else left it in order to enter non-church related occupations. In fact, a 1962 inventory disclosed that after 25 years, only ten of the more than 200 students who had enrolled in the seminary were still functioning as pastors. Once accustomed to urban life, many students of rural background did not return to the agriculturally rich, but unhealthy and economically depressed areas from which they had come.

Solution: In 1962 the Seminary was moved from the capital city to a rural area closer to the majority of churches and more geographically accessible to the leaders of local congregations. By now the denomination numbered 10,000 communicant members with a total community estimated between 30,000 and 40,000 members. A network of 65 organized congregations included ten in the major cities of Quezaltenango and Guatemala City. In addition there were 140 unorganized preaching points.

Problem: The genuine leaders in the rural areas could not go even a few miles to attend a residence programme because of job and family responsibilities.

Solution: In 1963, the seminary leaders took the daring step of minimizing the residence programme in order to begin an extension system. They organized several regional centres located so that nearly all who desired could attend. These professors met for a three-hour seminar each week with students. The seminary paid student travel expenses. Periodically during the school year, once a month at first, meetings were held at the central campus for all the students from all the centres. Thus, the extension movement was born.

Problem: "Take home" studies used by the extension students included lengthy reading assignments. These, however, were simply not being digested, especially by the less academically oriented rural students.

Solution: To meet this challenge, the faculty developed a series of workbooks utilizing inductive methology for the study of the Bible and traditional theological textbooks. They geared them especially for individual study. As time passed elements of programmed instruction and open education were incorporated into the programme.

Problem: Immense diversity in the educational and socioeconomic levels of the students was evident. Persons of equally keen leadership and spiritual qualifications possessed radically different cultural heritages, social levels, and academic backgrounds.

Solution: The very flexibility of a decentralized pattern allowed "breathing space" for multi-cultural and multi-social diversity. However, academic differences made it necessary to build a multi-level structure into the curriculum design itself. This enabled students to build their theological studies upon the highest level of secular education previously attained, whether at the level of primary, secondary or university education. Thus, while all students covered the same basic assignments together, the more advanced students were expected to go "a second and third mile" in reading assignments, reports and projects.

Problem: Particularly in the rural areas, many gifted leaders with innate intelligence had such meagre academic training that they could not even do the sixth-grade-level work required for the most basic courses.

Solution: To meet this need for "pre-theological education", a second extension programme was established on a nationwide basis to help not only prospective seminary candidates but also other interested persons complete their primary schooling and receive their government-recognized primary school diploma. With the passing of time, similar government programmes have been initiated making this second system unnecessary.

Nearly all of the above steps met with opposition from one segment or another of the Presbyterian Church of Guatemala. However, by 1966, not only had a coherent extension programme emerged, but it was beginning to attract continent-wide attention. With no increase in funds, the student body of the Presbyterian Seminary had increased from 7 to 200 taught by 3 full-time and 12 part-time faculty members. And many of the evident needs of the churches were being met.

By training persons where they lived, the seminary was able to reach into various sub-cultures without uprooting persons from their environments. Thus, it was able to enlist and equip for ministry those persons best suited and gifted for such ministry. The extension study proved more difficult than expected, because it placed a great demand for personal discipline on the student, yet it also proved to be valuable as a vast screening process. It filtered out unequipped or unmotivated candidates without exposing them to the trauma of re-entry into their previous environment. Although the average age of the student body climbed into the thirties, the number of younger students also increased. The quality of academic work improved over that of the residence programme, due largely to the greater maturity of students and the consistency resulting from the development of life-long personal study habits. In addition, a full theological education was made available to many lay leaders in the congregations who wanted to deepen their faith and understanding without committing themselves to candidacy for ordination.

The Guatemalan model had now assumed definitive form: self-instructional home-study materials for daily preparations, decentralized weekly seminars of students and teachers, periodic extended meetings at a central location of students from any or all centres.

As the extension movement developed beyond its Guatemalan base, too often it was promoted as a set formula. The product was elevated and the process was ignored. Too often a clone of the creature born in Guatemala was adopted as a panacea for the ills of theological education.

New challenges

Meanwhile in Guatemala, the next decade was one of consolidation, "plateauing", even stagnation. The time and energy of the missionary and national personnel who had produced a major breakthrough were absorbed in editing and producing the quarterly

Extension Seminary, writing numerous articles expounding and defending TEE, leading many workshops around the world, directing a training programme for Latin American theological educators on the site of the Guatemalan campus. Needed developments were postponed. Few additional professors were trained specifically for the Presbyterian Seminary. As a result too much of the teaching remained in the hands of overworked expatriate missionary personnel and their national colleagues. They were forced to range over wide areas to cover their centres each week. The needed revision of courses hurriedly constructed in the early and mid-1960s was put off for lack of time. Often the printing date for new or revised courses was set back for lack of time to do final editing or proofreading. The incorporation of Indian leaders with limited Spanish language fluency into the seminary programme was also delayed and serious re-thinking of the place of residence education within the Presbyterian Church was resisted.

In the mid-1970s, the administration and faculty faced squarely a number of issues:

1. *Adjunct professors:* The geographical expansion of the Presbyterian Church, which generated the need for increasingly far-flung centres, and the world energy crisis, which made the cost of servicing those centres formidable, combined to bring about the expansion of the teaching staff to include adjunct professors. These are teachers, certified by the seminary, who teach a course or two in the areas in which they live. Many are pastors of local congregations who have graduated from the seminary. As teaching elders (in the Presbyterian tradition) they receive no economic remuneration for teaching in one centre, but are paid if they tend a second centre. These adjunct professors are trained and supervised by the full-time staff of the seminary. Their incorporation into the extension programme has allowed the seminary enrolment nearly to double and brought the training programme into even closer conjunction with the churches at the grassroots level.

2. *Additional extension:* Although extension did succeed in incorporating "Spanish-fluent" Indians into the seminary programme, it excluded not only those without a primary education, but also those with limited Spanish fluency. Finally, a process was devised in 1975 to meet this problem. An extension programme for Mam-speaking Indian leaders was developed. With the help of a specially devised Mam-Spanish theological glossary, the Indian leaders studied the

famous six-volume SEAN compendium of pastoral theology based on the life of Jesus in the Gospel of St Matthew. While lessons were prepared in Spanish, the seminar meetings were conducted in the Mam language. Completion of the entire course led to a certificate and met the academic qualifications for ordination set by the newly formed Mam Presbytery. In addition, the certificate was recognized by the seminary as equivalent to five of the fifteen courses required for graduation. Now Indian leaders had access to theological training which incorporated them into the mainstream of ecclesiastical and national life.

3. *Accelerated advancement:* While theological education by extension did extend the resources of theological education to the people, at the same time it usually extended the time necessary to complete the requirements for a diploma or degree. Slower assimilation of content coupled with more immediate application probably provided more efficient education and effective ministry. However, the expanded length of time needed to complete the total course sequence also produced impatience, frustration, and even discouragement, particularly to those who were candidates for ordination vows. To meet this problem, intensive courses are offered at the seminary campus or even occasionally in strategic urban centres. This allows students to be exposed to visiting or guest professors, thus broadening the horizons of the students who, because of their rootedness, may be in danger of parochialism. Students are also permitted to study in residence at the seminary campus. This has always been true, but until recently no money was available from the synod to subsidize students. Recently, the emphasis on residence study has intensified as a concentrated effort has been made to accelerate the education of selected students by subsidizing their full-time study.

Ideological issues

The original purpose of extension was the training of mature leaders for ministry in the growing but scattered Presbyterian congregations of Guatemala. With the passing of time, it became apparent that TEE carried powerful side effects of a liberating nature. Prof. Jacobs maintained that TEE has demonstrated that it is not only a vehicle for leadership development and the subsequent growth of existing church structures, but that it is also a vehicle for the renewal and beneficial change of both ecclesiastical and social structures.

First, in regard to educational methodology, TEE tends to free students from intellectual domestication. Rather than limiting the student to the role of a passive receptacle of information imparted by an authoritative teacher, it permits and encourages active participation and stimulates theological reflection on the part of each student. "There is communication and the interchange of ideas in which each person both learns and contributes new knowledge" wrote Prof. Jacobs. The very fact that TEE opens theological education to students who are actively involved in ministry transforms many centres into gatherings of colleagues in ministry. Each of them, with roots deep in the social reality of Guatemala, has something unique and valuable to contribute to the others.

Second, in regard to theological content, TEE tends towards a holistic approach. It overcomes the dichotomy that results when the categories of traditional evangelical pietism are divorced from concrete, earthly realities. Prof. Jacobs pointed out that TEE keeps students in contact with "people in their misery". In fact, many of the students themselves are immersed in the poverty and are victims of the oppression that racks Guatemala. They also adhere to traditional evangelical theology. "We are not saying that we ought to discard spiritual, abstract, traditional language in order to be mastered by a purely material language" wrote Prof. Jacobs. "No, what we want to say is that TEE does not divorce these two factors, rather, it combines them." She argued that it was impossible for the Christian to become involved with the concrete material reality of people in their misery without being aware of the nature of neighbour love. It is dynamically spiritual in its origin, yet expresses itself in specific action. She writes:

> It is impossible to speak of the multiple problems of people in their misery — their hunger, their sickness — without need of a gigantic faith, that although abstract, is capable of saying to this mountain "Be taken up and cast into the sea" (Matt. 17:20) ... and it is impossible to speak of service, to struggle against earthly evils, without believing in the existence of a just and all-powerful God, who is ready to execute the promise of liberation and capable of sending plagues to do it.

TEE is also an agent of change in that it challenges the divisions that splinter and compartmentalize the people of God. Two of these divisions, in particular, are being confronted by TEE in Guatemala.

First, the geographical extension to communities where actual and potential church leaders live has opened theological education to many married women, active in Sunday school teaching and women's societies, but previously unable to attend the residence school because of family responsibilities. Married women had usually only studied if their husbands were enrolled full-time as residence students. TEE has produced a flowering of increasingly capable female leadership in a denomination that excludes women from ordination as elders or pastors, while at the same time allowing them to teach in the denomination's theological schools.

Second, TEE has opened up theological education to the laity. In fact, about 80% of the students thus far have not been candidates for ordination. Thus, those who have been ordained have been educated not in isolation from the lay leaders of their church, but among them. This has lessened the distance between clergy and laity, activated the laity, and made the candidates for ordination intensely aware of the issues faced by lay persons. Recently the president of the board of the seminary, a distinguished elder and prominent local businessman, became an extension student.

Continuing tensions

Reviewing the impact of the extension movement on the Presbyterian Church in Guatemala, it is apparent that it has succeeded in its initial goal. It has produced trained leaders for large numbers of congregations previously lacking such leadership and in so doing has accelerated the numerical growth, cultural extension, and geographical expansion of the church. It has enriched the lives of countless persons. It has provided a model for a worldwide movement.

At the same time, because TEE has been an agent for change, it has created tensions within its own denomination. Instead of simply strengthening the educational, theological, and structural *status quo,* it has called that *status quo* into question at those points where it is a hindrance to ministry by the people.

1. The educational methodology has produced a dialogical and collegial style of leadership that questions the efficacy of authoritarian and hierarchical leadership patterns.

2. The interaction of evangelical pietism with the concrete realities of the Guatemalan situation, as the students experience it, has brought into focus new concerns: the meaning of God's justice and

righteousness; the nature of salvation as liberation; the apolitical stance of the church amid pervasive corruption and violence; the place of human rights in the witness of the church; faith and ideology; the relationship of church and kingdom; the ordination of women; historic Presbyterianism vis-à-vis renewed Roman Catholicism and maturing Pentecostalism. More traditional sectors of the church remain unready to grapple with these concerns, and at times unwilling.

3. The extension of theological education to minority groups, women and laity has raised the competency level of these persons to the point where they constitute a threat to the automatic passive acceptance of the pronouncements handed down by theologically trained males of the predominant socio-cultural group within the church leadership.

At the time of writing the extension movement within the Presbyterian Church stands in jeopardy. The ascendancy of parochial and rigid traditionalists to denominational leadership threatens the existence of theological education by extension at the very seminary which gave it birth. The new wine of TEE has stretched old skins to the point where they can be kept from bursting only by setting them in cement. The loss of leadership to death, transfer, and retirement, plus the change of other strategic leadership posts at national and international levels weakens the vanguard role that the seminary has traditionally assumed. Cruel warfare between a repressive, military-dominated government and popular, liberation movements plays havoc with the coordination of transportation and communication systems upon which TEE depends. A deteriorating economy drives up the prices of paper, books and gasoline while diminishing the power of the church and its students to support a far-reaching extension system.

It has been characteristic of the leadership of the Presbyterian Seminary to find new and creative solutions to pressing problems. Those solutions have been an incalculable blessing to the world Christian movement. Once again the challenge is before them.

Study by Extension for All Nations

Passing on the faith

MICHAEL CROWLEY

"You know that every year the numbers of people are increasing; the churches need help. Above all they need teaching at a higher educational level. Before the people had no education at all; now it is different, with many of the people being educated in the schools and needing Bible teaching at this level." So wrote Mario L. Marino, a Mataco Indian, Anglican bishop of the Mataco people of northern Argentina. No doubt church leaders all over the world would share a similar concern for the teaching needs of their churches. An extension programme under the strange name of SEAN has attempted to do something about this in Latin America.

The name SEAN is taken from the third person plural of the Spanish verb "to be" found in 2 Timothy 2:2, where the instruction is given to Timothy to hand on the apostle's teaching to faithful people who will in turn be able to teach others. The choosing of the name and text by the initial group of extension writers highlighted their intention of doing something about the teaching and mobilizing of Christians in the local churches of the southern cone of South America. The project was born in 1971 when the then Anglican bishop of northern Argentina asked missionary Anthony Barratt to set up an extension programme to teach the churches. Conveniently,

• Michael P. S. Crowley, a UK missionary of the South American Missionary Society, is a newcomer to the SEAN staff. The Latin American address of SEAN is: Casilla 561, Viña del Mar, Chile. The international office of SEAN is at Allen Gardiner House, Pembury Road, Tunbridge Wells, Kent TN2 3QU, United Kingdom.

the word SEAN also served as a title for this Anglican extension programme (Seminario por Extension Anglicano). The interdenominational and international character of the programme soon brought about a third meaning for the name: Study by Extension for All Nations!
Based in Tucumán, Argentina, Anthony Barratt set about the task with characteristic enthusiasm, pulled together a small group of course writers, and began to write. Ten years later the achievements and possibilities of this ministry evoke praise and hope. What began so modestly in the hot suburbs of a city in northern Argentina is now being used in many parts of the world. SEAN texts find acceptance because they conform to the demands of extension programmes that train Christians within their workaday situations in a way which is economical, adaptable, and expandable.

Church leaders and pastors in Latin America
The number of Protestant pastors in Latin America is conservatively estimated at 100,000, of whom only 20 per cent have received formal theological training. The vast majority have received less than a full secondary education and must cope with the challenges of the church in Latin America in the last quarter of the twentieth century.
The 400 or so Latin American Bible institutes and seminaries are totally inadequate to meet existing training needs. Most pastors are mature family men who are restricted by inadequate education, social immobility, and lack of financial resources, but they have emerged as spiritual leaders in their churches. Conversely, the young, single seminarian is often not acceptable to a local congregation, even if he is willing to devote himself to Christ's humble service there. These salient facts have been accepted by many people concerned with theological training in Latin America. The question now is not the suitability of theological education by extension but whether the right extension programmes exist.
The growth of SEAN with limited financial resources and personnel was not so much due to missionary endeavour, but rather to the grassroots acceptance of the courses produced and their utilization under local initiative. Over the ten-year period of SEAN in Argentina, its programmes were adopted by all the mainstream denominations for use in training their members. Extension programmes cannot be imposed on the churches. Good texts, well tested, written in a local situation or with a particular local need in mind, will prove their

worth by local success. For example, a six-book compendium based on St Matthew's Gospel aims to teach each student the following:
— a thorough knowledge of the life and ministry of Christ in its historical, social and political setting;
— an analysis of the Gospel of St Matthew and its relationship with the other gospels;
— a grounding in the fundamentals of the Old Testament and how it relates to the coming of Christ and his ministry;
— the techniques of simple Bible text analysis, so students can tackle the scriptures in personal study;
— an outline of systematic theology;
— an appreciation of the teachings of mainstream Christianity and the teachings of sects that the students are likely to encounter;
— techniques of study, thinking and application (often not learnt in previous education);
— practical and pastoral theology with special emphasis on the ministry in the local church — Bible study (personal and private), worship and liturgy, preparation of simple sermons/messages, evangelism (personal and team).

Students normally undertake the study of two books a year, with exam and evaluation at the end of each book. Completion of each book provides an opportunity for all the local groups and congregations to meet for evaluation and fellowship. Certificates are awarded, and most conscientious students are congratulated!

A local programme in Viña del Mar, Chile, using the St Matthew Compendium

SEAN set up in 1980 an extension programme for the Anglican churches in the Valparaiso-Viña del Mar region of Chile, beginning with a series of evening classes for the local Christians who would be tutors for their study groups. The tutor course does not assume teaching skills or academic achievement on the part of the would-be tutors. The manual "How to be a tutor" leads the tutor carefully through each study group session, encouraging him or her to create an atmosphere where each student can participate and share experiences related to the lessons studied.

The extension programme started with eight participating churches and 100 students. During 1980 they completed books one and two of the "Compendium of Pastoral Theology", nearly all of them achieving 90 per cent marks in the assessment exams.

Enthusiasm was high, and these students have gone on to books three and four. New groups are studying books one and two. The aim of having a continuous flow of Christians training in the churches is becoming a reality. The tutors are gaining in confidence and learning first-hand the skills of group dynamics. This local programme has benefited the churches enormously, and it has also provided a working model for other regions and dioceses of the Anglican church.

This model of a local extension programme has previously been used in other Latin American republics. One Pentecostal extension seminary in Argentina enrolled 1,200 students in 1980, and 75 per cent have already completed the full SEAN basic course of six books. This programme, normally called "the Matthew course", has proved to be acceptable among seminary and Bible training centres of the Presbyterian, Baptist, Anglican, Pentecostal and Lutheran churches throughout Latin America.

A programme at intermediate level

With the move of the SEAN team from Tucumán, Argentina, to Viña del Mar, Chile, in 1980 a providential meeting of forces came about. The team discovered that a group of Anglican pastors and leaders were using, as part of their theological training, texts supplied by Logoi, which is an international, interdenominational group committed to improving the theological resources and training of pastors in Latin America. Logoi has built up an enrolment of 2,000 students who participate in the programme by studying and sitting an exam on each of the texts provided. Unfortunately, most of the pastors, being unused to academic study, found this beyond their capabilities.

The SEAN team, thinking primarily of local pastors in the Valparíso-Viña area of Chile, set about writing semi-programmed study guides to help the students through their texts and prepare for the exams. These guides proved to be of enormous benefit, as they not only guided the students through the texts but began to teach the pastors how to read efficiently and break down complex material in their training. After the local success of these guides, Logoi asked if all the participating pastors in Latin America could use them. This was readily agreed to and the guides became an integral part of the SEAN/Logoi Programme.

This development fits in with the plans SEAN had for the development of their extension programme on an intermediate level.

Students having completed a basic Bible course (like the SEAN Abundant Life Course) and the six-book pastoral theology are now able to go on to the SEAN/Logoi Programme, which upon completion will prepare them up to university level for ministry in the church. Further advanced studies for capable students are planned to take them to degree level in theology.

The present scheme of study covers all important areas of theology and pastoral studies: Old and New Testament, systemic theology, biblical exegesis and commentary, church history, pastoral counselling and psychology. During the three-year period of the programme each student will receive over 40 texts, providing vital resources for ministry in Latin America, where education standards are rising. The programme involves about five hours of home study and a weekly tutorial for assessment and discussion. The weekly tutorial is also an opportunity for visiting theological teachers to elaborate on the theme of study. In many areas such people do not exist, but future plans may involve the use of tapes whereby theological instructors/pastors can reinforce the students' work.

Literacy

From the very beginning SEAN has been concerned to meet the students at their own cultural and conceptual level and to raise that level gradually through the programme. Illiteracy is still a problem. Where a church member is motivated to learn but handicapped by illiteracy, the use of the simple Alfalit Course from Costa Rica has proved to be an ideal starting point for an integrated literacy/theological programme. In Argentina, motivated students have progressed from illiteracy to a fifth-grade basic educational level by the use of existing courses. It is hoped and planned that an adequate literacy programme will be a vital part of SEAN, so that no church member will be prevented from advancing educationally and in the knowledge of faith. Those who are already experienced in the use of the SEAN texts and tutorials will thus be able to provide a literacy programme in their own churches, where such is needed.

St Paul course

There was a need to provide an additional programme for students who have completed their basic orientation (the Abundant Life Course) but who are not ready to start the St Matthew course. With this in mind the team has completed the first half of a programmed course on the life of St Paul. Using new techniques and visual presentation, the programmed text hopes to reach thousands of Christians whose reading and writing skills are limited. The first part of this elementary but very stimulating course deals with St Paul's life up to the Jerusalem Council in Acts 15. Students complete the programmed studies on the major events in Paul's life at home. In the weekly tutorial they study in depth Paul's letter to the Galatians. In addition a visual commentary will present their increasing knowledge of Paul's life and Gospel in a vivid way.

The second part of the course will cover the remainder of Paul's life and his mission in the Roman world, his experience of Christ, and his relationship with his churches. The tutorials will draw out the central ideas in his teaching and relate them to the students' own society and environment.

The entire course will be covered in six to nine months after an initial literacy programme, if necessary, and the completion of the Abundant Life Course. The successful completion of these courses will give students adequate preparation and background for starting the St Matthew pastoral theology programme.

Courses in evangelism

In response to the great need for teaching and instruction in methods of evangelism SEAN is encouraging the use of a new, visual approach to Christian witness and proclamation of the gospel. Courses have been run in Santiago and Viña del Mar to train local pastors and leaders in evangelism so they in turn can help train their congregations. The trainees learn simple techniques of visual, dramatic or musical presentation of the gospel in an open air situation and then utilize small teams of supporting church members to discuss the implications of the presentation with interested people who have stopped to listen. The results have been encouraging, and the SEAN team hope this model can be developed as an integral part of the extension programme.

Additional materials

The Abundant Life Course, originally published in Argentina in the early 1970s, provides 18 programmed lessons for new believers. It teaches about the new birth and relationship of the believer with Christ, the reality of the body of Christ and its responsibilities. It thus provides training for total church membership. It is used successfully in rural and suburban areas among people with limited formal education and also with university students. The text is accompanied by a counsellor's manual, so local church leaders are able to use it for the training and teaching of new believers.

A programmed tutors' training course was designed to train tutors of the St Matthew Compendium as they guide their tutorial groups through the first book of the Compendium. This on-the-job method makes the training as realistic as could be desired. More experienced tutors can observe and assist if necessary, but it is not essential. The tutor of the group is not a teacher or instructor but the person who provides the momentum and atmosphere for the whole group to participate in discussion.

"How to Preach", a three-month, programmed course with a detailed tutor's manual, teaches helpful skills for competent preaching in the local church. Students who have completed a course like the St Matthew Compendium do not lack material for preaching. The aim of the course is to mobilize local members in the ministry of teaching and preaching in services and evangelism.

"How to Lead a Meeting" is a companion text to the preacher's course. It aims to equip more church members competently to lead services and meetings in the local church and to encourage more active and disciplined participation in the church by all who are gifted to assist in leadership and worship.

The production and use of SEAN courses

The SEAN writing centre in Viña del Mar does not have the latest figures for the number of churches and students using SEAN materials, but at a conservative estimate 30,000 students have completed at least book one of the St Matthew course.

The production and distribution of all the SEAN courses is separate from the writing and testing of the courses. Formerly the centre in Tucumán, Argentina, was the base for writing, drawing on writers from other parts of Argentina, Paraguay and Chile. With the move in 1980 to Viña del Mar the whole of the production of the SEAN courses was given over to an interdenominational commission of Alliance, Mennonite/Pentecostal, Anglican and Baptist churches who produce and supply all participating churches in Chile. In each country a similar commission is responsible for this work, thus freeing the central team for the writing and testing of new courses. This arrangement has proved very satisfactory. Each commission agrees to pay SEAN 10 per cent cooperation fees, which are used for the writing of new courses.

The SEAN method and team

The method of writing has always involved the submission of ideas and texts to the team for scrutiny and change where necessary. Courses have often been produced amidst local problems, shortage of personnel, lack of secretarial help, and limited funds, but well-researched and well-written texts have emerged from these makeshift conditions, which adds to their authenticity. Prepared with sound programming principles, the texts have been tested repeatedly to make sure they are as clear and effective as possible. Knowing that many students lack education opportunities and are trying to study in difficult social conditions, all those involved in writing SEAN texts are motivated to refine their skills. Their enthusiasm is fuelled by their experience of local conditions in a way that immunity and isolation from the local situation could never have produced.

The group of team writers involved in producing the St Matthew course in Tucumán collectively possessed over 100 years of experience in the local church as well as extensive pastoral, educational and theological experience. Extension ministry must be an amalgam of educational and theological insight tempered by local understanding and experience. Such a combination of skills is hard to find. Each writer is expected to know the local needs and have sufficient training to mould any curriculum to the real situations of their students. SEAN has been committed not only to the teaching of theological concepts but to the vital task of developing and enlarging the capacities of the students to learn, evaluate and relate such concepts to their situations. SEAN holds strongly to the proposition that scripture *is* vitally relevant; our task is to make sure the truth of the revelation we seek to teach is directed to the context of the students' life and experience.

No one writes outside the team. All efforts are monitored by the others in the team; each course is a team effort, resulting from pooled ideas and experience. Often courses have been written by several writers corresponding between Latin American countries. This is not always ideal, but it does allow the use of writing skills scattered geographically to be pooled in the production of a course.

It has to be said that preparing courses involves a great deal of application and dedication. All SEAN course writers have been actively involved in ministry in the local church whilst contributing to the SEAN programme. It is essential that course writers be involved in and draw on experience from the local church situation while setting aside adequate time for preparation and research. SEAN has always depended upon a central, experienced team (whether or not located in one area), devoted to course writing and preparation and assisted by others who are able to contribute as time permits.

SEAN International

The international interest in the SEAN programmes continues to increase. Having proved their worth in Latin America, they have been able to fill the needs of theological extension in other areas of the world where educational and financial resources are limited. The St Matthew Compendium is being used in the USA, Canada, Great Britain and Indonesia. At the time of writing its greatest potential is with the TAFTEE extension programme in India. Translated and reworked in nine Indian languages, these programmed courses will be a contribution by the Latin American churches to their brothers and sisters in India. The course is also being translated for use in Nepal, the Republic of Gabon, and Zululand in South Africa. More recently plans are going ahead to translate and transculturalize SEAN texts for use in Eastern Europe in six languages, including Russian.

With the growing international use of SEAN texts there has been an increasing need to coordinate and facilitate their use. It has proved difficult to direct and monitor such international interest from a provincial town in South America, and there has been a growing awareness that a basic English text of all the SEAN courses is needed that can be used for translation and transculturalization. With these points in mind it has been decided to try to set up a SEAN International Commission, based in the United Kingdom, to be responsible for the international/interdenominational use of the SEAN texts and for the writing and testing of future basic English texts. There will continue to be close liaison with this commission and the SEAN/Logoi writing ministry based in Chile. Using the techniques and methods proven in the southern cone of South America, both centres will interchange material and experience to further the advance of this extension ministry worldwide. SEAN International will not develop into a promotion ministry but will try to serve the church by responding to local needs, helping to set up local programmes, explaining the use of the texts, and endeavouring to write and test new materials when no suitable texts are available.

Some may question the advisability of translating and transculturalizing programmed texts. One of the SEAN conditions for translation rights is that the edition in the new language be thoroughly retested and reculturalized. When this is done properly, as we found in the case of the St Matthew Compendium, 90 per cent of the students are able to achieve 90 per cent of the objectives, i. e. the same as for the original Spanish edition. A second point in favour of the international use of the SEAN texts is that the courses concentrate on the text of the Bible, leaving the application open-ended, to be discussed in the weekly group meetings. This also means that the texts are suitable for all denominations, and no denominational bias is written into the courses, whatever the personal views of the writers.

Extension Bible Institute (Northern Honduras)

Theological education and evangelism by extension

GEORGE PATTERSON

Pastoral education on a poverty level

In the mid-1960s the Conservative Baptist Home Mission Society operated a resident Bible Institute hoping to train pastors who could spark growing, reproducing churches in our northern Honduras field. We suffered the traditional problems, for the traditional reasons. Single young students would leave the arduous physical work of their poor villages, to live in clean rooms, gain weight on a wholesome, worm-free diet, discover books, wear shoes and clean clothes, and enjoy the prestige of "preaching". They refused to return to the poverty of the villages, which desperately needed pastors. We made it a "requirement" to go, but they still didn't pastor in the biblical sense; they only preached, making "hearers only". Their newly acquired urban mentality despised their poor country brothers' stammered scripture reading, spontaneous shouting and discussion during worship, pigs sleeping under the pews, toothless song leaders slurring through their own "home-made" hymns. They dreamed only of big city churches or secular jobs with regular salaries or a post with the mission and a chance to go to the USA.

We needed an alternative, a training programme that would result in new churches. We proposed TEE (theological education by exten-

---

• The Rev. George Patterson, a US missionary, is the founder and Director of the Extension Bible Institute, Apartado 164, La Ceiba, Honduras. His TEE methology has spread to all continents, and his comic-book texts are used throughout Latin America. For further information read his *Church Planting through Obedience Oriented Education,* William Carey Library, 1705 N. Sierra Bonita Avenue, Pasadena, California 91104, USA.

sion). A sharp controversy resulted; the resident graduates refused to cooperate with an extension programme; the missionaries were divided. I remember asking myself: "With whom will I work? With someone like José, who is educated but will work only where he can get a good salary, within the restricted confines of our own crippling traditions? Or with someone like Armando, who is teaching himself to read? He is crude, but open to new methods." I chose Armando and alienated the majority of our former pastors. The leaders of the national association of churches determined publicly to put an end to our "modernistic doctrine" and began separating the churches from fellowship with us. After a hurricane of criticism and tears had passed, only three tiny rural churches remained loyal.

Due to years of "raising the standard of pastoral education" in Latin America *no* theological textbooks existed on the level of those people whom God had given us. We wrote feverishly. We "programmed" self-study texts painstakingly. No one studied them. "Too hard!" What could they read, people from a town with *no* books, *no* newspapers, and *no* magazines? For them, reading was a tedious punishment, like crawling to a saint on your knees with a candle. One day in the train I noticed that they *were* reading something. Photonovels! We started writing comic book texts, pocket-sized so the people (who needed glasses and had no electricity) could carry them while they worked during the day. Little by little, they began to read. We kept the texts *short*. Each person proceeded at his own pace. Older, family people began to study.

Integrating education and evangelism

Our basic curriculum, out of sheer necessity, took the form of a congregation progress chart, a check list of the activities ordered for a church by the Lord Jesus Christ and his apostles. The essential elements of traditional pastoral courses were brought in only where they contributed to a church's obedience to these commands. This stripped the course of all non-essentials. Every unit had two parallel rails: the word and the work, the doctrine and the dúty, the theory and the practice, the blueprint and the building. Every student leaves the extension class with a form entitled "Plans". The teacher jots assignments on it for both tracks — studies to read and work to do — and keeps a carbon copy to verify work done at the next meeting.

Given our mission objective—to start many village churches— our greatest need was to train people to witness effectively for Christ on a personal basis. We provided simple studies on the life, teaching, death and resurrection of Christ, with good response. But the new growth provoked a reaction; many preferred an outside evangelist for "special meetings" to the hard work of personal evangelism. We heard the angry protest: "But they're not really saved unless they raise their hand and go forward!" They had made this US decision-getting rite into a rigid sacrament necessary to salvation. One church had developed a course of studies for its members to teach their friends at home, with such good results that it soon became our largest church. But then it fell into the trap, called a professional revivalist for special meetings, and discontinued personal evangelism. They got a lot of "decisions", but soon attendance dropped to two families. We pumped a lot of doctrine about Christ and the gospels into the curriculum; they resurrected their courses for non-believers and soon were growing rapidly again, only to continue repeating the cycle over the years.

Campus Crusade came with a lot of money to teach our men to get "decisions". They got a lot of decisions but made no disciples. It took months to teach our men the difference. To help the churches to grow again, we injected heavy doses of the doctrine of salvation into the curriculum, not to teach it simply for the love of theology but to erase the imported pattern of evangelism.

Relating education to a local church

As Baptists, we couldn't consider a congregation as an obedient church until its members were baptized. So we gave the assignment to the students: Baptize! A bomb exploded. They were baptizing people who were not legally married. Virtually no couples in our poor villages are legally married; many cannot legalize their common-law marriage for lack of a birth certificate.

Doña R. announced she would leave her common-law husband (who refused to marry her in a civil ceremony) in order to be baptized and obey Christ. The church ordered her to remain with him, in recognition of their five children and years of living as man and wife —but refused to baptize her because she was in "fornication". We added Bible study on fornication in the curriculum and the church baptized her, but not without a serious division.

Don N. asked to be baptized, but the church refused because he was not *legally* married. His common-law wife refused on the grounds that they really were married, although *illegally,* by a

Catholic priest. "To repeat it", she argued, "would be the same as confessing to living in prostitution all these years!" We added biblical doctrine on marriage to the curriculum, but the pastor took a hard line, refused to study the booklet, and continued to harangue don N.: "Make your wife accept marriage, for the salvation of your soul and hers!" Don N. had a nervous breakdown and left the church permanently.

Don P. had four children by his common-law wife. I told him he must marry her legally. She refused. He promised to live with her faithfully as man and wife before God, so we baptized him. A month later don P. came to town all excited. "I got legally married!" he cried, "Now I'm free from fornication!"

"Great!" we responded. "How did you convince her?"

"I didn't. The missionary from [another denomination] said my baptism was invalid because I was in sin. So I married a señorita from his church and he rebaptized me. Now I'm preaching in his church in that village."

The hypocrisy of abandoning his wife and children in the name of Christian holiness offended his neighbours and brought our church to an infamous end. A month later we returned with a truck to pick up unused building materials for a chapel and never returned. We added biblical studies on baptism and church membership to our curriculum, but too late to avoid division within our movement which exists to this day.

The new churches raised another controversial question: Who has the right to baptize and to serve the Lord's Supper? The national association of churches claimed: "Only an ordained pastor with a three-year Bible Institute diploma." Our extension Bible Institute countered: "A church can license a lay pastor for this, in order to obey the commands of Christ." The association stood firm and condemned the extension training and the idea of lay pastors. In a climactic meeting Antonio C., a lay pastor studying with us, stood in tears and tore his lay pastoral credentials to shreds. "This is worth nothing then," he said, and left the church permanently.

But the fact remained that the extension students were out-pastoring the traditionally trained men on every count. Their churches were growing and raising up daughter churches, and they had fewer problems. But this seemed only to provoke more criticism of extension education; some churches continue to send their people away to study in residence, even though those who return prove relatively ill-equipped to pastor a church, compared to those who have studied by extension. The institutionally trained tend to perpetuate "preaching points" rather than churches. When they come to a church, they usually stop all the activities the church has been learning through the extension students' assignments, and simply preach. And preach. And preach. Church after church has fallen into this paralyzing trap; some have ceased to exist. We deal with the biblical doctrine of the church in our curriculum to combat this, but the shadow of traditional education still haunts us.

Obedience-oriented education

Our educational philosophy demands obedience to the Lord Jesus Christ. He seeks disciples who obey his commands. The curriculum for new students (and new churches) revolves around seven basic commands of Christ: repent and believe, be baptized, love, celebrate the Lord's Supper, pray daily, give sacrificially, and make disciples. This orientation requires that we teach people to discern three levels of authority: *commands of God* in the New Testament, which are always obeyed in the simplest, most direct way; *apostolic practices,* things mentioned but not commanded in the New Testament, for which we do not have the authority to require adherence nor to prohibit it; *human customs,* with no biblical basis, which we must change or eliminate if they impede obedience.

Our traditionally trained pastors see this hermeneutic as a threat. We violate their tradition. There have been sharp arguments concerning the difference between a *disciple* and a mere Bible *student.* Our philosophy holds that the difference is absolute. The disciple follows Christ; the student raises up schools. The disciple puts the Christian life and duty first; the student gives top priority to correct interpretation of scripture. There is at least no argument as to which of the two scripture supports. Jesus never commanded us to "go and make scholars". At this point we had to introduce educational philosophy and teaching methods into our curriculum, something for which our semi-literate people show little interest.

To make sure our extension students are obedient disciples requires continual two-way communication with their churches. Our teaching gets to the churches through the extension students; the results in terms of growth and church activities come back to us through the students' reports. These reports, which include church goals for the year, are essential to gearing our teaching and text preparation to present needs and goals. Many of the students resent the needed paper work. Several churches have been paralyzed because no one knew their state, or their goals, to help them. Requiring these reports provoked the criticism that we were "controlling the churches". One of the traditionally trained pastors visited many of our churches warning of this control and urging the churches to break off their submission to our authority. He offered to take over and "reform" our extension programme in the name of the association of churches. Because of this influence many churches discontinued their only pastoral training programme. We injected into the curriculum more teaching on the doctrine of the body of Christ, unity, mutual help and love, searched our souls and made a lot of visits, struggling for our very existence as an extension programme.

New churches through extension chains

Theological education by extension means more to us than simply spreading out our classrooms. We take the word "extension" seriously; every student is required to pass on what is learnt to other pastoral students; and every church is asked to raise up new churches. This is the kind of "apostolic succession" we find in 2 Tim. 2:2. This transfers the ministry from the hands of the missionary to the hands of the local pastor, to the hands of the people. It means ministry by the people. But not all are agreed. The older pastors do not want the work to grow out of their hands or out of their control. More than once one of them has walked for hours or days over the mountains in order to prohibit some new extension worker in a remote area leading a spontaneous, grassroots, Spirit-moved work. We had to introduce missionary methods into the curriculum and reinforce the concept of extension chains. One pastor does not interfere with the people in another pastor's field; one teacher does not order another teacher's students.

The concept of extension chains enables the rapid reproduction of churches. A church sends extension students to raise up daughter churches, which send their extension students to raise up their own daughter churches, and so on, until you have great-great-granddaughter churches. The method makes spontaneous reproduction possible. But it does not *cause* it. God does not bless methods. God blesses only *obedience,* done in faith and love. We cannot *make* the church grow. We can only provide an educational structure which will plant the seed and water it, but only God gives the increase. We yielded to the temptation to push our students to use "methods" to get growth. We scolded and stormed and stifled it. We had to stop pushing; we added to the curriculum the biblical doctrine of the Holy Spirit's work in the body and in the individual; and we are learning to leave the results to the Lord.

The church is a living being, a dynamic, living body whose head is Christ. It has all the potential of any created organism to grow and reproduce; each local church is a link in the chain of reproduction — or else a non-reproductive parasite on the body. The greatest enemy to this dynamic is the do-it-all teacher or the we're-the-only-ones church. Good pastoral education will make the more educated into humble servants — the kind who put everyone else to work and delegate responsibilities to their own students. Bad pastoral education makes the person with the most education into a domineering octopus, holding on to the members with a hundred arms, controlling the work. Some of these types will spring up no matter what we teach, and they always break the extension chain. They cannot pass on the baton.

Our chains often break. Bad teaching, laziness, death, and nomadism require continual reorganization. Best growth results where the churches are one or two links removed from the missionary or national educator, not so far as to delay communication for several months. The chains require constant supervision. Even so, the administration costs much less than a traditional Bible institute or church planting programme would. Our chains have produced 64 congregations with trained pastors; many teachers are labouring as unpaid volunteers. Only one seminary graduate has been required for curriculum development and to start the teaching in the first link of the chains. Most of the churches are small, rural congregations with less than 20 active, baptized adult members.

One-to-one instruction

Although we occasionally teach some general theme to a large group, our official extension classes are small, usually with one student, at most three. To mobilize people for ministry requires individual attention, specific work assignments and a confident, loving relationship between teacher and student. To extend the chains requires teacher-student links born of confident loving relationships between *churches.* These Paul-Timothy relationships must be cultivated; the scriptures command it.

To raise up a daughter church requires that a teacher help the students with a thousand details. The teacher must accompany the student frequently in the work, and show by example what to do. The teacher must teach the Bible *biblically*. The students do the same for their own students in the daughter churches; they train two or three elders or future pastors who in turn teach their own people. The extension teacher, an "outsider" from the mother church, does not pastor the daughter church. The extension teacher is a missionary who trains local leaders; they raise up and pastor their own church. This concept is reinforced by including in the curriculum relevant church history and a knowledge of apostolic practices. Many of our churches started with no public preaching; the extension teacher only evangelizes and instructs those who do the rest. But often extension workers yield to the temptation of the "preaching point". They start public preaching services, by-pass their students, take over their work and then wonder why they see no need to prepare for the ministry and become discouraged. The cure involves studying and applying the teaching principles in the Acts and Epistles, as well as church administration. Good administration requires everyone to have one's own clearly defined area of responsibility and ministry. The place to develop this concept is within a proper teacher-student relationship, in which the teacher takes full responsibility for the student's effective ministry.

Obedience-oriented education and social work

Obedience to Christ requires giving top priority to loving our neighbour in a *practical* way. This requires much biblical teaching on love and stewardship. We train our churches to give medical care to the needy, promote cooperatives among the poor, and initiate other community projects. But traditional missions and well-meaning agencies with a contrary philosophy of ministry often undo our training. A well-meaning team from the Christian Medical Association, for example, gave free medicine and treatment in one of our villages; for years afterwards we could not get them to go back to our own programme which required sacrifice, money and initiative on the church's part. We are now teaching health, basic medicine and agriculture by extension through our deacons, so that each church will minister in the name of Christ to its own community.

Some of our churches have resisted this social work as being too "liberal". In reality they want the mission to give everything to them freely, without their giving or sacrificing at all. Some followed Christ for the bread he gave them, but turned back when he told them what it really meant to follow him. Some of us missionaries have given out bread too freely and too long. We now have to include in our curriculum all those unpopular teachings of Christ for his disciples about carrying a cross, giving our lives, sacrificing for others, laying not up treasures in this world, etc. and to really hold our students to it.

TEEE—Theological Education and Evangelism by Extension

The marriage between pastoral education and basic discipling of unbelievers strengthens both ministries. It also produces many children, in the form of new disciples and churches. It also has the approval (if not an imperative) of scripture. It was the only way Christ and his apostles taught those who were to pastor his church.

It is easy to develop. Simply gear your education to the urgent needs of each student's church; see that the student helps meet those needs. You won't neglect any vital area; the needs seem to have a way of multiplying so fast that you soon realize you are teaching almost everything, just to meet the most urgent needs! This requires continual revision of the curriculum by someone who knows what a pastor needs. If you can't do it alone, team up with someone who can help you.

But don't do it unless you are willing to make a great sacrifice. Making obedient disciples is dangerous for everyone involved. It means asking God for the cross God wants us to bear. It means avoiding traditions and provoking opposition from the traditionalists. Your students will rebel when they see that you want them to be disciples with a military mentality (2 Tim. 2:2-4). But the rewards are worth it, if what Christ said about the kingdom of heaven is true.

Surely the mathematics involved in reaching the millions of unchurched communities requires a strategy that has room for the spontaneous reproduction of churches with a corresponding philosophy of education.

Theological Community of Chile

Extension training
for indigenous church leaders

AGUSTÍN AND ROSARIO BATLLE

History and description

The theological community of Chile started its TEE programme as an organized teaching institution in 1974, after a series of conversations by authorized representatives of various Chilean churches meeting in Santiago. The TEE programmes serve three kinds of students and are called: "congregational", "continuing studies", and "basic pastoral".

The *congregational programme* is open to any church member regardless of previous studies or spiritual experience. It is an occasional study programme, and it takes place in the churches themselves. At the end of each subject the participants receive a recognition card. The *continuing studies programme* is for lay leaders (church officers, lay preachers, Sunday school teachers, youth leaders). It has bi-weekly or monthly seminars and takes place in permanent locations in different parts of the country called study centres. A certificate is given upon completion of each course. The *basic pastoral programme* is a five-year programme of studies for pastors and candidates for the Christian ministry. It also takes place in permanent locations in different parts of the country in study centres. A diploma is given upon completion of the programme of studies.

• The Batlles directed the Chile extension programme from 1974 to 1980, when they moved to Kenya as consultants to the Organization of African Independent Churches for the development of extension training. The address of the Chile extension programme is Casilla 13596, Santiago, Chile.

The first two programmes follow a latent curriculum, varied and prepared on the way, according to the needs of the participants. The basic pastoral programme follows a homogeneous, functional curriculum, prepared in dialogue with the participants. It includes 60 subjects or courses.

The study centres are located in existing church buildings belonging to the churches represented by the TEE participants. Each study centre has:

— a coordinator-promotor, who is part of the study group and the person who keeps the study centre activities going on in terms of local administration, promotion, student registration, receiving and distributing the TEE texts, contacts with the TEE office in Santiago; s/he is one of the key persons;

— a seminar leader or facilitator, who is in charge of the teaching activities for the continuing studies and basic pastoral programmes; s/he is a seminary graduate (B.D., M.Div. or Ph.D.); some facilitators are from the same area where the study centres are located, and some come from abroad; for the congregational programme, most of the facilitators are products of the same TEE programme;

— its own mini-library (100-150 books) to reinforce the teaching-learning activities; each library has a student in charge; each study centre must contribute two new books a year to enrich the library.

The TEE programme produces its own texts in a small format with nine lessons (called "units"), programmed or semi-programmed, per study subject. The TEE staff recognizes that there are many, very well prepared TEE lesson materials produced in different places in Latin America; however, the staff believes that the writing of effective materials should be done in the country. Even if we deal with the same people and the same language, each country is different; there are also differences within the same country. Regular workshops for facilitators are held to give skills on how to use the TEE texts and on teaching methodology.

One of the problems faced by Chilean churches is that they lack their own Christian literature. They have been depending on imported written material. An extension series publication at the popular level was initiated in 1979 by the TEE programme. Three books have already been published and almost exhausted: *Jesus Present Today, How to Prepare Sermons,* and *Paul and his Teachings*

Today. These books are a further development of subjects studied at the study centres. This series is also a challenge and a motivation to staff members to contribute to the production of that kind of literature.

Analysis of the context and goals of the programme

The Chilean socio-economic situation: According to Chilean research sources, unemployment in large cities is very serious, as reflected in the following statistics: 1965-70, 6.1 per cent; 1975, 16.20 per cent; 1977, 16.25 per cent. In the rural areas unemployment is 25-30 per cent. This is not only a Chilean phenomenon; it is similar all over Latin America.

In spite of government claims about better salaries, the workers complain about decreasing salaries. For example, the average income received during 1974-80 was half the average income received during 1965-70. Seventy per cent of the population have such a low income that they are unable to acquire the minimum requirements listed by FAO and WHO. This means that most of the people do not get the minimum nutrition needed to function in society. Unemployment and low income have their repercussions in nutrition practices. The majority of the poor people eat once a day; consequently, there is a high rate of child malnutrition.

In 1977 there were 512,865 families living in shanty towns and 58,695 families without a place to live. This means a shortage of 571,560 housing units. The problem still remains because there is no interest among investors in low-income housing, while high-income housing has mushroomed in the affluent neighbourhoods. Large shopping centres have sprouted in high-income neighbourhoods completely stocked with imported goods at prohibitive prices.

This reality has a direct effect on the mental and physical health of a very high percentage of the population, increasing tensions and broken homes. The situation of the poor has not improved.

The banishing of all political parties in September 1973 by the present government has eradicated a long tradition of democracy. Any political affiliation different from that of the government has been considered a threat; therefore it must be destroyed. That is the reason all higher-education centres have military officers as directors.

Chilean ecclesial situation: There are two types of churches in Chile: first, the traditional or mission churches that constitute a minority and, second, the independent or indigenous churches that constitute the vast majority of Protestants (close to a million members). Divisions among Chilean Protestants did not originate within this context, but were brought in from the outside. The TEE programme is at this moment a cohesive agent.

If the independent pastor is paternalistic, it is because the majority of his congregation are labourers and unemployed, never having had the privilege of feeling themselves persons and making their own decisions. They have always been patronized. They have always done assigned tasks without knowing why and for what purpose their work would be used, as blind machines which are rented and used to benefit the owner. The struggle to subsist forces labourers to produce without any free expression, which is a domesticating and numbing experience. The independent pastor, in the last instance, represents the *patrón,* who does not permit anyone to touch his property. He rejects the educated pastor for fear of losing his people to him, and at the same time does not permit his people to receive any theological instruction. "For the written law condemns to death, but the Spirit gives life" (2 Cor. 3:6) is what he says and teaches. At the same time independent people fear being manipulated by outsiders, which is reflected in their introversion and non-dialogue. They accept being manipulated by their pastors but not by outsiders.

Foreign cultural patterns have been assimilated by the historic Protestant churches, which have accepted the paternalistic forms that were present a hundred years ago when they were being founded. It is deplorable that the traditional pastor, who has been formed in the foreign tradition, has reacted against indigenous values, assimilating a whole religious culture that he has tried to transplant forcefully among his members. This pastor then tries to preach the gospel with patterns which once responded to a certain historical moment in a determined geographical place, but which are not adequate to reach Chileans now in an effective and convincing way. The appropriation of a foreign culture without considering the completely different customs and ways of life of the people reflects a mentality which is incapable of reaching independent people who are more liberated in their worship than the historic churches. These independent people did not and do not react against the foreigners' faith but against their forms of expression in Chile. As Pepe Pato (a Chilean philosophic comic strip character) says: "Worship is a matter of the cradle."

Experience has taught us that independent people, in spite of having been viewed with suspicion and considered incorrigible by historic church people, are capable and intelligent persons who have had very limited opportunities. They are not second-category Christians, but persons who are sufficiently honest with themselves to express their faith without denying their own indigenous cultural values. This can be perceived only when one shares their table, their hospitality, their pulpit. Within these experiences is born genuine dialogue. These experiences give us the opportunity to know them, to set out and grow together with them, to avail ourselves of their religious experience, their immense biblical storage, their evangelistic methods, their healing of souls. Three fundamental principles are implied in this experience: "respect", "freedom to say their word", and "mutuality in learning", to use Freire's terminology.

The goals of the TEE programme are: first, to serve the whole Chilean church without regard to denomination or confession; second, to prepare the church adequately in the understanding of Christian truth as it is revealed in the Bible and most perfectly in Jesus Christ and as it responds to the contemporary needs of the Chilean church and society; third, to create fellowship and ecumenical attitudes among Christians.

Theology of ministry undergirding the programme

This TEE programme is an interdenominational teaching organization which recognizes the responsibility common to all Christian churches to be adequately prepared in the understanding and teaching of the Christian truth revealed in the Bible and in Jesus Christ, who is the content of our faith and of the church's mission. It seeks to offer theological training to the churches to help them present the gospel of Jesus Christ in the most faithful way, placing emphasis on the value of the testimony of this gospel in the face of the cultural currents and the socio-economic and political changes taking place in the country and developing an integral and globalizing ministry in response to the present historical juncture. It encourages and enables men and women to give as much as they can of themselves to serve the church and a society in which pluralism is not accepted. This programme also tries to nurture in the students' minds a global and ecumenical spirit, enabling them to be collaborators of God's kingdom, which has no barriers or discrimination.

Educational philosophy and methods

The theological educational process is based, first, on Christian values (the Bible, especially Jesus' teachings) and, second, on the contemporary andragogical approach to education, in which the experience of adults is valued as a rich ingredient for learning. The Unesco recommendations on the development of adult education (Tokyo 1972 and Nairobi 1976) are known and studied by the staff, because both documents contain fundamental theoretical and practical contributions of great value to TEE work.

Characteristics of the TEE programme are:

1. Priority is given to the educationally less privileged. In Chile we confront the reality, mainly with the Pentecostal tradition, of people lacking any training to develop a contemporary ministry.
2. We recognize and value the fact that each adult, in virtue of his/her experience, is a bearer of knowledge which permits him/her to be a learner and educator simultaneously. We encourage and facilitate an interest for reading, cultural aspirations, and analysis and development of the human being at all levels. We seek to foment an increasingly critical, prophetic and liberating conscience. Emphasis is given to immediate practice in the concrete situation of the student of that which has been learned. Active participation of the students in all the phases of the educational process which concerns them is promoted.
3. We seek learning through conversational communication based on a free and liberating spirit that permits the development of a dialectic in the student-teacher relationship. This participation in frank and open dialogue helps to develop abilities and knowledge that the participants can contribute to their own churches and society.
4. With a schedule of regular seminars or "encounters" the TEE participants acquire the habit of studying. The TEE programme is aware of the importance of "life-long education and learning" to help the participants through continual interaction between their thoughts and actions.

The TEE staff is involved in a programme of self-development which deals with interests and skills needed as they emerge from practice. Included is participation in programmes given by institutions specialized in adult education.

Evaluation, lessons, and future projections

The TEE programme was organized in 1974. Five years later it entered the evaluation stage. The type of evaluation chosen was internal or "self-evaluation", in which all persons involved in the teaching-learning process (from students to donor agencies) participated. The Latin American Centre of Adult Education of Santiago (CLEA) was the external consultant of the evaluation process, which was coordinated by an integrated team provided by CLEA and the TEE programme.

Only the continuing studies and basic pastoral programmes were evaluated at that time. The external consultant was a Chilean educational specialist, who understood the limitations and reality in which we had to work and who had no pre-established models. All the TEE participants plus the executive committee and board of directors of the theological community, church heads, and donor agencies had the opportunity to become involved, give their opinions, criticize, and suggest solutions. This evaluation was a learning experience in itself for everyone and has led the programme to become more objective concerning the magnitude of our difficult and overwhelming task, but with a taste of believing hope through our faith in Jesus Christ, our Saviour, who calls us to find him in our most needy brother and sister.

The TEE programme at the close of 1978 had 2,600 participants from 40 churches (3 traditional and 37 independent). The year 1979 ended with 4,228. The year 1980 ended with 3,200, a decrease due to the fact that many churches used the TEE texts without being served directly by TEE personnel and thus were not included in the ledger. The majority of the TEE participants are located in the southern part of Chile and belong to independent churches.

If the Chilean independent churches have accepted this programme, it is due to their having seen in it not a paternalistic attitude but a commitment of "quixotic" and "irrational" devotion, as Paul would say (1 Cor. 2:14). They have responded to the Christian and non-proselytizing philosophy of the programme and have opened their arms to the support offered to them, because it accepts them, for the first time in their lives, as persons. A TEE programme which is carried out in this manner captures the hearts of those that know and live it.

Latin American Biblical Seminary

Distance education in a revolutionary situation

IRENE WESTLING FOULKES and RUBÉN LORES

The experience of poverty, dependence and exploitation in Latin America imposes on theological institutions a new agenda and a new way of doing theology which takes as its point of departure that kind of experience and the struggles it generates. This starting point, radically different from that of most theologians in North America and Europe, necessarily leads to a rejection of theological orientations and emphases that perpetuate oppression.

Searching for the meaning of the word of God in a continent of poverty and exploitation, we have discovered that we must also question a prevalent pattern of theological education in residence institutions, a legacy of foreign missions which is unworkable without perpetuating an excessive dependence on foreign resources. A system of theological education which requires that a ministerial candidate reside for three or four years in a costly institution supported by others producing no income for oneself or the family is a contradiction, particularly in our situation.

We were searching for a new model of non-residential theological education that could serve a large geographical area, on a post-secondary level, and which could offer an open curriculum of ministerial education fitted for our context. Thus the Latin American

• Dr Foulkes has been Professor of Greek and New Testament at the Latin American Biblical Seminary since 1955 and has worked with PRODIADIS since its inception in 1976. The Rev. Rubén Lores, a former rector of the LABS, developed the original design of PRODIADIS and now works full-time on the preparation of materials. The address of the Seminary is Apartado 901, San José, Costa Rica.

Biblical Seminary (LABS) of San José, Costa Rica, launched in 1976 its Diversified Programme at a Distance (PRODIADIS).

A new approach

This programme of theological education at a distance is similar to an open-university programme and equivalent to LABS' well-known residential course leading to the bachelor and licenciate degrees. For the vast majority of people, the urban situation, no less than the rural, is desperate, even for the struggling few who have made it through secondary school. In order to obtain a theological education at university level, candidates must somehow be provided with a programme that allows them to continue in their jobs and in their professional or technical education. The churches are poor too, and few of them will offer a full-time, professional-level salary; often the candidate for theological education must also prepare for employment in another field. Many such candidates are already exercising multiple ministerial functions in their churches. Technical, professional and business people are providing pastoral services both in the churches and in para-ecclesiastical ministries.

The *distance* dimension means that neither students nor professors are obliged to travel from their home base to be together, and indeed they many never meet. It also means, however, the positive incorporation of resources available at a distance from the seminary but close to the students: tutors, adjunct professors, and local theological and secular institutions to be included in the programme. The *diversified* character of PRODIADIS has to do with, among other things, the curriculum design: it can incorporate a wide variety of current and past academic training, non-formal education, and life experience of educational value. In this way the curriculum is individualized at the outset, as the candidate's prior education and experience are evaluated and academic credit is defined and applied towards the theological programme. A basic aim of PRODIADIS is to break away from the standardized curriculum straitjacket by recognizing that mature candidates presently active in ministry have already attained some of the goals that theological education is supposed to help them reach.

The 253 students presently enrolled in the programme display extremely varied backgrounds. They range in age from 18 to 60, and in educational experience from bare secondary school to five or six years of professional training. Some are graduates of biblical and theological programmes and now seek to obtain a degree on a more advanced level; others had to interrupt residence studies in order to seek employment, either in the church or elsewhere. Some former residence students of the Latin American Biblical Seminary are in this group, and they now see that their withdrawal from the residence programme in San José is not the end of their hopes for a theological education. A significant percentage of the students are preparing for or already exercising the liberal professions. Their calling to some form of ministry is no less real than that of those who envision full-time employment within the church, and perhaps much more realistic. Because of this variety in background, these "new" students are working on programmes of study that range from the maximum bachelor's degree requirements of 40 courses/units to a minimum of eight for a few who already have a large number of transfer credits or non-formal educational credits. Launched less than four years ago, the programme has already graduated its first bachelor in theology, a pastor who had to drop out of the residence programme when he was transferred to a rural church. The first student to earn the licenciate in theology (Th.M.) is a Cuban pastor who directs a theological institution in Cuba. He finished his degree by combining studies at a distance with five months' residence at the LABS in Costa Rica. In this way the traditional programme does double duty, providing the distance student with one more option for completing his training.

An open curriculum

Only an open curriculum is adaptable to such a diversity of needs, and PRODIADIS defines its curriculum simply as a set of four basic areas, with a specific number of units required in each area. The aim of the *instrumental area* is to see that the student acquires the general background and specific tools necessary for doing theology: research methodology, language arts, and a critical approach to society, history, and philosophy. These goals can be met in many different ways, and the student who demonstrates that he or she already knows how to use the tools of literary research, for example, is given credit for a unit in this area. The *formative area* has to do with personality development and the spiritual characteristics required for ministry. The bulk of the programme is found in the *informative and vocational areas,* where students take courses and develop projects in theology, Bible and pastoral subjects.

A catalogue of 20 courses (rather limited at this initial moment in the development of PRODIADIS) on various levels is offered to the students, who are free to begin their studies at the point of most concern to them, usually a point directly related to their current experience. Only in courses with specific prerequisites, or those designed for an advanced level, is matriculation limited. The independent student, who has to depend on internal motivation for continued application to the task, is thus stimulated to build one's own programme according to one's needs and interests.

Most of the learning material for the courses offered in the catalogue have taken the form of study guides called *modules,* in which the professor presents the subject to the students, dialogues with them about it, introduces them to articles and texts, stimulates them to interpret and criticize the teaching, and requires them to do original work of analysis and synthesis on the basis of their new input and in reference to their own situation. Guidelines and a report format have also been developed to help the student acquire the skills required for critical reading. Distilled from teaching experiences with students in the residence programme (many of whom are part-time students similar in background to PRODIADIS students), the modules have in some cases been incorporated back into the residence format as valuable teaching aids. The publication of 40 additional modules is projected for the next three years.

The distance student, unlike the residence student, is required to include projects in his curriculum. The equivalent of one or more course units, these action/reflection projects are to be designed by the students in response to their analysis of a particular need in their church or community. A project manual provides the students with the basic information they need to design and carry out various kinds of projects.

They can include a wide variety of activities to meet felt needs of the community. The student must describe and document these activities fully, as well as set up and report on the means of evaluating their effectiveness. The student must also write a reflection paper in which he or she integrates theological, ideological and strategic insights gained by this experience.

Making it work

How can we make such a programme work? How can we avoid its becoming just a correspondence course? Live dialogue, group experience, good libraries, and thorough-going evaluation are all essential for a worthwhile theological education. In stressing these aspects, however, traditional theological education has too often forgotten one over-riding criterion of effective education: vital involvement with the environment for which the education is supposed to prepare the student to minister. This is no excuse, of course, for denying the other aspects, and PRODIADIS aims to combine the best of both worlds by developing a variety of means to provide the student with personnel and library resources. The students themselves are part of the answer to their own problem, as they are stimulated and guided to seek out resources in their own locale that can help them accomplish their programme. For instance, even in the matter of obtaining theological books and journals PRODIADIS helps the students discover in their own city where the quality theological book deposits are — often related to the Catholic Church or to sociopolitical organizations and hidden away in offices, convents and obscure institutes.

Only in its initial stage at present, but with high priority, is a network of relationships between PRODIADIS and other institutions and individuals. One small denominational seminary in another country, for instance, has taken the initiative in approaching PRODIADIS about pooling resources in order to offer the higher level licenciate degree that the seminary could not hope to offer with only its own facilities. A study centre has been formed in a South American country to provide contextual theological education. Combining locally produced courses with PRODIADIS modules, the initial results are very positive. Other such relationships are being worked out in several countries. The objective of this aspect of the development of PRODIADIS is to provide services both to individual students through the resources available near their place of residence and to seminaries, church groups, and study programmes that can use the resources of PRODIADIS better to serve their own constituencies.

It is planned that the distance students will relate to a large number of people in the course of their theological education: adjunct professors in their locale named by the LABS, tutors they will seek out themselves, fellow students with whom they will be put in contact by the PRODIADIS office, study centre personnel in allied institutions, approved supervisors for their action reflection projects. Professors travelling from San José will also serve in short encounters with

PRODIADIS students in various countries, as well as in longer seminars or courses. Many students in the course of their total career with PRODIADIS will be able to include an intensive summer course, or in some cases a whole semester or year of study in San José, or in some other residence seminary. The diversified quality of PRODIADIS can apply to every aspect of the programme.

No less important than concerns with curriculum and students is the basic question of dependence on outside financing in theological education. While in its initiation PRODIADIS depends heavily on grants and subsidized personnel, it is hoped that this seed money will produce a self-developing organism that can continue to grow on its own. PRODIADIS charges realistic prices for its services, aware that this uncommon practice in a dependent church environment is a step towards ending dependence by building a programme that the Latin American church itself can sustain without foreign aid.

The emergence of PRODIADIS within the extension movement as a new way of doing university-level theological education testifies to the creative possibilities inherent in an approach which takes seriously the challenge of both contextual ministerial formation and contemporary educational methodology.

A critical overview

While all aspects of the programme seem to be developing well at this stage, we are not tempted at all to present PRODIADIS as a success story. We may have passed the experimental stage to become a permanent and promising outreach of the Latin American Biblical Seminary. There are many persons throughout Latin America who are looking to PRODIADIS as the only access to the kind of theological education they feel they need. But our experience during the past five years has given us many insights into the problems and situations we are facing. The areas of concern are many.

1. Teaching modules have been developed at a much slower pace than anticipated. While the publishing of 20 modules is not a small accomplishment for an institution which has developed little literature in the past, we can hardly speak realistically of an open curriculum with such a limited selection for the students to choose from. The goal was 1981 is eight modules.

2. In producing modules we have been limited so far to courses already in existence in our residence programme. Therefore, very little has been done to enhance PRODIADIS by offering courses

which go beyond the traditional seminary curriculum. We are not surprised that this is so, because of our mutual interdependence with the residence programme. We feel that our residence curriculum is one of the best offered by any residence institution, in spite of constraints at the academic and traditional levels due to our relationship with the National University of Costa Rica. But we must move beyond this point soon to gain more credibility as a new modality that can offer educational experiences out of the context where the students live and work rather than out of the drawing board of seminary professors who gained their experiences at the seminaries where they were taught in other times and locations.

An additional area of concern at this point is the fact that PRODIADIS, as it was originally designed, called for the input of many persons and institutions outside the LABS. In fact, the first proposal was made to the Association of Theological Schools, Northern Region (ALET), with the hope that the programme would be developed by a consortium of institutions. Due to the logistic problems in setting up such an organization, the LABS was encouraged to develop the programme on its own and work out in due time bilateral arrangements with other institutions. We are very keen that this may happen soon so that the programme may be enriched by the experience of people and institutions who are doing theological education in other contexts.

3. We are eager to see more creativity in producing additional educational material in keeping with our stated philosophy of doing theology in a context of oppression. It is not difficult to handle the rhetoric about oppression and exploitation. It is quite another matter to produce teaching materials out of our evangelical background that will have liberating effects on professors and students alike and, above all, will prepare both for a more effective, liberating ministry. Some progress has been made in this qualitative aspect, but the need is urgent.

4. The fact that we were not able to produce the project manual until recently has been a major set-back in the programme. The action/reflection projects envisioned in the PRODIADIS design represent one concrete effort to go beyond book learning in theological education. While there is much book learning involved in designing and carrying out projects, this approach seeks to force the students into the kind of liberating praxis that will bring them face to face with the reality in which they live and work. During the next two or

three years we will test out in actual practice this way of learning theology by doing theology.

5. The problem of trying to do theology from within each context, while at the same time projecting an international programme from Costa Rica to other Latin American nations, keeps coming up. It is true that the components of oppression, poverty and exploitation tend to homogenize the context. But the differences also are many. And people are different in each country. They need and want to manage their own act. We seek to deal with this problem by giving the students as much freedom as possible to develop alternative assignments that will allow them, and in fact that will require them to work in context. We also hope that learning by doing, through action/reflection projects, will help. Yet another way will be by increasing the network of relationships that will allow students to work on educational experiences developed by people in their immediate context.

6. PRODIADIS is now an essential part of an institution that has a dynamic, flourishing residence programme. This is a very positive development that has caught the attention of many people. We are determined to maintain and strengthen the mutual advantages for both programmes. This does not mean, however, that this relationship can be taken for granted. We must continually work on it so that the enrichment continues without illegitimate constraints on either programme and without unhealthy protectionism. At the initial stages of PRODIADIS it is easy to see how the programme would benefit from the richness of our long history of residence teaching. But in the future, when PRODIADIS is more fully developed and the number of students increases, we must be sure that this mutual enrichment continues without undue limitations.

7. Another aspect that must come under review soon is the number of staff involved in PRODIADIS. So far the number of personnel has been kept limited on purpose. We have not been interested in developing a large parallel faculty for a programme that was designed to render a service. Growth was planned to come about by the demand for services. But there is no question that the growth of this as of any similar programme is determined in part by the number of people who are available to work on it. In a small institution (90 residence students) with two degree programmes, most of the personnel is related to our residence programme. Only a few professors have dedicated a substantial part of their time to PRODIADIS.

No particular tension has developed on this account, but this fact calls for reflection, since it affects the long-range goals of PRO-DIADIS. We have no doubt that at the right time the right decisions will be made, but the problem has to be faced realistically and with an open mind.

8. We do not dare ignore the danger of providing elitist education by designing a programme for post-secondary level. Of course, our teaching materials are available to anyone. Theological educators can use our material and adapt it to any level they wish. But the fact remains that PRODIADIS itself only enrolls students who can meet the educational requirements for university level work. While the reasons for our doing this have a firm basis on historic, strategic, and relational grounds, we continue to be concerned about the ultimate goal of our programme. There are relatively few people who will enjoy the privilege of this kind of education, and we would like to be sure that the kind of teaching we provide will challenge them and enable them to work effectively at the grassroots level.

9. Another hurdle that we must face in the development of PRO-DIADIS is institutional jealousy. Is PRODIADIS really fulfilling a needed service, wanted and welcomed by the population it serves? Or is it simply the outreach of an international institution that is seeking to enlarge its turf? While it is our desire to complement other local programmes, we can easily see how other institutions could view the expansion of PRODIADIS into their "territories" as competition for their programmes. We mean to work sincerely on this problem by making as many bilateral arrangements as possible with all sorts of institutions and denominations. PRODIADIS indeed seeks to fulfill real, felt needs of the people who use it, including the leadership of churches and institutions.

10. We must continue to work on many logistic problems that are slowing down the programme and hinder its efficient operation. Communication through mail is always slow and limited. Sending professors where clusters of students exist in different countries is expensive and subject to the very limited time the professors have available. Difficulty in getting textbooks is a real headache. A book widely available in one country may be totally unknown in a number of other key countries. A major textbook may go out of print after the first edition, never to appear again. Book prices are becoming exorbitant, and lack of dollar currency is making it almost impossible to import foreign books in many countries.

11. The limited number of students who have enrolled in the programme so far is seen by some of us as a blessing. A much larger number of students would put undue pressure on the institution at a time when we need to spend more time on the basic development of the programme. The fact remains, however, that this number is much too limited in view of the large potential of the programme and the great need that exists. Intentionally, no formal promotional programme has been launched, for the reason noted above. It remains to be seen how the system will work when the active student body increases into the thousands.

Our hope is that growth will be gradual so that if and when the time comes for the Latin American Biblical Seminary to revolve around a distance programme, rather than a residence programme, the relationship will be as meaningful and as mutually beneficial as it is at present.

Bible Study Centre
for People's Pastoral Action (Brazil)

The use of the Bible among the common people

CARLOS MESTERS

Introducing the issue: three basic situations

In Brazil there are many groups meeting to focus on the Bible. In this case the motivating occasion for the group is some pious exercise or special event: a feast day, a novena, a brotherhood week. The people meet on the parish level. There is no real community context involved. The word of God is the only thing that brings them together. They want to reflect on God's word and put it into practice.

Some groups are meeting within a broader context. They are meeting on the level of the community and its life. I once went to give a course to the people in such a community. In the evening the people got together to organize the course and establish basic guidelines. In such groups you generally get questions such as these: "How do you explain the apocalypse? What does the serpent stand for? What about the fight between David and Goliath?" The questions, you see, are limited to the Bible as such. No hint of their own concerns, no hint of real-life problems, no hint of reality, no hint of problems dealing with economic, social and political life. Even though they are meeting as a community, the real-life problems of the people are not brought up.

• This article was adapted from a paper on the same topic presented by the author at the International Congress of Theology held at Sao Paulo in February 1980 and published in *The Challenge of Basic Christian Communities*, edited by Sergio Torres and John Eagleson, Maryknoll, Orbis Books, 1981. It is used with permission. The writer is the Director of the Bible Study Centre for People's Pastoral Action, Caixa Postal 64, 23900 Angra des Reis, RJ, Brazil.

To introduce the third situation, I am going to tell you a typical story about my experience in this area. I was invited to give a course in Ceara, in north-east Brazil. The group was made up of about ninety farmers from the backlands and the riverbanks. Most of them couldn't read. In the evening we met to get things organized. They asked me about a dozen basic questions, but these are the ones I remember:

— What about these community activities we are engaged in? Are they just the priest's idea? Are they communism? Or do they come from the word of God?

— What about our fight for land? (Most of them had no land. But they had plenty of problems and fights on their hands.) What about our labour struggles and our attempts to learn something about politics? What does the word of God have to say about all that?

— What about the gospel message? Does it have to do just with prayer, or is it something more than that?

— The other day, in a place where there was a big fight going on between the landlord and his tenants, this priest came, said mass, and explained the gospel in a way that made the landlord right. Then the local priest of the parish read the same gospel and explained it in a way that made the tenant farmers right. So who really is right?

— The landlord gives catechism lessons that teach subservience and bondage. In our community we have a catechetics of liberation, and the landlord persecutes us for it. So how do we settle the matter and figure it all out? We want to know whether the Bible is on our side or not!

Here we have three basic situations. In the first situation the group involved comes together solely for the sake of discussing the Bible; the Bible is the only thing that unites them and they stick to it. In the second situation the people focus on the Bible, too, but they come together as a community. In the third situation we have a community of people meeting around the Bible who inject concrete reality and their own situation into the discussion. Their struggle as a people enters the picture. So we can formulate the following basic picture:

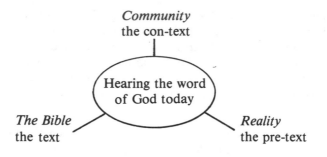

We find three elements in the common people's interpretation of the Bible: the Bible itself, the community, and reality (i.e. the real-life situation of the people and the surrounding world). With these three elements they seek to hear what the word of God is saying. And for them the word of God is not just the Bible. The word of God is within reality and it can be discovered there with the help of the Bible. When one of the three elements is missing, however, interpretation of the Bible makes no progress and enters into crisis. The Bible loses its function.

When the three elements are present and enter the process of interpretation, then you get the situation that I encountered when I gave a course in Ceara. The people asked me to tell them the stories of Abraham, Moses, Jeremiah, and Jesus. That is what I did. But in their group discussions and full meetings, the Bible disappeared. They hardly ever talked about the Bible. Instead they talked about real life and their concrete struggles. So at the nightly review the local priest asked them what they had learned that day. They quickly got to talking about real life. No one said anything about the Bible. Ye gods, I thought to myself, where did I go wrong? This is supposed to be a course on the Bible and all they talk about is real life. Should I feel upset and frustrated, or should I be satisfied? Well, I decided to take it easy and feel satisfied because the Bible had achieved its purpose. Like salt, it had disappeared into the pot and spiced the whole meal.

It's like what happens when you take a sponge and dip it in a little bowl of water. The water is soaked up and disappears inside the sponge. At the end of the nightly review the people were asked what they had learned from the biblical explanations. They squeezed the sponge a bit and let a few drops of water out. I could see that the sponge was filled with water. At the final ceremony for the week, which lasted four hours, they squeezed the sponge completely and everything inside came out. I realized that when the three elements are integrated — Bible, community, real-life situation — then the word of God becomes a reinforcement, a stimulus for hope and courage. Bit by bit it helps people to overcome their fears.

Conclusions

1. When the community takes shape on the basis of the real-life problems of the people, then the discovery of the Bible is an enormous reinforcement.

2. When the community takes shape only around the reading of the Bible, then it faces a crisis as soon as it must move on to social and political issues.

3. When the group closes itself up in the letter of the biblical text and does not bring in the life of the community or the reality of the people's struggles, then it has no future and will eventually die.

4. These three factors or situations characterize the use of the Bible by the common people and reveal the complexity involved. The three situations can be successive stages in a single ongoing process, or they can be antagonistic situations that obstruct and exclude each other. It all depends on how the process is conducted.

5. It doesn't matter much where you start. You can start with the Bible, or with the given community, or with the real-life situation of the people and their problems. The important thing is to do all you can to include all three factors.

Some obstacles and how the people are surmounting them

It is not always easy to integrate all three factors in the interpretation of the Bible. There are many obstacles along the way that the people are trying to surmount in various ways.

Many people don't know how to read, and the Bible is a book! Sometimes no one in the group knows how to read. They are inventing ways to get around this problem. They are using song and story, pictures and little plays. They are thus making up their own version of the "Bible of the poor". Thanks to songs, for example, many people who have never read the Bible know almost every story in it.

Another obstacle is slavery to the letter or fundamentalism. This usually occurs when the Bible is read in dissociation from a real-life community and concrete situation. The circle closes and the letter becomes a source of further oppression rather than of liberation.

The Bible is ambiguous. It can be a force for liberation or a force for oppression. If it is treated like a finished monument that cannot be touched, that must be taken literally as it is, then it will be an oppressive force.

Three things can help to overcome this obstacle. The first is the good sense of the people. In one community composed of blacks and other farmers the people were reading the Old Testament text that forbade the eating of pork. The people raised the question: "What is God telling us today through this text?" Their conclusion was: "Through this text God today is ordering us to eat the flesh of pork." How did they arrive at such a contrary conclusion? They explained: "God is concerned first and foremost with life and health. In those times eating the flesh of pork was very dangerous to people's health. It was prohibited in God's name because people's lives had to be protected. Today we know how to take care of pork meat, and the only thing we have to feed our children are the piglets in our yards. So in this text God is bidding us to eat the flesh of pork."

A second thing of great importance in breaking through enslavement to the letter is the ongoing action of a local church that takes sides with the poor. The ongoing movement of the church in this direction is helping to ensure that questions focused exclusively on the letter of the biblical text gradually give way to others. Literalist questions are falling from the tree like dry leaves to make room for new buds. The larger complex of a local church that sides with the poor and joins their fight for justice is very important in correctly channelling the people's interpretation of the Bible.

The third thing has to do with various devices of a fairly simple kind. For example, we can show people that many of the things we talk about in words cannot be taken literally. Symbolism is an integral part of human language. In many instances the first step towards liberation comes for people when they realize that they need not always take the biblical text literally. They discover that "the letter kills, the Spirit gives life". This realization unlocks the lid and lets new creativity out.

Another problem or obstacle is the people's conception of time. Often folks will ask questions like these: "Did Abraham come before or after Jesus Christ? Did David live before or after Cabral discovered America? Was it Jesus Christ who created the world?"

Such questions may seem to indicate a great deal of confusion to us, but I think not. Apart from a certain amount of ignorance about the content of the Bible, I don't think it is a matter of confusion at all. Instead it is an expression of their circular conception of time. In such a conception you don't know exactly what comes at the beginning and what comes at the end. A simple explanation will not suffice to change this view of time, because it is a cultural problem rather than a problem of mere ignorance. In their minds the people simply don't have a peg on which to hang a concept of linear time.

How do we help them to overcome this obstacle? How do we unroll the carpet of time in their consciousness? Perhaps the best way we can help is to help them discover their own ongoing journey in their lives today. We can help them to recover the memory of their own history, of struggles lost and forgotten. We can help them to begin to recount their own history. In Goias a group of farm workers was asked: "How did the Bible come about?" An old farmer gave this reply: "I know. It was something like this. Suppose fifty years from now someone asks how our community arose. The people will reply: In the beginning there was nothing here...." Thanks to his own concrete journey in life, the old farm worker perceived that the Bible had arisen from narrative accounts, from stories people told to others about their history. He realized that the Bible was the collective memory that gave a people its identity.

You often hear people say something like this: "I don't know anything. You or Father should do the talking. You're the ones who know things. We folks don't know anything." In the past we members of the clergy expropriated the Bible and got a monopoly on its interpretation. We took the Bible out of the hands of the common people, locked it with a key, and then threw the key away. But the people have found the key and are beginning again to interpret the Bible. And they are using the only tool they have at hand: their own lives, experiences and struggles.

Biblical exegetes, using their heads and their studies, can come fairly close to Abraham; but their feet are a long way from Abraham. The common people are very close to Abraham with their feet. They are living the same sort of situation. Their life-process is of the same nature and they can identify with him. When they read his history in the Bible, it becomes a mirror for them. They look in that mirror, see their own faces, and say: "We are Abraham!" In a real sense they are reading their own history, and this becomes a source of much inspiration and encouragement. One time a farm worker said this to me: "Now I get it. We are Abraham, and if he got there then we will too!" From the history of Abraham he and his people are drawing the motives for their courage today.

Now here is where the danger comes in. Some teacher or learned expert may come along. It might be a pastoral minister, a catechist, or an exegete. This expert may arrive with his or her more learned and sophisticated approach and once again expropriate the gains won by the people. Once again they grow silent and dependent in the presence of the teacher or expert. Our method is logical. It involves a reasoning process, a careful line of argument. We say it is scientific. When the people get together to interpret the Bible, they do not proceed by logical reasoning but by the association of ideas. One person says one thing; somebody else says another thing. We tend to think this approach has little value, but actually it is just as scientific as our approach! What approach do psychoanalysts use when they settle their patients into a chair or a couch? They use the free association of ideas. And this method is actually better than our "logical" method. Our method is one for teaching information; the other is one for helping people to discover things themselves.

Another obstacle that crops up at times is the lack of tact on the part of pastoral workers among the people. They are in a hurry and have no patience. They ride roughshod over some of the natural resistance that people have to our interpretations of the Bible. One time a nun went to give a course on the Old Testament. Half way through she had to close down the course because no one was showing up. The people said: "Sister is destroying the Bible!" A certain priest offered an explanation of the Exodus. Many people never came back. "He is putting an end to miracles," they complained.

Meddling with the faith of the people is very serious business. You must have deep respect and a delicate touch. You must try to feel as they would and intuit their possible reaction to what you are going to say. The people should be allowed to grow from the soil of their own faith and their own character. They should not be dragged along by our aggressive questions.

Another obstacle is erudite language, abstruse words. We talk a difficult idiom, and the language of translations is difficult. Today, thank God, various efforts are being made to translate the Bible into more popular terms. Nothing could be more desirable. People now feel that they are getting the point at least. The first and most basic requirement is that people talk in such a way that their listeners can understand them. It sounds simple enough, but often it is very hard to do.

Another important point is that we must not lose the poetry of the Bible. We must not reduce it to concepts. The Bible is full of poetry, and poetry is more than a matter of words. It is the whole way of seeing and grasping life.

Another problem crops up on the grassroots level with "fundamentalist" groups. They head for people's homes with the Bible in their hands and make it clear that they have the only right answer. This leads to a defensive reaction and sectarian apologetics. It is hard to foster any ecumenism around the Bible in such an atmosphere.

In some areas, however, practical biblical ecumenism is growing from other starting points. Roman Catholics and Protestants are meeting each other and working together in labour unions, in fights for land ownership, and in other real-life struggles. Gradually other sectarian issues are taking a back seat to practical ecumenism.

Characteristics of the people's interpretation of the Bible

In a sense we can say that the tabernacle of the church is to be found where the people come together around the word of God. That could be called the church's "holy of holies". Remember that no one was allowed to enter the holy of holies except the high priest, and he was allowed in only once a year! In this holy of holies no one is master — except God and the people. It is there that the Holy Spirit is at work, and where the Spirit is at work, there is freedom. The deepest and ultimate roots of the freedom sought by all are to be found there, in those small community groups where the people meet around the word of God. One song in Ceara has this line: "It is the tabernacle of the people. Don't anyone touch it!" Certain characteristics are surfacing in this tabernacle, and I should like to point them out here.

The things I am going to mention now are not fully developed and widespread. They are more like the first traces of dawn in the night sky. We are dipping our finger into the batter to savour how the cake will taste when it is baked and ready. The following characteristics are just beginning to surface here and there in the ongoing journey of various communities. I think they are very important.

In the eyes of the common people the word of God, the gospel message, is much broader than just the text itself. The gospel message is a bit of everything: Bible, community, reality. For the common people the word of God is not just in the Bible; it is also in the community and in their real-life situation. The function of the Bible, read in a community context, is to help them to discover where God is calling them in the hubbub of real life. It is as if the word of God were hidden within history, within their struggles. When they discover it, it is big news. It's like a light flicking on in their brains. When one leper in Acre made this discovery, he exclaimed: "I have been raised from the dead!" He used the idea of resurrection to express the discovery he had made.

Theologians say that reality is a *locus theologicus*. The common people say: "God speaks, mixed into things." A tinker defined the church this way: "The church is us exchanging ideas with each other to discover the idea of the Holy Spirit in the people." If it hadn't come from Antonio Pascal, I would have said it came from St Augustine. But it came from Antonio Pascal. It is us exchanging ideas with each other to discover the idea of the Holy Spirit in the people. Not in the church, in the people!

So you see, when they read the Bible, basically they are not trying to interpret the Bible; they are trying to interpret life with the help of the Bible. They are altering the whole business. They are shifting the axis of interpretation.

The common people are recovering the unity or oneness of creation and salvation, which is certainly true in the Bible itself. The Bible doesn't begin with Abraham. It begins with creation. Abraham is not called to form some separated group apart. Abraham is called to recover for all peoples the blessing lost by the sin of Adam. This is the oneness between life and faith, between transforming (political) activity and evangelization, that the people are concretely achieving in their praxis.

The Bible was taken out of the people's hands. Now they are taking it back. They are expropriating the expropriators: "It is our book! It was written for us!" It had always been "Father's book", it seemed. Now it is the people's book again.

That gives them a new way of seeing, new eyes. They feel at home with the Bible and they begin to link it with their lives. So we get something very interesting. They are mixing life in with the Bible, and the Bible in with life. One helps them to interpret the other. And often the Bible is what starts them developing a more critical awareness of reality. They say, for example: "*We* are Abraham! *We* are in Egypt! *We* are in bondage! *We* are David!" With the biblical data they begin to reflect on their real-life situation. The process gradually prompts them to seek a more objective knowledge of reality and to look for a more suitable tool of analysis elsewhere. But it is often the word of God that starts them moving.

The rediscovery of the Bible as "our book" gives rise to a sense of commitment and a militancy that can overcome the world. Once they discover that God is with them in their struggles, no one can really stop them or deter them. One farm worker from Goias concluded a letter this way: "When the time comes for me to bear my witness, I will do so without any fear of dying." That is the kind of strength that is surfacing. A sort of resurrection is taking place, as I suggested earlier.

We who always had the Bible in hand find it difficult to imagine and comprehend the sense of novelty, the gratitude, the joy, and the commitment that goes with their reading of the Bible. But that is why these people generally read the Bible in the context of some liturgical celebration. Their reading is a prayer exercise. Rarely will you find a group that reads the Bible simply for better understanding. Almost always their reading is associated with reflection on God present here and now, and hence with prayer. They live in a spirit of gratefulness for God's gift.

Another characteristic which I hinted at already is the fact that the Bible is not just history for the people; it is also a mirror. Once upon a time we used to talk about the Bible as "letter" and "symbol". Today we might do well to talk about it as "history" and "mirror". The common people are using it as a mirror to comprehend their own lives as a people.

We who study a great deal have a lot more trouble trying to grasp the point of images and symbols. If we want to get a handle on symbolic language, we have to go through a whole process of "demythologizing". We have to go through a long process of study to get the point of the symbol. To us images are opaque glasses; we can't see through them at all. To see at all, we have to punch out the glass and smash it. To the common people in Brazil, an image or symbol is a pair of glasses with a little dust or frost on it. They just wipe them a bit and everything is as clear as day.

I don't think we pay enough attention to this educational item. We are awfully "Europeanized" in our training. Take the question of the historicity of a text. I think you have to approach it very differently, or worry about it differently, when you are dealing with ordinary people. Very often pastoral workers are talking about the Bible and they ask questions like these: "Did that really happen? Did Jesus walk on top of the water? Were there only five loaves and two fishes?" They think that this is the most important problem that the people have with the text in front of them. I don't think so. Once, in Goias, we read the passage in the New Testament (Acts 17:19) where an angel of the Lord came and freed the apostles from jail. The pastoral worker asked his people: "Who was the angel?" One of the women present gave this answer: "Oh, I know. When Bishop Dom Pedro Casaldaliga was attacked in his house and the police surrounded it with machine guns, no one could get in or out and no one knew what was going on exactly. So this little girl sneaked in without being seen, got a little message from Pedro, ran to the airport, and hitched a ride to Goiana where the bishops were meeting. They got the message, set up a big fuss, and Dom Pedro was set free. So that little girl was the angel of the Lord. And it's really the same sort of thing."

The people don't always take things literally. They are far smarter than you would think. Our question, simply will have to take more account of the way ordinary people understand history. They are far more capable of understanding symbols than we assume.

Dislocations

Some speak about the irruption of the poor. When there are only five people in a room, then each one can be pretty much at ease. When 50 more people enter the room, then the original five find themselves a bit crowded and some moving around has to take place. Well, the common people have entered the precincts of biblical interpretation, and they are causing much shifting and dislocation.

First of all, the Bible itself has shifted its place and moved to the side of the poor. One could almost say that it has changed its class status. This is important. The place where the people read the Bible is a different place. We read the Bible something like the wealthy car owner who looks out over the top of his car and sees a nice chrome finish. The common people read the Bible something like the mechanic under the car who looks up and sees a very different view of the same car.

The common people are discovering things in the Bible that other readers don't find. At one session we were reading the following text: "I have heard the cries of my people." A woman who worked in a factory offered this commentary: "The Bible does not say that

God has heard the praying of the people. It says that God has heard the cries of his people. I don't mean that people shouldn't pray. I mean that people should imitate God. Very often we work to get people to go to church and pray first, and only then will we pay heed to their cries." You just won't find that sort of interpretation in books.

The Bible has changed its place, and the place where the common people read the Bible is different. It is the place where one can appreciate the real import of Jesus' remark: "I thank thee, Father.... that thou hast hidden these things from the wise and understanding and revealed them to babes; yea, Father, for such was thy gracious will" (Matt. 11:25-26). If you take sides with the poor, you will discern things in the Bible that an exegete does not see. All of us have a slight blind spot that prevents us from seeing certain things.

Another shift mentioned earlier has to do with the fact that the word of God has moved in a certain sense from the Bible to real life. It is in the Bible but it is also in real life — especially in real life. So we come to the following conclusion: the Bible is not the one and only history of salvation; it is a kind of "model experience". Every single people has *its own* history of salvation.

Clement of Alexandria said: "God saved the Jews in a Jewish way, the barbarians in a barbarian way." We could go on to say: "God saves Brazilians in a Brazilian way, blacks in a black way, Indians in an Indian way, Nicaraguans in a Nicaraguan way, and so on." Each people has its own unique history. Within that history it must discover the presence of God the Liberator who journeys by its side. The scope of this particular dislocation is most important.

Another dislocation is to be found in the fact that emphasis is not placed on the text's meaning in itself but rather on the meaning the text has for the people reading it. At the start people tend to draw any and every sort of meaning, however well or ill founded, from the text. Only gradually, as they proceed on their course in life, do they begin to develop an interest in the historical import and intrinsic meaning of the text. It is at this point that they can benefit greatly from a study of the material conditions of the people in biblical times, i. e. their religious, political, and socio-economic situation. But they do so in order to give a better grounding to the text's meaning "for us". In this framework scientific exegesis can reclaim its proper role and function, placing itself in the service of the biblical text's meaning "for us".

The common people are doing something else very important. They are reintroducing faith, community, and historical reality into the process of interpretation. When we studied the Bible back in the seminary in the old days, we didn't have to live as a real community or really know much about reality. We didn't even have to have faith. All we needed was enough brains to understand Greek and Hebrew and to follow the professor's line of reasoning.

Now the common people are helping us to realize that without faith, community, and reality we cannot possibly discover the meaning that God has put in that ancient tome for us today. Thus the common people are recovering something very important: the *sensus ecclesiae* ("sense of the church"). The community is the resonance chamber; the text is a violin string. When the people pluck the string (the biblical text), it resonates in the community and out comes the music. And that music sets the people dancing and singing. The community of faith is like a big pot in which Bible and community are cooked just right until they become one tasty dish.

The common people are also eliminating the alleged "neutrality" of scholarly exegesis. No such neutrality is possible. Technology is not neutral, and neither is exegesis.

The common people are giving us a clearer picture of concepts that have been excessively spiritualized. Let me give just one example. Some time ago Pope Paul VI delivered an address in which he warned priests not to become overly preoccupied with material things. He urged them to show greater concern for spiritual things. One farm worker in Goias had this comment: "Yes, the pope is quite right. Many priests concern themselves only with material things, such as building a church or decorating it. They forget spiritual things, such as food for the people!"

This is what the people are doing with such notions as grace, salvation, sin and so forth. They are dusting them off and showing us that these notions have to do with solid, concrete realities of life.

Finally, the common people are putting the Bible in its proper place, the place where God intended it to be. They are putting it in second place. Life takes first place! In so doing, the people are showing us the enormous importance of the Bible and, at the same time, its relative value — relative to life.

Problems, challenges, requirements

There are many problems, difficulties and failings associated with the interpretation of the Bible by the common people. But every good tree has a strong, solid limb that can be pruned when the time comes. The point is that its roots are okay. The common people are reading and interpreting the Bible as a new book that speaks to them here and now. And this basic view of the Bible is the view that the church fathers of the past had when they interpreted the Bible.

Here I simply want to enumerate a few further points that need greater attention:

1. There is a danger of subjectivistic interpretation. This can be combated in two ways: by more objective grounding in the literal sense of the Bible and by reading the Bible in community.

2. It is possible to read the Bible solely to find in it a confirmation of one's own ideas. In this case the biblical text loses its critical function. Community-based reading and interpretation help to overcome this tendentious use of the Bible. In addition, people must have a little humility and a little signal-light in their brains that calls them up short when they are tempted to absolutize their own ideas.

3. People may lack a critical sense in reading and interpreting the biblical text. They may be tempted to take the ancient text and apply it mechanically to today, without paying any serious attention to the difference in historical context.

4. The above three points underline the proper and necessary function of scientific exegesis. Exegesis is being called upon to concern itself, not with the questions it raises, but with the questions that the common people are raising. In many cases the exegete is like the person who had studied salt and knew all its chemical properties but didn't know how to cook with it. The common people don't know the properties of salt well, but they do know how to season a meal.

5. We need biblical interpretation that will reveal the material living conditions of the people in the Bible. We need a materialist reading and interpretation of the Bible, but not a narrow and confined reading. It must be broad and full.

6. We urgently need to give impetus to ecumenism on the grassroots level. It is a hard and challenging task, but a beginning has been made here and there.

7. The Bible is a book derived from a rural environment. Today we live in an urban environment. Rereading the Bible today here in Sao Paulo, in this urban reality, presents no easy task of interpretation.

8. There is the matter of revolutionary effectiveness and gratitude for the Father's gift. This is another matter that needs further exploration.

9. Criticism can be derived from the word of God to foster transforming action.

Bible Study Centre for People's Pastoral Action

In 1977 concerned Catholics and Protestants who shared the new vision of a church which was being recreated through the spontaneous formation of an estimated 80,000 basic ecclesial communities in Brazil joined together to create the Bible Study Centre for People's Pastoral Action. The aims of this Centre are:
— to stimulate the study of the Bible at the level of the people and from the perspective of the concrete life issues which they are facing;
— to provide biblical training and exchange of experiences among the various kinds of pastoral agents in order to strengthen their ministry and teaching among the people;
— to collect and organize material relevant for popular study of the Bible and implementation of popular pastoral action.

The Centre organizes periodic courses of various kinds for people who are involved in popular pastoral action: one-month-long courses for pastors, priests, religious and laity who have some knowledge and experience of the Bible; 10-day decentralized courses in various regions of Brazil; basic Bible courses at the parish and diocesan levels. Twice a year the small, mostly part-time staff and volunteers, gather for Bible study weeks to pray together, to deepen their knowledge of the Bible, and to share together their experience of the Bible and of its use in popular pastoral action.

The president of the executive committee is a Roman Catholic bishop. The secretary is a Presbyterian pastor, and the treasurer is a Methodist pastor. The director of the Centre is a Roman Catholic priest.

No longer is pastoral action the exclusive prerogative of professional, highly qualified priests, carried out in isolation from social realities. It is now regarded as the work of the entire Christian community, inspired by pastoral agents, who can be bishops, pastors, catechists, workers, peasants, men or women. The Bible Study Centre for People's Pastoral Action provides biblical training and materials for these agents so that they can strengthen the basic communities as they read the Bible from the perspective of the life issues of the people, relate their hopes to the promises of the gospel, and engage in concrete joint action with the wider human community.

Guyana Extension Seminary

A response to local needs for lay training

DALE A. BISNAUTH

The need for a programme of lay training was felt to be urgent. There were just not enough trained persons to provide leadership in Christian communities which were almost isolated from one another by the fact of geography. This was particularly so in the interior areas. Poor and irregular transportation facilities exacerbated the problem.

Almost every denomination suffered from the lack of trained pastors and priests to serve the scores of denominational parishes, districts and pastoral charges. Even if priests and pastors were readily available, smaller parishes would have experienced grave difficulties in maintaining them at an adequate level. Some congregations were too small for this and some parishes too poor. Meanwhile, many pastors and priests were itinerants who serviced congregations as best and as often as they could.

Clearly, this was not good enough in a situation in which Christians needed the kind of understanding of the faith that would help them to respond creatively to the needs of a developing society and to the need for a new sense of independence from metropolitan links and interdependence among sister churches within the region.

The task of equipping the church (the *laos*) to be the church in a newly politically independent and developing nation and to do so against a background of denominationalism and pietism was urgent. How were Christians to understand the implications of interfaith

• Dr Bisnauth is the Director of the Guyana Extension Seminary, 71 Murray Street, Georgetown, Guyana.

dialogue when they had not yet learned to distinguish between evangelism and proselytism? How were they to respond responsibly to economic development and matters relating to church-state relationships when they had not worked out the implications of the faith for social, economic and political demands?

Land, people, history

Guyana is situated on the northeast coast of South America with the Atlantic Ocean on the north, Surinam on the east, Brazil on the south and southwest, and Venezuela on the west.

The country sprawls over 83,000 square miles. Its population of about three-quarters of a million is concentrated mainly on the Guyanese coast, in pockets on the banks of the country's main rivers, and in the Rupununi savannahs in the far south.

Guyana boasts a national mix of some six races. Its people are of Amerindian, European, African, Indian, Portuguese and Chinese origins. Except for the indigenous Amerindians, the forebears of the Guyanese people came or were brought to these parts from the early seventeenth century onwards.

Guyana's economy is heavily agricultural. Sugar and rice are the pillars of the export trade. Bauxite is the major mineral resource industry, and forestry comprises another significant dimension of the export market. While there is no question that many Guyanese live in poverty, relatively speaking, the people as a whole are better off than many in the third world. The development of the hinterland both for its natural resources as well as for resettlement of people is a continuing thrust of the present government.

The country has a rich heritage of cultural traditions. How to put them together into what one writer calls a "mosaic" rather than into a "melting pot" is an important matter. In recent years, there has been a strong move to collect and preserve the old folklore and music of Guyana. The arts — poetry, music, dance, handcraft, graphic arts and architecture — have been fostered with a view to pulling out the essence of the Guyanese spirit using the talents and abilities of the Guyanese people. The steelband, the calypso, the sitar and tablah, and Indian dance and song have all become an integral part of the socio-cultural life of the nation. The church is now awakening to the possibilities inherent in using Guyanese art, music, poetry and literature in worship and teaching.

Guyana faces a series of difficult social problems which include family disintegration, racial disharmony, rising crime incidence, religious intolerance, alcoholism, and a general feeling among many of uncertainty about the future and/or a lack of faith and hope that Guyana can indeed be self-reliant. A renewed church with a trained laity can be an essential reconciling agent in Guyana.

Guyana is also multi-religious. The dominant religious groups are Christian and Hindu, with Muslims forming a somewhat smaller, but active group. The traditional Christian approach to Hindus or Muslims has been to see them as "pagan". Recently, there has been an attempt in Guyana to deal with this attitude and to foster religious understanding and common concerns for human need under the umbrella of the Guyana Inter-Religious Council formed early in 1976. Whether this body will be able to accomplish its avowed task, without division, remains to be seen.

The churches

The Christians are also a many-faceted group. Fourteen of the more mainline denominations are members of the Guyana Council of Churches. They include African Methodist Episcopal, African Methodist Episcopal Zion, Anglican, Church of God, Congregational Union, Guyana Missionary Baptist, Guyana Presbyterian (former Canadian Mission), Lutheran, Methodist, Moravian, Nazarene, Presbytery of Guyana (former Scots Mission), Roman Catholic and Salvation Army. In addition, the Council received an indigenous Amerindian group known as the Alleluia Church as an affiliate member of the Council of Churches. There are significant church groups that are not members of the Guyana Council of Churches: Assemblies of God, Church of Christ, Elim Church, Pilgrim Holiness (now called Wesleyan), New Testament Church of God, Regular Baptist, Seventh Day Adventist, Southern Baptist, plus many smaller groups.

Most of the churches in Guyana have experienced a similar pattern of development in which the church was established by means of missionary enterprise. This also entailed expatriate control of leadership and funds. Most of the churches have now become independent or autonomous, with little or no reliance on expatriate funds for the ongoing operations of the church. Training for the full-time ministry has developed in the Caribbean with Anglican, Roman Catholic and Presbyterian theological schools in Trinidad and Barbados, as well as an ecumenically-supported seminary for many of the Protestant bodies — the United Theological College of the West Indies in Jamaica.

Guyana Extension Seminary

The various Christian denominations in Guyana had been carrying on training programmes for diverse forms of ministry for many years. Catechists, deacons, lay readers, lay preachers, parish workers and the like had been the focus of training programmes, but the intention, in many cases, was to provide a semi-professional and sometimes salaried personnel. When overseas funds began to be withdrawn, some of these programmes withered either because of lack of persons to do the training or because there was resistance to a ministry of the laity in the true sense of the word.

The concept of training the laity as lay persons for significant ministry in the church had its roots in the 1970s when training and enrichment courses were provided for pastors and lay leaders through the then Extra-Mural Department of the United Theological College of the West Indies in Jamaica. By early 1972 it was decided on an informal basis that an ecumenical programme should begin and that it should be called Guyana Extension Seminary. This was held in New Amsterdam, 60 miles from the capital, Georgetown, largely because the prime movers of the programme at that time (Lutheran, Presbyterian and Roman Catholic among them) were resident in that area.

For about two years, until late 1974, the Guyana Extension Seminary in New Amsterdam offered about a dozen courses in Bible study, church history and preaching. Courses were taught by an ecumenical team of pastors on a one-per-week basis. After the programme ceased to function in late 1974, an evaluation revealed that a beginning had been made in developing a consciousness of the need for lay training on an ecumenical basis; that this need was being fulfilled; that while the programme met with good response from students from some denominations, other students did not maintain an adequate level of interest in the programme; that the study material was on an academic level that was unrealistic for many of the persons involved; that there was not a real consensus among the churches as to what sort of programme was desired or needed.

The Guyana Council of Churches, at the suggestion of the Lutheran Church in Guyana, agreed to call a person with skills in lay leadership training to work in Guyana to see what needs might be met. The Rev. Paul A. Tidemann, a pastor of the Lutheran Church in America, came to Guyana in September 1974 to fill this post on a part-time basis. Permission was given by the Council of Churches to form an ad hoc committee of representatives from every member denomination to work with Tidemann to determine what steps to take and make recommendations to the Council.

For a period of about six months, through June 1975, the Committee conducted a series of "research soundings" including written surveys from denominational heads, evaluations and discussions with representative lay persons from various parts of the country, contact with seminaries and extension programmes in the Caribbean and Central America, and conversations with representatives of the Caribbean Conference of Churches through its newly formed Agency for Renewal of the Church (ARC). The 14-member Guyana Council of Churches decided in early 1976 that the establishment of the Extension Seminary to train lay persons was a matter of urgent priority.

Unlike many programmes of theological education by extension, the Guyana Extension Seminary is not an "extended arm" of a formal, residential theological school. Experiences in the 1970s indicated that such an approach would be impracticable because the seminaries in the Caribbean are too far removed from Guyana to be able to extend themselves on a week-to-week basis. "Extension" in the Guyanese context means, therefore, that the *churches* in Guyana have extended their considerable resources of trained personnel, experience, and finances to train lay leaders as close to their places of work and residence as possible. "Extension" in Guyana also means that the 14 churches that form the Guyana Extension Seminary have extended themselves to one another. They appreciate the need of working cooperatively in such a venture. Some churches had not been able to train their people for years because of a dearth of personnel to do the work, while other denominations had been able to carry on rather sophisticated programmes for their lay leaders. A sharing of financial and personnel resources and experience in this manner enables the richness of Christian life and church work to be shared by all and for all.

In this sense the Guyana Extension Seminary has experimented in an area which few extension programmes have — in an ecumenical approach. In the early stages of development there had to be serious grappling with the issues of what kind of training could be done together. Now, in the actual experience of teaching and learning, it has been discovered that lay persons are tremendously excited about their ecumenical contacts — a first experience for many persons — and their sharing of traditions and ways of thinking. It is clear that in the approach to teaching and participation there must be an attitude of openness and understanding of the various emphases among the churches. The ecumenical dimension, far from weakening denominational loyalties, seems to foster greater appreciation for one's own Christian heritage. It also offers a practical demonstration of ways in which the churches can cooperate for the common good of the entire Christian community and for the nation and its people.

Objectives

The following objectives form a basis upon which the present and future programme of the Guyana Extension Seminary is carried out:

— to train lay persons to be effective leaders in congregations of the Christian churches which are without resident, full-time pastoral leaders; such lay persons will be used in leadership as the denominations individually decide;
— to train lay persons to fulfill specific types of leadership in any congregations, such as teacher, counsellor, worship leader, administrator, community organizer;
— to train lay persons to supplement the full-time ministry in a local congregation in order to free the pastor for supervisory activities among a cluster of congregations;
— to provide the training resource for all denominations that can be drawn upon for the basic training of persons in any aspect of ministry desired by the denomination;
— to make courses available to individual lay persons for personal enrichment in Christian faith or the development of specific skills;
— to be a touchstone for all clergy in Guyana where they can come for in-service training and enrichment;
— to conduct practical research into new forms of ministry to various aspects of the developing Guyanese society, such as national service, hinterland development programmes, agricultural development schemes, and to train persons to minister to these non-traditional gatherings of people;

— to be an influence in enabling the church to assume the forms and styles that it needs in order to communicate the gospel in this Guyanese/Caribbean society;

— to be a leaven within the entire church, ecumenically, to enable a more common understanding of the particular mission that the Christian church has to Guyanese society;

— to maintain relationships through the Guyana Council of Churches with the various theological seminaries in the Caribbean and with the Agency for Renewal of the Church of the Caribbean Conference of Churches in order both to provide data from our experience and to receive guidance and resource assistance.

Results

The GES operates on a regular basis through ten centres, nine of which are located on the coastlands, with the tenth at Linden on the Demerara River. Courses are also offered on the Berbice River. Here, the tutor/coordinator operates out of St Lust but travels by motor-boat to villages scattered on the river banks to hold classes with students. Special programmes are conducted in the Rupununi savannahs for Amerindian lay leaders of the Roman Catholic and Anglican churches.

Some 500 students from across 14 denominations have attended courses organized by the Guyana Extension Seminary. These come with the recommendation and blessing of their priests and pastors. Many of them are artisans, farmers, housewives, school teachers, and businessmen. Their common motive is to equip themselves for more effective service in the churches.

The tutors/coordinators are all persons who have had formal training in theological colleges. One is involved in the development of agriculture on church lands; the others are all pastors or priests.

It is difficult to assess the effectiveness of the work of the Guyana Extension Seminary. What is very evident is that there is a growing ecumenical spirit among those who share in GES courses. This spirit manifests itself in a willingness to promote and participate in ecumenical ventures sponsored by the Guyana Council of Churches and the Caribbean Conference of Churches. Given our history of narrow denominationalism, this is no mean development.

The churches are making increasing use of those who attend the GES. The Anglicans and Catholics lead in this regard. The African Methodist Episcopal Church has given recognition to some of its leaders who have been trained by the GES to the extent of giving them responsibility for directing parishes. Anglican and Presbyterian students have been ordained to the deaconate. But what is more important, the consensus is that those who attend the GES are much more alive as to what Christian discipleship entails. They bring this new sensitivity to whatever they do within the church, as well as to their witness at the work place and elsewhere as Christian citizens in a developing country.

Africa

Programming for ministry through theological education by extension

FRED HOLLAND

The setting

Theological education in Africa continued to have paternalistic influences long after the establishment of national, independent churches. This was probably due to arguments such as these, with their attendant fallacies: financial dependency (it appeared economical to send missionary teachers); theological fears (Dallas- or London-trained faculty would assure "sound" doctrine); national faculty shortage (overseas trained nationals often did not return home). The 1964-65 Theological Education Fund report, *Issues in Theological Education,* speaking of third world theological courses, states that they "show a rigid dependence upon forms created in the West". "It is not difficult to trace the ancestry of a particular curriculum back to its American, British, or Continental forebear" (TEF, 1966, page 32).

Ten years later Bishop Kauma of Uganda, the principal of Bishop Tucker Theological College, repeated this concern: "It is more than clear that in Africa many of our theological schools are outmoded. Many are modelled on the pattern of theological colleges of the mother church." He adds to that: "What is taught is answering questions that Africa is not asking."

While church leaders confronted and worked within the problems of government stability, church finances, nationalism, syncretism,

• Dr Holland served in Zimbabwe and Zambia 1955-1974, taught at Fuller Seminary and Wheaton College 1974-1981, and has recently returned to P.O. Box 711, Bulawayo, Zimbabwe. The address of Evangel Publishing House is P.O. Box 28963, Nairobi, Kenya.

urban needs, maintaining institutions and many more, the theological training schools presented little problem and were stable, somewhat prestigious and usually not in difficulty. Except for radicals who wanted reform, relevance, contextualization, or ministry performance, there was little to challenge these rigid forms. Schools, colleges, and seminaries on all levels carried on, little affected by the surrounding turbulence.

There were various attitudes held by the groups involved in these schools. It is true, of course, that the institutions differed greatly in their programmes and in the achievement of ministry-training goals. Missions tended to regard the theological schools as their last responsibility and of great significance in holding doctrinal soundness. The churches had mixed feelings about these schools but generally regarded them as sacred trusts. The students ranged from professional church people being further prepared for leadership positions, through local church workers finding time for biblical studies and teachers and professional people coming into church offices, to young people seeking preparation for social advancement. Teachers usually viewed as very serious and important their efforts at preparing church evangelists, teachers, pastors and other leaders. Depending on the situation, their attitudes ranged from a high degree of fulfilment to gross frustration.

The schools themselves ran from very basic Bible instruction programmes to high level graduate theological schools. The low entry level ability and young age of students, coupled with the results of extraction, were in many schools the major problems.

The awakening

If one talks of an awakening in theological education, the roots would certainly be found in the TEF with its concern for contextualization and in the Association of Evangelical Bible Institutes and Colleges in Africa and Madagascar (AEBICAM) with its concern for relevance and ministry performance. The organizations were similar; they were both broadening out to concerns for libraries, faculties, curriculum, and ministry in context; and they benefited from each other.

Within this awakening there was innovation in spite of the stagnation. Theological schools tend to resist change as do other institutions, and they also have a sense of sacred safeguarding. Many of the suggestions — of TEF through the area theological associations and of AEBICAM through regional fellowships — were received as the new alongside the old. The new partially satisfied the desire for change, while the old remained static and in place. New ideas were considered as experiments within the proven old. Curriculum changes from the Western subject/content dominated position led to additions such as a term or a year of in-ministry service. The success of such innovations did not usually lead to any drastic curriculum change but to curriculum expansion. The three-year course remained the same; the service involvement added a fourth year.

When Theological Education by Extension was introduced by the Committee to Assist Ministry Education overseas (CAMEO), it came first as an addition to the residential school. Those of us involved in theological schools had been wrestling with needs and problems, adding new ideas, respecting the old, and bearing our frustrations. TEE came as an answer to many of our problems. Variety in approach could be seen as extension being first *from* the residential school. As principal of our Bible school I started TEE to extend the ministry of our training programme. Many of the first TEE programmes in Africa were started as extensions of theological education *from* existing schools. A few TEE programmes were developed in opposition to inadequate schools. In such cases residential institutions were closed with great sighs of relief and some nostalgia. The Free Methodists did this with a school in the Transvaal that was failing to train the actual leadership of the church; they have developed a very extensive and effective extension school that meets their needs. Some independent churches or churches without resident schools have started TEE directly under the church as an acceptable form of training for ordination.

The TEE model
The basic TEE model for Africa came from the Presbyterian Seminary of Guatemala, as it was observed and reported in its early days of operation by J.F. Hopewell and was promoted worldwide through the CAMEO workshops. Various tripartite models have been used, with the rail fence model (as introduced by Ted Ward of Michigan State University) being most popular. During my teaching at the School of World Mission in Pasadena another model with a fourth part emerged as a result of discussion on the static nature of the fence and the need for a more dynamic expression.

The four-part railway model includes the three parts of the fence model but adds the dimension of spiritual formation. Without repeating what has been so widely publicized let me simply state that the four parts are to work together in a cybernetic, self-correcting and functional way. The participant learns from service experience and from the cognitive input of home study, and this is integrated and multiplied by regular seminar discussions. We have added a planned concern for spiritual formation. The new model appears thus:

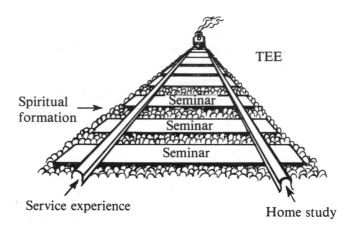

All theological education should rest on the foundation of the building of men and women of God — spiritual formation. The church moves forward with practical theological education that relates learning and doing and the development of being.

The leadership problem

In Africa both churches and missions realized that there were thousands of leaders of local worshipping groups who had inadeqate, if any, training for their ministry involvement. The existing programmes were not training enough people, seemed not to be training the right people, and/or were not training people to do the right things. Numerous surveys by research organizations, such as Daystar in Kenya, confirmed that these were the real problems. Not only did we lack local group leaders, but church leaders on all levels lacked full training to perform their assignments adequately.

As we considered the TEE model, we realized that we had people in leadership roles at all levels who needed theological training. They were already in service. TEE suggests that this is the proper place for training — *in* the ministry, not in isolation from the ministry. We had then one part of the model in abundance — the people in service.

Again as we considered the model we realized that the potential to lead the seminar sessions was at hand. There were trained pastors, theological educators, and many good, capable senior workers who could become extension centre leaders. It seemed practical to utilize local leaders and avoid expensive, difficult travel. Workshops on the role of the seminar leader were conducted in South, Central, West and East Africa directly aimed at giving TEE basics and training discussion leaders. A small practical booklet, *Teaching Through TEE*, subtitled *Help for Leaders in Theological Education by Extension in Africa*, has sold thousands of copies. So we had two parts of the model — the people in service and the seminar leaders.

The problem for Africa was obvious as we looked at the model again — there were no suitable home study books. Those of us doing TEE soon discovered that the strengths of the system were easily lost when one part was weak, missing, or misused. Books for TEE were not available. Letters crossed Africa and the oceans in search of suitable TEE study books, but there were few. The programmed books used in Latin America were in Spanish, were aimed at that culture, and were on the seminary level. Others tried using modified books or correspondence workbooks. Harold Alexander of World-Team prepared a series of workbooks in French. But still we had no TEE books suitable for the grassroots need in Africa.

The foundation that makes the service experience, home study, and seminar discussions into acceptable ministry training is spiritual formation, which encourages devotion to God, dedication to service, and growth in personal holiness. It is a planned-for part of the model. It does not simply happen while TEE is done. Spiritual formation is the positive response to all that God is calling us to be.

The Africa solution

To overcome the problem — absence of TEE books — we made some decisions. We would aim at the thousands of local leaders. There were other needs on the college and seminary level, but there were some good higher-level schools that could be utilized. We felt we must produce the missing study books, i.e. a complete Bible school curriculum of programmed textbooks. We wanted to make possible the expansion to all areas of Africa materials for an adequate and high quality theological education through extension.

The first obvious need was for people trained in instructional technology, particularly in programming. There had been some secular uses of programmed instruction (PI) on the continent. Dr Cromoski of the Programming Centre at New York University had visited Ghana and worked with government programmes. Clive Lawless of the Open University in England had used PI while a secondary school teacher in Malawi. The Post Office Department of Zambia used PI in worker training, as did the gold and copper mines there and in other countries. An oil company in Kenya produced a programmed text to assist local shop-keepers. A centre had been established by the United Nations to experiment with the use of programming on the African continent.

The Association of Evangelical Bible Institutes and Colleges of Africa and Madagascar was formed in 1966, and became the agency that provided for TEE expansion throughout Africa. The association had no particular membership in its early days. No one was excluded and participation in workshops and projects was very broad. The first few years of its operation concentrated on gathering theological educators together for sharing and reflection, and the discussions were very beneficial. After the first CAMEO-sponsored workshops AEBICAM applied much of its energy to TEE. TEE was considered an extension of existing schools and not a separate approach or a competitor. AEBICAM made many friends in the early workshops among people who did not usually attend evangelical conferences. Some of these — Lutherans, Anglicans, Presbyterians, and other mainline denominations — became a part of the textbook project. AEBICAM served uniquely from its birth until it later became the theological commission of the more defined Association of Evangelicals of Africa and Madagascar (AEAM).

Assisting in the dissemination of TEE concepts and relating to a broad and large group of theological institutions put AEBICAM in the position of being the anticipated source of PI materials. Letters were continually received that said one thing: We want to start TEE. Where do we get the materials?

As the executive secretary of AEBICAM and involved in one of the first TEE operations, I sought answers. AEBICAM was more than just a TEE organization and specifically more than an agency for the production of PI books for TEE. I was not interested in extension as another method but was concerned with the church and the development of its leadership. Another organization for the production of PI books was needed and came into being. It did not start as a duly constituted body but rather emerged as a project. TEXT-Africa was the name given to an activity to produce Theological Education by eXtension Texts for Africa.

It came about this way. My wife and I conducted extension centres in Zambia in 1970 from Choma Bible Institute. We had experimented with other non-formal approaches with some satisfaction. This included short-term courses (for which we gathered approximately 100 local pastors and leaders), correspondence courses, and a mobile Bible Institute (where the teachers stayed at a centre for four or five weeks and had half-day classes). TEE seemed to combine the best of what we wanted to see with the least amount of disadvantage. We were excited about the prospects!

We soon realized that if we were to write programmed lessons, we needed more training. The church was committed to supporting extension and approved my going to the University of Illinois (Chicago Circle) for special study under Susan Markle. This prepared me to begin and try programming. Upon returning to Zambia I experimented with various PI formats, frame lengths, response styles, and confirmation formats. Programming was both fun and tedious. My wife and I worked together and soon had actually prepared some self-paced, home study lessons suitable for church leaders to use in our extension programme. We used a Volkswagen camper to cover a four-day 105-mile circuit of five centres in which 70 students were enrolled. As we travelled, we wrote lessons that would be used two weeks later. The proximity of writing and use helped the learning process for new programmers. Methods that did not work were changed until a form that did work emerged.

The number of PI requests increased, so we decided to share our discoveries with others and then share the books produced. The first effort was a five-week production workshop in Salisbury. Subjects were assigned for content research prior to the workshop. Teams of church leaders and missionary theological educators worked together. The materials produced by each group were to become the property of all. Four basic principles guided us. First, the content was to be evangelical. This meant that we accepted the Bible as authoritative and presented salvation through faith in Jesus as Saviour and Lord. It also meant that we were non-sectarian. Since

Calvinists, Wesleyans, Pentecostals and others were cooperating, we wanted materials acceptable on a broad doctrinal spectrum. Second, the content was to be culturally relevant to Africa. Africans participated in developing the content and approaches of the courses. We tried to answer the questions that were being asked by the pastors. We dealt with the ancestors and spirits and faced the problems of urban change. We attempted to speak in context. Third, the original lessons were in a basic 1500-word English vocabulary, with limited sentence length to aid translators in preparing materials at the level of functional literacy. This does not mean that the content was simple or immature. Our target group was defined as mature, Christian, adult, literate church leaders. The fourth area of content concern dictated a linear programming style that did not involve a great deal of page turning or searching for places to get information or confirmation.

Through experimentation we discovered what worked best for our target group. We did away with scrambled responses and confirmation sections at the end of daily lessons and inserted the confirmation of answers in the opening of the input in the successive frames. I later asked a group of professional programmers to comment on this, and they confirmed that it was sound programming.

Programme evaluation

The concept of TEE people working as a coordinated production team worked beyond our dreams. Workshop participants committed themselves to a long-term project. All the subjects of a three-year Bible curriculum were to be produced, more than 40 of them.

PI production workshops were held in Zimbabwe, Nigeria, Kenya and South Africa. Follow-up meetings helped the programmers with problems and provided additional input. At the same time basic TEE workshops were scheduled in all parts of the continent. In the writers' workshops 97 writers became involved in writing teams and· this has sent 26 books through publication. Another ten are in various stages of completion.

As soon as the first books were published we began receiving requests for translation. We extended full permission with non-profit rights for translation and production in order to make the books available for TEE as widely as possible. Since the books were written in Africa with African content, the basic worldview was animistic. We supplied a four-page translation guide to assure that the programming flow was not disturbed. Some difficulty in word usage arose in areas of Muslim influence. Illustrations created problems because objects referred to were not customary in some areas. Our translation guide showed how to change the illustration form without losing the meaning. Perhaps the greatest translation problem was the repetitive use of specific words, as opposed to the use of synonyms to avoid repetition. Translators tended to mix the synonyms, or not use them when required. Our guide helps to point out what the learning objective is and why its wording is critical. If the translator sees the significance of the objective, the general PI flow is better preserved. Although we supply the basic English copy, we recommend that the translated material also be tested.

Now the 26 published books are being translated and used in more than 100 languages, including New Guinea Pidgin, Palauan, Thai, Urdu, Cebuano, Gujarati, Bengali and Arctic English. This speaks well for at least three things. First, we see that Christians can work together. Second, African writers recognize the church of Jesus Christ as being bigger than their own denominations, and they have given themselves to such a difficult task and have participated so faithfully. Some beautiful fellowship came out of the long days of working together in the five-week workshop periods. Third, considering the scope of the project and the amount of work completed, it is a tribute and continued testimony to God's faithfulness.

To evaluate the project one can look at two indicators. From a publisher's position the books have sold well. The Evangel Publishing House, relating to the Pentecostal Assemblies of Canada, have been extremely cooperative. In 1970 they also began to receive requests for TEE books. Being the largest religious publishers in Africa, they have distributors and agents in all areas and are aware of the needs. Their managers, Calvin Bombay and Calvin Ratz, offered to publish the first few books on a trial basis. Many extension schools wanted only a few copies of the basic English text to use for translation. Such a market does not provide for large press runs which lower cost. The first press run was 4,000 copies and these sold in less than six months. Pre-publication standing orders made it possible to increase the original press runs to 7-8,000. Some English TEE programmes ordered large quantities. In terms of publishing and sales the project has been successful despite the fact that the prices are kept as low as possible to make them widely available.

The second area for evaluating the success of the project is the extended use of the books. It is recognized that they may be used, not because they are good, but because there is nothing else available. We do, however, receive a continuous flow of letters from TEE leaders and students expressing appreciation. We also ask for and receive critical evaluations. There is a continually expanding market. The books are used, because of their animistic bias, with Indians in Latin America, Aborigines in Australia, Native American Indians in Canada, Eskimos in Alaska, Mountain Tribals in Taiwan, and Islanders of Micronesia. While we recognize their shortcomings and extreme simplicity, we are gratified at the wide acceptance and use of the books. It is estimated in a survey done by Harold Dalton of the Pentecostal Holiness Church missions office that up to 70,000 persons may currently be using the books in continuing TEE study. Evangel Publishing House alone has printed 250,000 of these texts.

Problem areas

We looked first at the African setting that called the TEXT-Africa project into being. Then we described briefly the mechanics and scope of the project. What remains and may be the most helpful is an evaluation of our programming for TEE among leaders. Some qualitative value may be deduced from the broad use and acceptance of the books themselves. We have also done some critical evaluating of the PI quality and its effectiveness. A general survey of users has supplied statistics on acceptability. Critical pre-publication readers supply corrective criticisms, and unsolicited user comments supply data. Arnold Labrentz, editorial manager of Evangel Publishing House, has had close contact with the manuscripts for publication and with user reports. For his M.A. research project he designed a 17-page research tool and administered it to a representative sample group of 395 TEE students. The data has been computer-entered and cross-referenced for statistical evaluation of specific indicators. Some of the findings reveal the level of lesson retention:

Text	Course studied		Fact retention	Objective involvement
	Before 1977	After 1977		
Following Jesus	91	130	68%	45%
Bringing people to Jesus	96	133	76%	44%
Talking with God	83	69	72%	84%

The retention of specific facts is high after the passing of considerable time. The ministry use of the material is acceptable. This does not indicate the percent of students in the ministry but the use of specific task abilities taught.

Of 36 questions on the survey regarding church member problems of cultural concern, most were either taught in the books and/or discussed in the seminar. Two areas, divorce and deception, were rated highest as not having been taught, but only 37.2 per cent of leaders said it was not taught (they did not remember that it was in the book), while more than 60 per cent did remember it. Of the above-mentioned 36 categories, eleven were in the 30 percentile range of the negative, 13 in the 20 percentile range, and 5 in the 10-20 percentile range of the negative. Five were below 10 per cent. This means that information in most of the 36 categories was retained by from 60 per cent to over 90 per cent of the group. It should be pointed out that some of the subjects were handled in greater detail in some of the study books that the students had not yet studied.

Other data revealed that 95.8 per cent were helped with their personal problems. Only 4.8 per cent wanted the TEE courses to be taken faster. The age spread of the 395 students in TEE surveyed was: 19 years or less, 2.7 per cent; 20-29 years, 23.2 per cent; 30-44 years, 52.5 per cent; 45 or over, 21.6 per cent; no response, 5.1 per cent. Sixty-six per cent were male and 34 per cent were female; 60.8 per cent were the pastor, only leader, or a deacon/elder of their church; 22.3 per cent were church officers or Sunday school teachers or workers. Fifty-two percent attended nine or more sessions out of ten; 21.6 per cent attended less than five meetings. Ninety-three percent of the groups met at least once each week, while only 7 per cent met less than once weekly. Of the 395 students only 8.4 per cent (33 people) had taken the course in English.

The survey indicates that we must continue to strive for relevance and to bring the lessons to the problem-solving level of learning. More careful testing will help in some areas. More seminar leader training is needed. As the full implications of the survey unfold, we should be able to improve the relevance of the programmed instruction.

Three other areas of concern are indicated in the unsolicited criticisms we receive.

Academic level: Some people are dissatisfied with the academic level of the content. A decision was made to aim our texts at the largest segment of untrained local leaders. Personal contact and surveys have shown them to be mature, adult, capable men and women, with little formal education but functional literacy. Our writers direct their programmes to this target group, and testing assures that we present the lessons so that this group can comprehend the content. The two areas of complaint are (1) the content level is too low, and (2) the content level is too difficult. The answer to the first complaint, regarding simplicity, is that we programme for our target group's entry level. We programme for learners to achieve, not for an amount of material to be covered. The simple, directly stated objectives often surprise subject matter experts when they see our comprehensive examinations. The material is given in small bits, but, as an African proverb says: "You can eat an elephant if you do it one bite at a time."

The second complaint can be answered in a similar way, but it gives us more concern. We may be permitting writers' concern for content to exceed our actual testing level. There is a great need and a challenge to those in leadership training for the programming of college/seminary level material for use in a pan-Africa extension seminary.

Doctrinal acceptance: Another area of concern relates to doctrinal acceptance. Writers are instructed to say what the Bible says and not bring their own theology to it. At this point the usual reply is that what is said is not what is meant, or it doesn't mean that today, or it will not be understood. Our instruction — and we have been stretched theologically in this project — is to stay with the wording of the text and the bounds of hermeneutics. It is difficult! Several things help the process without compromise of scripture. The directness and level of our writing helps avoid doctrinal issues. The limited vocabulary avoids theological terms. We have planned not to programme a theology text until one can be done that can realistically be called an African biblical theology.

We are helped further by a series of content controls. First, we have critical readers from various doctrinal persuasions read the texts before publication. Their responses affect the final editing and usually involve a word here or there. Second, we keep office master copies in which typos, errors, and complaints are recorded for consideration and correction prior to reprinting. Third, seminar leaders are taught to discuss problem areas. The text may give an answer but indicate that class discussion will give clarification. The scope of a statement such as Paul's, "I wish that you all spoke in tongues", do not get an elaborate supporting explanation, nor are they explained away. Instead there is the suggestion that they be discussed in the seminar.

Another issue under this second area of concern — doctrinal acceptance — emerges here and relates to James Goff's early criticism of evangelical brain washing (*Risk,* Vol. 7, No. 2, 1971). It is inappropriate for a dominating culture to impose limiting content on a recipient culture; this strangles the potential for a truly local contextualization and application of scripture to cultural needs. We have attempted to avoid this by insisting on African involvement in the development of content, by not programming a theology course, and by having the text acceptable across a broad theological spectrum. This does mean that we avoid theology. It does mean that we state biblical truth in non-technical terms, and this allows church leaders in the peer group of the seminar, within the context of their own church and cultural backgrounds, to determine meaning. The freedom of the seminar session resolves many of the problems.

Effectiveness of the programming: A final area of concern relates to the effectiveness of our programming. Some of our inadequacies have been corrected by our continued research and insistence on testing and field validation. As a writer completes a daily segment, it is tested and revised until it works. Each of the books has ten weeks of lessons, with each week of five days having a unifying theme. When the ten weeks are completed, they are used in an actual TEE field situation, hopefully with more than 50 students. Validation forms are used to record every individual response of every student. This process involves examination of each frame response — so that if there are 50 testees and each day has approximately 15 frames, we would have recorded 37,500 responses (50 students x 15 frames x 5 days x 10 weeks = 37,500 entries). Such testing assures us of a high degree of student achievement. We keep testing and revising until we achieve our standard. Our cognitive input level of acceptance is that 90 percent of the target group gain 90 percent of the objectives on a criterion test consisting of all teaching points. We continually watch for problems and seek to improve in each new text.

The church does not move forward by TEE or any other method. God is glorified among the people when his Son becomes known as Lord and Saviour. If TEE helps to produce leaders for the church who achieve this result, then TEE should be used. The emphasis must be on the goal and not on the method. My passion is the church. My concern is its leadership. The present method is TEE.

Fambidzano (Zimbabwe)

African Independent churches adopt theological education by extension

PETER M. MAKAMBA

As early as 1920, African Independent churches began to emerge in Zimbabwe. Bishops Makamba, Mtisi and Masuka were the first of the Shona leaders to join the South African Zionists in 1921. These three planted Zionism in Zimbabwe and converted and baptized several people including the late Rev. S. Mutendi. From this small nucleus several independent groups arose as early as 1930, particularly among the Shona-speaking people. These churches operated mainly in the rural areas, but later on spread to urban areas. At present they have a total membership of approximately 70,000.

The selection and training of leaders

Most of the founders of these churches never underwent any form of training. Makamba, Masuka and presumably Mtisi had no catechetical training and never joined any mission church as full church members. They regarded themselves as having been converted to Christianity for the first time in 1921 when they were baptized as Zionists. According to them the Spirit led them into action and, being charismatically gifted, they led their respective churches.

But to say that in these churches there is no training is very misleading. As soon as a person joins the church movement, the leadership regards him as a trainee. He is given the doctrinal teachings of the particular church and is expected to watch and imitate closely the life of other Christians who joined the church before

---

• The Rev. Peter M. Makamba is the current Principal and former General Secretary of Fambidzano, P.O. Box 127, Fort Victoria, Zimbabwe.

him. Real training takes place during evening services. Here younger Christians preach first and the older ones come last, during which time they try to pinpoint mistakes made by the younger Christians, at the same time suggesting good methods of preaching. It is only after the leadership is satisfied with one's ability, conduct and loyalty to the church that one is assigned a specific task, like being in charge of a congregation. The selection of leaders was regarded as the work of the Holy Spirit. No person was ordained to any office before the prophets (those who speak in tongues) were consulted so as to be sure of the person's rightful place in the church hierarchy. Even the founders of the respective churches profess to have received directive visions before starting their church movements. As time went on, the procedure changed. Seniority of membership became important; the longer the time one stays in the church, the greater the chances for being selected for a post.

At present the ability of an individual is considered before selection to any post. This ability must not be evaluated according to Western standards where, in most cases, university qualification is the minimum requirement. One who is well versed in the Bible, with a good command of church doctrine, who lives a good Christian life, is considered the most able person and is eligible for selection. Of course these churches are beginning to have a few people with high academic attainments, but these rarely hold responsible positions in the church since they are employed outside.

There are various patterns of leadership in the Independent churches. The founder of the church regards his leadership as something that came directly from God. God vested him with the power and wisdom to found and lead the church. This became clear through revelations of the Holy Spirit which he experienced before starting his church movement. This is one type of leadership.

The Independents' strong emphasis on healing by faith alone has led to another type of leadership. When a church member receives the power of healing the sick, people from all over the country flock to him for help with their ailments. Unbelievers who come to him are made Christians first before they receive help. Gradually a big group develops around him and he becomes so busy that he has no time to attend services with the other members of his church. Instead he administers his own services at his homestead with those whom he heals. In this way he builds his leadership and eventually becomes autonomous. This kind of leadership usually falls away as soon as the power of healing disappears.

The most respected way of receiving leadership in the Independent churches is through the principal leader. The principal leader selects and ordains someone to lead a section of his church that is far from his homestead. The ordained man remains loyal to the principal leader. This kind of man is usually called *Muongamiri* (the one who calls others together).

The ballot system is not common in the Independent churches. At the end of his life the principal leader appoints someone to lead the church. It could be his blood son, if he is a committed Christian, or any church member. The appointment of the son of the principal leader is preferred because such an appointment allows continuous use of the "Jerusalem"[1] already erected by the founder of the church. Also, it is believed that the Spirit of God which worked through the principal leader will now work through his son and in this way provide the same leadership as before.

Every church has its own system of establishing its leadership, and the system changes according to the factors present at the time. Nevertheless, there remains a vast difference from the mission-type clergy with its extensive theological training as a precondition for promotion to the highest ranks. In the Independent churches kinship ties and seniority of membership, religious zeal, conformity to group norms, charismatic power, social standing, and Bible knowledge are the bases for appointment and promotion in the leadership hierarchy. Through the influence of a few people who have attained higher theological education, and more particularly through Fambidzano, the Independent churches are beginning to lay emphasis on theological training as a precondition for promotion to the highest ranks. But this is still at its initial stage, and it will take time to be understood and accepted as the basis for promotion.

A new endeavour

Having studied the history and training needs of the Independent churches, Dr M.L. Daneel, currently professor of missiology at the University of South Africa, decided to launch an experimental work among the Shona Independent churches in Zimbabwe. After a period

---

[1] In the context of the Independent churches the homestead of the principal leader is called "Jerusalem". This is where the first church building is erected. If another man is made leader, who is not the principal leader's son, it means that a new Jerusalem is to be built.

of preparation in Holland and a trip to the United States to determine the prospects of future financial aid, he travelled to Zimbabwe. Soon after he had settled at Morgenster Mission of the Dutch Reformed Church, he contacted Independent church leaders whom he had known during his earlier research in 1965-1967.

His proposals for a joint theological training centre were discussed at length at the various church headquarters. Most leaders responded enthusiastically to the prospect of theological training for their leadership. They generally underscored the basic idea that they themselves should take the responsibility for such a venture, even though they were aware that financial and administrative problems were bound to arise. The ecumenical aspect of the project troubled some, especially the leaders of the spirit-type churches. A few Zionists openly declared that it would be impossible for them to be trained by people who did not give as central a place to the manifestations of the Holy Spirit as they did. They thought it wiser for each church to establish its own theological school, without, however, venturing suggestions as to the implementation of such an idea in practice. The Ethiopian-type churches were less hesitant about interchurch cooperation. Yet they were fully aware of the fact that the lack of prophetic activities in their ranks caused zealous Zionists and Apostles to regard them as not fully Christian.

Numerous questions concerning the building of a school, future identity and autonomy of each church, administration of funds and ultimate control of the theological school were raised. Yet it was clear that the envisaged centre had captured the imagination of many Independents and that they were eager to see the proposed plans materialize.

Formation of the African Independent Churches' Conference

During the weekend of 28-30 July 1972, the first joint meeting was held in the Bikita district. We camped on the banks of the Rozva river and conducted open-air meetings in typical Independent church style. Each of the attendant churches was supposed to be represented by three official delegates, but for the 20 church groups attending we eventually counted more than 150 conference participants.

The major aim of this conference was to discuss proposals for the formation of an association and to gauge the response of delegates to the proposals in an "experimental" ecumenical situation. The need for Christian unity and interchurch cooperation with reference to John 17:21,23 was expounded, and it was suggested that an association could contribute towards the realization of this ideal. During several marathon sessions we discussed the possible basis, objectives and organization of an association. It was generally agreed that a representative body of the Independent churches should seek to promote theological education for its office-bearers and to promote interchurch relations.

The theological conditions for a church to obtain membership were discussed at length. Generally it was agreed that in order to qualify a church should:

a) accept and propagate the word of God (Old and New Testament);
b) believe in God the Father, Jesus Christ his Son, and the Holy Spirit;
c) practise baptism in the name of the triune God;
d) have a council which exercises church discipline;
e) and practise holy communion.

Towards the end of the conference the delegates of twelve churches supported the idea of an association and favoured immediate formation of such a body. On Saturday evening, 29 July 1972, the *Fambidzano Yamakereke Avatema* (literally cooperation of the churches of black people), referred to in English as the African Independent Churches Conference, was founded.

The objectives of the association read as follows:

a) the theological education of members of the African Independent churches through the establishment of a theological training school, Bible correspondence courses, and refresher courses;
b) the establishment of a scholarship fund for theological education;
c) the promotion of interchurch relations through conferences and assistance in the problems and needs of member churches of the conference.

Training programme

After many failures with regard to the securing of a land lease in the rural area where a theological school was to be built, we aimed at a programme of theological training by extension with a team of lecturers developing theological courses adapted to the needs of the Independent churches and teaching Independent church students in the surrounding districts. With this in mind we converted an old storeroom in Fort Victoria into an administrative centre for the programme. A few lecturers were appointed to start developing both extension training and correspondence courses.

Preparations for the opening of rural extension centres were also made. Discussions were conducted with the district officers as well as local chiefs in order to secure permission to operate in the rural areas. After many months of struggle, with more delays than we originally expected, signs of success began to appear. Our teaching team went out for the first time to teach at the extension centres in August 1973. We started with three centres: one in Bikita, one in Gutu and one in Victoria District. The enrolment was 22. To start with, Old Testament, New Testament, homiletics, ethics and church history were introduced at the centres, and these were taught once a week at every one.

Our correspondence courses were also welcomed. We started by giving courses on Genesis and Exodus and later developed some more from the various books of the Bible. Quite a number of people resident in urban and rural areas of both Independent and other churches followed these courses. Although the pace of participants living out in the tribal areas was slower, enthusiasm for the correspondence courses continued to grow.

In 1974 more people became interested in the training programme; as a result two more centres were added to make five: two in the Gutu district, two in Bikita and one in the Victoria district. About 50 students, including several women, attended the classes. We noticed signs of a growing appreciation among the students themselves for the training they were receiving. Later in the year, there were requests to extend our teaching to three more centres: in Buhera, further south in Victoria, and in Zaka. But as it was, the teaching team was covering 700 miles each week, which left them little time for drafting reports and preparing new lessons. Fatigue had already proved to be a major obstacle in this kind of work. Thus we couldn't properly respond to the growing demand unless more teachers were appointed.

Under these circumstances one couldn't expect model lessons to be worked out. We were breaking new ground for the Shona Independents at last, and it needed more time before a complete syllabus was developed. What we were really doing was teaching a few Independents some of the rudiments of church history, homiletics and ethics and introducing them to a more systematic study of Old and New Testament than they were used to. Of course, to the Western theologian this approach might have appeared oversimplified and fragmented. To the potential Independent church leader out in the tribal area, however, such lessons meant a tremendous increase in knowledge, a whole set of new tools with which to work. To the few educationally advanced students the four lessons each week proved to be too little, but to the majority of participants the new facts provided were about as much as they could absorb.

Enthusiasm for our lessons continued to grow. In 1975 about 60 students enrolled for extension training and 100 students for correspondence courses.

In 1976 Fambidzano experienced rapid growth and a significant expansion of its sphere of influence. It had acquired a fleet of vehicles suited for operations in both urban and rural areas. More students (100) enrolled than in any of the preceding years, and an additional office was acquired. About 50 students completed their two-year course and were awarded certificates. From these graduates Fambidzano began to draw teacher assistants.

In the same year, the work was affected by the intensification of the guerrilla war. As the chances of driving over landmines became more real, we decided to use landmine-proofed trucks. This did not take us far. There were innumerable explosive devices on the roads so that moving in the tribal areas became both costly and time-consuming.

Every week the lecturers reported back at the office on their latest experiences. Consideration was also regularly given to the indications from students on the situation in their areas, helping us make an ongoing assessment of the viability of our working methods. After serious consideration, at the end of 1976 we decided to confine our activities to the office in town and to revise and print TEE training material.

During 1977, 1978 and 1979, about nine studies were revised and printed. A book entitled *Introduction to the New Testament* (written in Shona) was also produced, which at the moment is awaiting printing.

The temporary closure of our rural centres did not mean the end of our activities in the tribal areas. A new system of messengers providing lessons to the students and bringing answer sheets to the office for correction was firmly established. In practice it proved difficult to stay in touch with all the students. Assistant lecturers in particular travelled long distances on foot. Additional assistants had to be employed to help distribute new and collect completed lessons.

Despite numerous snags the new system eventually functioned smoothly, and lessons poured into the office regularly for correction and comment. Few students dropped out, and their enthusiasm did not dim.

In addition we introduced a new extension centre in the form of night classes in the Mucheke Township of Fort Victoria. Attendence was sporadic, but members of a variety of churches that were not affiliated to Fambidzano participated. This had the effect of improved relations between the leaders and members of a number of churches outside Fambidzano.

In 1980, after Zimbabwe attained its independence, Fambidzano resumed its activities in the rural areas. After acquiring the needed permission to work in the tribal areas, a good number of extension centres (seven), with an enrolment of 100, were reopened. In urban areas, particularly Salisbury, six centres were reopened with an enrolment of 40 students. Real progress in the establishment of extension centres was noticed in 1981. Eighteen centres were operating: ten in Victoria Province, six in Salisbury and two in Charter District. The enrolment was high (250), compared to the preceding years. During these two years correspondence students also increased. About 150 students joined, making the total number of students following correspondence courses 600.

Impact of the Fambidzano training programme on the Independent churches

Early this year, our teaching team was assigned to do a field survey on the effect of Fambidzano's training programme on the Independent churches. The team set out to determine how the students themselves evaluated the ecumenical aspect of TEE programmes, whether friction between trained students and their superiors was noticeable, whether there were changes in preaching and in pastoral care, to see if there was a correlation between training and spiritual growth, in the understanding of fundamental biblical truths concerning salvation, grace, the trinity of God, etc. and the possible influence of trained ministry on church growth patterns. Although some of the results of this survey were of an impressionistic nature, a notion was obtained of the validity of observations made in the past, and valuable new insights were achieved.

The students generally were highly appreciative of the cooperation that has been established among the Independent churches. One of the students, an influential *Mutopia*, said: "In the past we (the African churches) accused each other, and the resentment ran deep. I myself never wanted to attend the services of the Zionists, and the Zionists never attended the *Topia* meetings. But that has now changed because of the knowledge received through biblical studies of *Fambidzano*. Now we are like the followers of one man who cooperate with each other. We also see a great improvement in our relations with the mission churches. There is still a great deal of strife among those churches not affiliated to Fambidzano."

One of the problems we have anticipated all along was that some of the students may use their new status to oppose or undermine the authority of their leaders. Special care was therefore taken to instruct the students to be tactful in their approach to the elders and to help them build their respective churches rather than cause conflict and division through the advocacy of radical changes. Apparently this strategy has paid off. The team reported that just about all the Independent church leaders interviewed approved of the work Fambidzano students were doing. Their appreciation was reflected in that they tended to promote Fambidzano graduates to the ministry and commented favourably on improved preaching techniques. I have also noticed during my regular visits to the Independent churches' headquarters that the crisis of authority which we expected in the leader-student relationship is not to be found. Instead, the students are loyal to their leaders, and the leaders in turn appreciate them by publicly denouncing unsystematic preaching. That the training programme has generally functioned as a constructive and not as a divisive force in the Independent churches fills one with gratitude.

From the comments of students it appears that they benefit most from their studies through the improvement of their preaching. Virtually all of them have become more critical in evaluating the sermons in their churches. They spend more time preparing their own messages, analyzing texts and trying to restrict themselves to the central theme of the biblical portion they are dealing with. Said one of the students: "At first we did not know what we were doing. We simply preached what we wanted without knowing what it all amounted to. It always happened that one would end up preaching something quite different from what the selected text implied. Each Zionist service usually comprises quite a number of sermons—one man choosing a passage from Matthew, another a text from the

Psalms, and the following one a text from Revelation. This causes confusion... Now that we apply better methods, our people understand the Bible better. As leader of my own congregation, I now discuss before the service what subject we are to preach about. We get the appropriate references from a concordance. Therefore the central message for a particular service remains the same. This works much better than the old practice of everybody just preaching from unrelated portions in the Bible.''

What this student has in fact achieved is the introduction of a session of Bible study and exegesis of certain texts as a preliminary to the weekly church service. This certainly must lead towards greater coherence and depth in the presentation of God's word during a Sunday service.

Quite a number of students have experienced spiritual growth as a result of participation in the TEE programme. They specifically mention regular Bible study and an intensified prayer life as the signs of spiritual progress. Mrs Forichi, wife of Bishop Forichi of the Zion Christian Church, stated that she never prayed regularly nor did she understand Christianity before she got involved in the Fambidzano training programme. She said: "I attended church because my husband was a bishop and he needed support. But I seldom understood what was being preached. My husband had taught me to read Titus 2:1-15. This chapter deals with obedience of a woman towards her husband. I did not really know who Christ was nor what he had done for me. Light came to me while following Fambidzano courses. My life changed completely. Before I took the course, I never prayed in the morning or evening, and I never read my Bible. Now I do so regularly, having realized that the Bible is a book full of guidance and life.''

The views of students on doctrinal issues reflected several misconceptions. Some were at a loss when they were required to describe the Trinity. The most obvious tendency was an over-riding focus on the Holy Spirit and an inclination to attribute a lesser position to Jesus the Son than to God the Father. Legalistic tendencies were apparent in the views of those who emphasized church affiliation and obedience to church rules as a condition for eternal life, rather than salvation through God's grace and individual faith. A full confession of sins to the church leader was of over-riding importance for the forgiveness of sins. To some at least the attitude of the church leader had such an important influence on the forgiveness of sins that the free grace of God in his direct relationship to the individual was of little existential influence.

The teaching team's survey highlighted the need for the inclusion of a course on systematic theology in the Fambidzano training programme. One was drafted some time ago, but we have been hesitant to introduce it. Doctrinal issues have been a bone of contention in the Independent churches, and an early introduction of such a subject would have caused friction. But having discussed the composition of the course with the leaders, we feel that it is time to have it in our curriculum. This will include a first-year survey of the history of dogma and a second-year focus on doctrines most relevant to the Independent churches.

Lutheran synod and
Roman Catholic diocese of Arusha

Training village ministries in Tanzania

BUMIJA MSHANA and DEAN PETERSON

The Arusha region programme of theological education by extension began in January 1974 after nearly a year of preparation. It offers a three-year course in Christian theology for congregational servants. The first two classes graduated in 1976 and 1979, and the current class is scheduled for graduation in 1982. Each of the first two classes numbered under 40 students, and we expect a graduation of 70 in 1982. The programme is a modest attempt to train people at the grassroots level for ministry in the villages of the Arusha region, and it is currently seen as a contribution in the areas of theological education and evangelism. Of great importance is the fact that from the start there has been significant and growing cooperation between Lutherans and Catholics. The involvement of these churches in one educational programme has already strengthened our ties to mutual benefit.

Context and goals

Tanzania's total population numbers 17 million; the Arusha region presently has a population of one million people with an expected increase to two million by the turn of the century. This region is one of the largest in Tanzania, covering 310 miles from north to

• The Rev. Bumija Mshana was a parish pastor and taught at the Lutheran Theological College, Makumira, before becoming the Principal of the Extension Seminary of Arusha Synod. The Rev. Dean Peterson, a Lutheran missionary from the US, has played an important role in the development of the Extension Seminary, Oldonyosambu, P.O. Box 1396, Arusha, Tanzania.

south and 240 miles from east to west. Lutherans in this region number 45,000 (21,000 adults and 24,000 children), who worship and witness in 40 congregations with approximately 150 preaching points. There are 49 ordained Lutheran pastors, four of whom are expatriates. The Arusha diocese of the Roman Catholic Church numbers approximately 20,000 in 18 parishes with some 60 preaching points. Though the region has a variety of ethnic groups, Swahili is the common language for education and trade. Among the adult populaton of the region, the last statistics regarding literacy tell us that there are 52,800 illiterate men and 84,400 illiterate women. Christian communities in the Arusha region do not number over 70,000, less than 7 per cent of the total population. The others are mainly traditional religionists and Muslims with the former definitely in the majority.

The ecclesial context which gave rise to this venture includes the following factors. First, there is a multi-level ministry in the parishes of the region. From the beginning both Lutherans and Catholics have had several levels of ministry, such as pastors/priests, evangelists/catechists, parish workers/sisters, etc. With the exception of the pastors/priests, these congregational servants have seldom had the theological training necessary for nurturing and equipping the people of God for their role in church and community. Though the churches involved may ordain a graduate of the extension seminary to the higher levels of the ministry, this is not the express purpose of the extension programme. Rather, it is seen as a way to train any of this multi-level ministry who are presently serving a parish in some capacity and who are best reached through an extension programme.

Second, the pattern for growth in the churches is parish-centred. That is, the several preaching points of a congregation usually expand in the direction of need in order to establish new preaching points which in time become new congregations. Thus the expansion of the church into new areas exceeds the number of trained workers. The extension programme is designed to meet this need by providing training for the servants of these rapidly growing congregations. Many of the students earn at least part of their living other than through church employment, hence the programme must suit their schedules as well as the needs of the congregations they serve. The need for such a programme is evidenced by the pattern of evangelism. Though the Christian community in the Arusha region is expanding into new geographical areas and each year the number of Christians increases, in relation to the growth rate of the total population the growth of the church is minimal indeed. Considering this slow rate of growth, it is evident that more attention needs to be directed to the congregations' evangelistic efforts. Ways to encounter people with Christianity as a viable option and ways to effectively nurture small Christian communities are high priorities in the life of the churches, because they take seriously their mandate to witness and to serve.

Third, Tanzanians are presently hard-pressed economically; hence it is fitting that a means of training provide basic services without undue financial burden. The extension programme as practised in the Arusha region does this.

Fourth, Tanzania's policy of villagization emphasizes basic social services on-the-spot — the utilization of local indigenous personnel whom the village can afford as opposed to expertise from the outside. In 1974 in the "Directives on the Implementation of Self-Reliance" the National Executive Committee of Tanzania had this to say:

> Up to now we have totally failed to rid ourselves of the unfortunate habit of giving more esteem to someone who has higher education.... In our employment policies performance in the classroom has been the only yardstick.... Very often, however, it has happened that both in our thinking and in our action we have been unduly influenced by international standards.... We have not succeeded in liberating ourselves mentally, nor in having self-confidence, nor in selecting that which is most suitable to our objectives, instead of continuing to ape the system of other people whose economy and mode of life is totally different from ours.

Western churches have tended to assume that theological schools can prepare people for ministry, whereas in African culture leaders are often selected on the basis of service and maturity rather than education alone. This challenges the African churches to experiment with types of theological education which encourage and accommodate African patterns of leadership. The concept of "Ujamaa" in Tanzania is too complex for simple definition, but inherent in the concept is the conviction that the local village is endowed with the necessary talents for mutual benefit. The church can be in the forefront of this attempt to give high priority to experience and maturity when it comes to choosing leaders. An "extension" programme is one way of accommodating this pattern of leadership in African culture.

The ecclesial atmosphere most conducive to an extension programme such as ours is one in which the ministry is understood within the context of the calling, through baptism, of the whole people of God. The various levels of ministry are seen as contributing to the nurture and vocation of the whole body of Christ, thus preparing for evangelism and service in his name. Where this goal is at home in the life of the church, a sincere attempt to equip the people for ministry is welcomed and encouraged. Given the minority status of the Christian church in the Arusha region today, there is no way to present Christ as a live option to the masses apart from utilizing the love and talents of the whole people of God. It would seem that several other churches in Tanzania as a whole recognize the value of extension programmes as tools for equipping God's people for ministry. The Anglican Church of Tanzania is currently running theological education by extension programmes in four dioceses. The Baptists of East Africa have deemed it necessary to "extend" the services of their seminary in a programme having three sub-centres and currently reaching 150 people, three-fourths of whom are ordained.

Programme and curriculum

The three-year course combines home study, weekly sub-centre meetings, and semi-annual seminars of one month's duration. The semi-programmed lessons are the backbone of the home study and sub-centre discussions, whereas the two long seminars each year provide opportunity for more specialized courses and the utilization of local resources for teaching. Each week the student is expected to study at home from five to ten hours and to meet in guided discussion with a teacher and other sub-centre students for half a day. It is only at the semi-annual seminars that they are away from their homes and parishes. Rather than demanding a certain level of formal education as an entrance requirement, it was decided to insist on only two criteria: competence in Swahili and involvement in some form of service at the local level. This basically puts the process of selection in the hands of the local parish, which in turn is subject to the discretion of the district.

Since the lessons are in Swahili, actual feedback from the education sector has been minimal though significant. The Christian education staff of the Evangelical Lutheran Church in Tanzania has been both helpful and supportive. Of value to us in our gleaning from the professionals concerning programmed lessons are the following: (1) the material must be divided into manageable units; (2) each unit should be built around clearly stated objectives and the expedition of the same; (3) a work section is necessary where the student can evidence a grasp of the objectives (or otherwise). These three factors have been of paramount importance to us in the preparation and use of lesson materials, and we have abundantly witnessed their value in the teaching/learning experience.

Concerning the content of the three-year programme in basic Christian theology, a theme for the year dominates the lessons as well as the seminars: first year, biblical; second year, historical; and third year, Christian theology in the African context. The lessons and teaching thereof are based on the conviction that God speaks to us where we are. Thus theology must take seriously the categories of our existence and give opportunity for the students to reflect on their own heritage and its encounter with the Christian faith. This is an important aspect of the lessons for the entire three-year course. The third year lessons are particularly designed for this, as they begin with a positive appraisal of traditional African religious/cultural beliefs and patterns and move on to dialogue with the Christian faith and its significance in the local and national context. There is a sense in which systematic theology is an exercise in the art of communication. To transmit the faith in ways which clarify and stimulate, to encourage an encounter from depth to depth, to reflect critically on faith's meaning in home and parish and nation — these are descriptions of what we aimed for specifically in the objectives of the third year lessons. To do this we began by choosing five themes from African religion and philosophy: creation and created things, sickness and health, the ladder of life, sacrifice and reconciliation, and curses and blessings. Since very little has been written in Swahili on this, we had to read, reflect, discuss and write. Each set of lessons begins with an exposition of one of these themes — with an attempt to be both positive and realistic. The next section encourages dialogue between these religious views and the biblical/historical faith, as studied during the first two years. What deserves to remain and enrich us? What conflicts with the pre-eminence of Jesus Christ? And most of all, what will our faith and parish look like if we take seriously this kind of a background? Thus most of the usual themes in systematic theology are dealt with as they arise out of a dialogue with the African religious themes. The third-year lessons look something like the diagram overleaf.

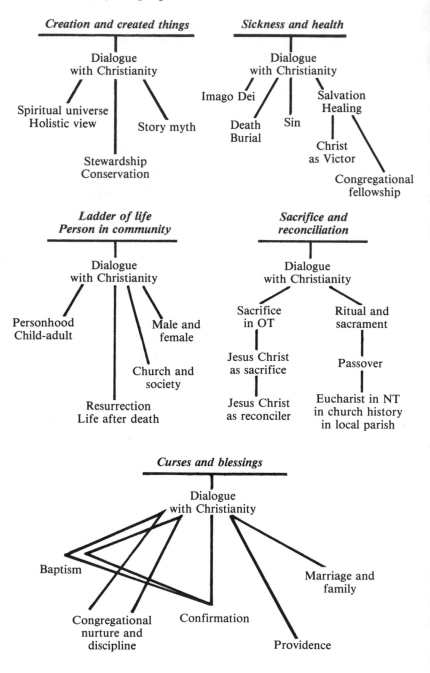

Many who teach theology in an African setting are acutely aware of aspects of traditional life and religion which enhance and enrich relationships both within and without the church. The emphases on person in community, on reconciliation in ritual and fellowship, on the unity of all life, etc. arc to be treasured and transmitted to future generations. Christian theologians are also acutely aware that there is no society or culture or religion which does not need to repent before the Lord of life. Part of our theological task is to see that this Lord is allowed to speak to us where we are, and this happens only if we take seriously the categories of our existence and open them to the probing, healing love of God.

Evaluation

An evaluation of the programme necessarily includes the negative as well as the positive. There are isolated instances where the students lack the necessary infrastructure as far as transportation is concerned. Where there is no scheduled public transport, the students are left to their own ingenuity and their legs, and this may pose a serious problem. Nevertheless, attendance even in these areas has been encouraging. During the past month, five students walked 13 miles each way to attend the weekly meetings because the local bus was in a state of disrepair. Another problem is the lack of relevant reading material in Swahili for those students who would like to dig deeper. We anticipate that an increasing number of Swahili publications will somewhat alleviate this problem in the future but we consider it to be a significant difficulty at present.

On the positive side, the extension programme greatly broadens the base as far as selection is concerned. We are able to train more people than would have been possible through a residential programme. There is a particular joy in being able to reach those who are often forgotten as far as any planned teaching programme is concerned. The churches abundantly testify that the students are truly assisted and encouraged in their work and living. Second, TEE in the Arusha region offers training with a minimum of social disturbance. Students continue to live and work within their normal surroundings and thus are able to combine learning and practise in a way that is conducive to growth and maturity. Third, TEE offers an economically viable programme for the congregations. Church workers continue to serve their congregations while being trained. The usual congregational remuneration applies, and they continue to be self-reliant as far as farm or business is concerned. Finally, TEE has provided a meeting point for Catholics and Lutherans heretofore not experienced. This close relationship is already contributing to respect and understanding in the local parish. On the diocesan level the extension programme has brought our attention to matters which demand our common understanding and effort. Presently our two churches are commencing a common research project in an area of mutual concern. It is the extension programme which brought this matter to the fore.

Botswana Theological Training Programme
Grassroots theology in Botswana

RICHARD SALES and JACOB LIPHOKO

Botswana has made incredible strides since independence in 1966 when there were virtually no tarred roads in the Bechuanaland Protectorate, as Botswana was known, and the number of high schools could be counted on the fingers of one hand. With a land area the size of France, in an arid wilderness dominated by the Kalahari Desert, the future of the new-born country looked very dim. It was particularly dim for the churches of Botswana, because no sooner had independence come than South Africa, their giant neighbour to the south, determined that persons from Botswana would be admitted to study only at theological colleges under government control, which excluded all the seminaries except the Dutch Reformed.

Within five years the shortage of pastors was being felt by nearly every denomination with a history of theological training. Some churches temporarily imported pastors and priests from other countries, but this was a situation that could not continue indefinitely. In other churches pastors were pressed to go on working long past retirement age, into their 70s and even 80s, in order that the churches should not be leaderless. Some adjustment had to be made. Completely untrained men were asked to lead smaller congregations in some areas. By 1974 in one of the largest denominations, the Con-

• Dr Sales was one of the founders of the BTTP and has worked with the programme since its inception in 1975. The Rev. Jacob Liphoko joined the staff in 1978; he is currently Chairman of the Botswana Council of Churches and a member of the Executive Committee of the Association of Southern African Theological Institutions. The headquarters of the BTTP is at P.O. Box 318, Gabarone, Botswana.

gregational Church, of 36 pastors in parish work, eight were ordained, 18 were semi-trained evangelists, and the remainder were untrained; only six were under the age of 60, and 14 were over 70.

During the years after independence, Botswana surprised everyone
by growing stronger. A major discovery of diamonds at Orapa took
place shortly after 1966, and a second diamond deposit was subsequently found at Jwaneng. A rich copper-nickel deposit led to the
building of the Selebi-Phikwe mine in 1970. At the same time, the
meat export industry was building up, and before long the fledgling
nation had balanced its modest budget. Revenues were pumped into
such necessities as education. High schools have multiplied until today there are twenty with a dozen community-sponsored secondary
schools. A university was begun in the late 1960s, and a faculty of
theology has been added to it in the last five years.

This relative prosperity was a mixed blessing to the churches.
Everyone with the minimum qualifications for theological study was
rapidly swallowed up by the demand for educated leadership at all
levels of government. Moreover, the increased funds in the country
were balanced by the inflation that has gripped the world, and the
churches found that the income from their members did not rise proportionately to the increased costs of pastors and services. The churches found themselves competing with the government and private
industry for scarce manpower. Government could offer double a
minister's stipend to a young man fresh from high school, at the
same time appealing to his idealism with the call for unity and
development.

The decision for extension

When the Theological Commission of the Christian Council met in
1973, these were the facts that faced the members, drawn from eight
denominations in the country, which served roughly one-third of the
total population. Not one of them was self-sufficient. None of them
had premises where theological training could be carried on, nor had
they the funds to acquire a site and build on it. None had a reservoir
of talented teachers in reserve. As one member of the Commission
put it: "If someone gave us a complete seminary and teachers, we
couldn't finance the maintenance crew."

Something had to be done. The Commission made its decision for
extension, not because members knew and understood what extension theology was, but because they saw clearly that for the time be-

ing, the people offering for the ministry in Botswana would have to continue to work at their jobs and study part-time. No one had any high school candidates in view.

Throughout 1974 one person was detailed to work on an outline of training, then to begin to put flesh to that outline, and finally to prepare units for the first year. Only when these had been tested and found valuable did the Commission decide to dissolve and form the Botswana Theological Training Programme (BTTP). The BTTP was formally launched on 10 December 1974 with five member churches — Anglican, Church of God in Christ, African Methodist Episcopal, Congregational and Lutheran. Of the remaining three, the Roman Catholics felt their major seminary in Lesotho would meet their needs; the Dutch Reformed and Methodist representatives were unable to obtain permission from parent bodies in South Africa. The original staff were a missionary working with the Congregational Church and an African Anglican priest who had taught in a seminary in South Africa.

Reflections on what the BTTP has meant

The launching of the Botswana Theological Training Programme broke the long-standing and expensive colonial tradition of training church leaders within the walls of a seminary. There, trained out of context, only a chosen few could benefit. This method stressed the academic at the expense of the pastoral, book knowledge against the ability to work with others. The successful elite emerging from this system find themselves on an attractive conveyor belt luring them to yet more irrelevent courses in Western universities.

The Botswana Theological Training Programme now can be seen as a necessary part of independent Africa, providing a challenge to Christian people and to their church leaders, an opportunity both to join the world and to be distinctively African in doing so. It offers training to people who would otherwise have no chance to serve God, their churches, and their society effectively.

In taking seriously the fact that no man or woman is an island, the programme takes cognizance of the local community in which a student lives and which to a large extent influences his/her attitudes and thinking, the family where his/her concerns are expressed and needs met, the congregation where he/she worships and which shapes ideas, and the work that he/she does for a living. Both in the preparation of materials and in teaching, these contexts are kept in mind. The materials constantly ask for meanings appropriate to the student's own life. The group meetings, where the information is digested, are open and flexible so that what deeply concerns a student becomes the matter of discussion. Understandings are tested at work, in the home, and in church, and evaluations are made constantly. Sometimes these evaluations lead to a change in the materials studied, at other times to a change in the student.

Students are encouraged to study together, rather than individually, to enable them to handle, digest, and grow through what they have read and done. Local study groups are encouraged, and this has achieved two goals:

— the students experience solidarity, which leads to mutual concern and team work;
— the age-long dream of ecumenical cooperation is realized wherever a study group is composed of persons from different denominations.

There is a third result which we are beginning to discover. In Africa, women and men usually form friendships among the same sex, leading to misunderstandings between sexes. Theological training in the past has been for men only and has not broken this barrier down. BTTP study groups bring women and men together for study at a deep level where mutual respect and understanding can take place.

It must be said that the BTTP, though founded with the idea of training ministers and upgrading laity, forced open other areas that were not foreseen in 1974. For example, BTTP started out, like residential seminaries, looking at paper qualifications before admitting people. But it was soon evident that many mature people had gone far beyond their original study qualifications. Also the students continued to show a high and increasing motivation to study from beginning to end. Perhaps this is because of group loyalty; perhaps because they are not studying simply to get a certificate to earn money; maybe it has something to do with comradeship with the tutor, rather than a teacher-student feeling. And those who complete the programme take a quite different attitude towards the work of ministry, preferring to work consultatively rather than through dominance.

BTTP offers different levels for different needs

BTTP works on three levels. Some enroll to take the full ordination course for five years; such people expect to serve their churches at the end in either a full-time capacity or as supplementary or voluntary priests or ministers. In the same groups are people who have no intention of studying five years. They want to gain specific skills for ministry in their churches: preaching, teaching, administration or counselling. Such people may study for two or three years to get what they want. In 1978 the BTTP began work on a course in the vernacular for rural church leaders lacking the background to study in English. This is a two-year course in lay leadership training.

All students study at home and only meet with their tutor once a fortnight to discuss and digest their materials and experiences. Those who are in the second, third, fourth and fifth years learn skills they must practise in their local congregations. Because the programme exists for the churches, it takes its connection with them very seriously. Most of the students are referred to the BTTP by their churches after the needs in the churches have been analyzed. Parish priests and pastors are engaged with student groups in their areas.

Student progress is assessed thrice yearly. Half the mark derives from their group work and half from a written examination. The final examinations each year are moderated externally with two active ministers and three university lecturers as external examiners, the latter taking the final years of study.

Since the BTTP operates entirely by extension, it publishes a monthly newsletter for students to remind them of the wider membership, and once each year all students from all over the country come together for three days to what we call the convocation. Here they meet in groups according to years of study to discuss their joys and sorrows and also to evaluate the usefulness of their materials so that these can be improved. These evaluations are taken seriously and serve as a regular check in the revision of courses. Outside speakers bring additional viewpoints to students, and they share together in worship as well as fellowship. It is here, too, that people completing courses are awarded their recognition.

The BTTP is a servant of the churches that determine its policies. It is not envisaged that we will be lured to a traditional seminary structure, even if we should find, in the next few years, that this could be afforded. With BTTP, the learning process is closely connected with the learner. We believe that the students learn better by *experiencing* something, then stopping to *identify* what has happened, then moving on to *analyze* the experience, and finally by *planning* what to do about it. The method, begun with a tutor present, gives the student the ability to work independently even after formal studies have finished.

We envisage that students who have studied with us will be able to form groups wherever they are and thus continue the learning process for themselves and others. At present two of our former students are employed as denominational religious educators; many are serving their congregations as part-time ministers; and others take other responsibilities in the different ministries of their churches.

The three-legged cooking pot

Many analogies had been coined for the experience of learning by extension. We speak of the three-legged cooking pot. One leg represents home study. Without that there is little to build upon. It can be compared to eating a meal. You cannot grow without eating, and you cannot learn without taking in new material. The second leg is group study. It can be compared to digesting the food. Here relationships and understandings are made and welded to previous experience. Old ideas are aired, considered, perhaps built upon, perhaps discarded. It is at this point that BTTP places the tutor, to act as a catalyst in the learning process. The third leg is practical. To make an idea your own you must use it and learn what it means in the doing. This is like the exercise taken after a meal, to ensure that the food goes to important body functions, not fat. We tell students and church people that a cooking pot is of great value so long as it has three legs. But let just one of those legs be missing or broken or foreshortened and the pot becomes scrap.

Home study

There are many ways of preparing materials for home study. These range from programming, a very complex and long-term process that ensures that every bit of what is presented is absorbed, to textbooks with study-guide questions. The latter can be done relatively quickly and simply. In practice the BTTP begins in the first year with a careful modular system of a page of reading followed by a page of questions and exercises. Six pages make a week's work in one subject. It is not programmed instruction, but it comes close because each page is absorbed carefully. In the second and subsequent years, more is expected of the student and less guided absorption is provided. In the last year of the five-year course students provide study materials for each other on topics of their choice as the year progresses.

Group meetings

Enough has been said already to indicate the importance we have placed on group study. Botswana is sparsely populated, and the groups have never included more than five persons and often are composed of two or three. In general, for maximum benefit to all, we feel that a group of from four to six would probably be ideal so that there are sufficient experiences to share and sufficient pressure upon all to participate at as deep a level as possible. We have discovered that materials appropriate to a tenth-grade education are applicable to persons with a university background. What is different is the discussion and the conceptual world into which such people integrate their learnings. This is not to say that persons with wider backgrounds should not receive appropriate materials in the first instance, but the level of learning is determined not by the complexity of the materials so much as by the mode of digestion of those materials. In this regard all those who have met regularly with first-year groups continue to express amazement that no two discussions are the same, although BTTP has now had at least 50 meetings.

Practical work

The weakest part of our monitoring has been the practical application of learning in church and society. It is simply impossible for tutors to know what happens in a hundred congregations all over the country on a given Sunday. Here, too, we have found that church leaders have not been as helpful charting the progress of students as they might have been. Our information on student progress comes to us in the subsequent group meetings when excited people speak of what they have found out through using their new skills and information. Although BTTP is unable to monitor these experiences directly, we can easily tell when a student has not used new knowledge. He or she tends to slip into a frame of mind not unlike the typical high school student as examination time comes around. Those who know what they know because they have used it regularly have few qualms about tests or other measures of attainment.

The tutor in BTTP

For those who have written and "taught" the materials, extension theology is a new and exciting experience. We are continually probed by issues that come up in discussions beyond our knowledge, continually discovering nuances and meanings in things we had felt we understood thoroughly. Unlike the lecturer, the extension tutor is a generalist. He or she will often find questions arising naturally in every area of theological, and indeed of liberal arts study, and it is just as well that the tutor is not expected to be a walking encyclopaedia but rather a gadfly, a stimulator of discussion, a participant-observer in the process which has been set in motion. Discussion is sharing. It is a situation that recalls the Lord's words: "Where two or three are gathered in my name, there I will be in the midst." For learning presupposes a teacher, and the group teacher appears to be the Holy Spirit. Many times people have said after a group meeting: "The group complimented me on having known the answer to that issue, but it was new to me, too." Something happens in group meetings that is beyond what anyone in the group knows beforehand.

Grassroots No. 1

We first realized we were involved in something new when, as tutors discussing together what happened the week before, one of us mentioned that he had never before heard a particular text dealt with as a student in his group did. We realized that something new was emerging, fragmentary and unsystematic, but real for all of that. Out of the mixture of basic information on such matters as the Bible and church history, with people in their environment and with their own distinctive backgrounds, new insights were coming forth.

We decided to term this emerging amalgamation "grassroots African theology" and were astonished when we could find no mention of it in the studies we read on African and third world theology. Certainly what we were and are finding is that when the gospel meets a person and that person is encouraged to engage the whole of himself or herself with it, something dynamic and new develops. Some insights are crude; others enormously comprehensive; and like a person's faith they grow and change before our eyes. At first we thought we ought to write down what we had found, but the sheer volume of material overwhelmed us. Because Botswana is in a state of rapid social change, and because our students themselves change and develop new insights, we realized that to try and draw a line and say: "This is what people's theology in Botswana is", would be wrong by the time we had written it. What we were experiencing was a gift to us, the opportunity to watch people come to grips in different ways over time with the enriching gospel. What they had discovered for themselves was theirs to use to enrich others who had their own discoveries to make. It was also a gift to us, for we were privileged to make discoveries beyond our imaginings.

Grassroots No. 2

The second grassroots aspect of theology in Botswana is equally dramatic to the tutors. We had all read that the Puritans and other dissident churches in England in the seventeenth and eighteenth centuries literally "chose God-fearing men from the midst" of the gathered congregations and ordained them as ministers, those who were gifted and devout and knowledgeable. This never seemed appropriate in a country like Botswana, where education was such a minority privilege. The best one could do was to select young people with potential and educate them in the few schools available before sending them to seminaries where they could become "knowledgeable" persons.

But with the advent of the BTTP we found ourselves doing exactly that, finding people, both men and women who had worked for some years in their churches, who had amply demonstrated their devotion, and lifting them up in their congregations to become skilful preachers and teachers and ministers. In the process we found that because people lacked formal education this did not by any means imply they lacked wisdom or profound experience of faith. We saw that our reliance on measurements of academic excellence had blinded us to the kinds of excellence they were exemplifying. Perhaps in the West, with its universal education and easy access to information, it is reasonable to regard people without academic preparation as lacking in some regard. This is emphatically not the case in Africa. Keenly active minds, deeply reflective personalities, and exceptional abilities may lie hidden to the casual observer behind the wall of language simply because a man or woman never had the chance to attend high school.

By taking the theological school to the student we have discovered extraordinary people in remote places. One such man told us in broken English that he wanted to take the ordination course. We were sceptical for two reasons. The first was that he lived far from any established group and would virtually have to study alone most of the time. The second was that he laboured over the language of his desired studies. But he was determined, and since his church desired that he be trained, we gave him materials and set up a "special student" category for him. The Lord alone knows how many hours he struggled with unfamiliar words in a setting devoid of stimulation for such study. But he continued and managed somehow to pass each test for more than two years before BTTP itself started to work in the desert. As a farmer in a continual drought situation he was sometimes forced to travel with his cattle for a month or more in search of water under temporary shelter. Yet he persevered and managed to complete his course. He is now a pastor. His is one of the most dramatic cases. By the end of his study he had not only made use of every teacher, nurse, and government worker to aid him, but so interested several of them in what he was doing that they, in turn, joined the BTTP!

Grassroots No. 3

The third grassroots aspect of BTTP has been mentioned already. It is the first opportunity women have had in this country to study for the ministry or for various skilled tasks in the church. Bearing in mind that when candidates were accepted for the ministry in the past, they had to give up their jobs and go to another country to study for three or more years, you will understand that even wives were generally left behind, both physically and intellectually. Yet women in Botswana form more than two-thirds of the active church membership.

We mentioned earlier that in rural African society friendship is normally between persons of the same sex. Men talk to men, and women to women. Several reasons have been advanced for the preponderance of women in the churches. Migrant labour, which until recently accounted for a substantial number of men between the ages of 18 and 50, is one factor; the demands of herding cattle in an arid land is another. But what this has meant is that the minister, as a male, has had personal relationships to the few men in his congregation, but only formal relationships to the vast majority. Because women were unable to go away for training and were usually overlooked in any case, they were unable to take leading roles in the churches. They formed women's associations and had their own church-within-the-church. When crises came up, they took their problems not to the pastor but to the pastor's wife, if she was available. She was not more informed about the faith than they but had status as the wife of the man who was informed, and she might ask her husband for advice. For years women chafed at the situation but could do nothing about it. Then, when BTTP came along, some sought admission. Church leaders were perplexed but could not find anything to object to in their request. A slow but very significant revolution is in the making today. About 30 per cent of the student body in 1981 is composed of women, and several of these women are enrolled for the full five years, often at their own expense. By no means all of the member churches (not to mention the independent churches from which several women come) are willing to ordain women on the completion of their studies, but the staff of BTTP believe this is only a matter of time. They can and will demonstrate their competence in church affairs (and some already have), and it may come as a shock to the men. They may find themselves, like Peter at the house of Cornelius, wondering, "can anyone forbid them... seing they have received the Holy Spirit as we have?" (Acts 10:47). The male church leaders will have to admit that for generations in Africa women have been diviners and religious practitioners everywhere but in the Christian church.

One of the tutors was accosted by a particularly energetic female student not long ago. She was angry, and he could imagine nothing he had done that would account for her anger. "Why", she cried, "did you wait so long before bringing us BTTP? My sisters are old, and I am old, and only now when I have so little time have you given me the chance to become an effective Christian." Her anger was only slightly feigned. She and many others now in their fifties are wistful that for so long they were denied the skills and information they craved.

Grassroots No. 4

As we write this, BTTP has been in operation for only seven short years. So far three dozen people have completed the courses. Yet already some signs of change are taking place. In one large congregation with three "branches" a team ministry is serving the parish on a voluntary basis. There is no professional over the three men (soon to be joined by one woman). Rather they have carried their classroom collaboration over into their work. None of these leaders is extraordinary. One of them is gifted in administration, another in proclamation, and the third in prayer. Together they make a powerful team, and the local church recognizes this very well. It has not been easy for them. They are pioneers in team ministry, and other nearby churches have derided their efforts. A motion was passed without the participation of their church to the effect that the congregation where they ministered should be divided into three parts and each assigned to one, to "fit the mould" that Christians in Botswana recognize. But this was defeated in the local church where they work together.

There are two things in their ministry that make them suspect in Botswana. The first is that it has been shown again and again that to put ministers together on an equal footing in a parish is equivalent to putting two roosters under one roof. But what is different here is the method of formation itself. Whereas in previous cases the ministers had been trained individually and reproduced the conditions of their training, these ministers had been trained cooperatively and just as faithfully reproduced the conditions of their training. The second suspicion arises out of the certainty in the minds of most Christians that the ministry, particularly the ordained ministry, must be professional to be adequate. These three are thus amateurs, dilettantes. But again, they see no necessity to be full-time in order to minister effectively to people. The others had trained to be professionals; these had trained to be volunteers.

The pressure of custom, a custom born not of the biblical witness nor of necessity but of a tradition rooted in the form of training for ministry used exclusively in Africa until now, is hard to bear. But they are bearing it, and we hope that there will be others in an increasing number to join them in the coming years, until the day will come when the idea that each congregation must be judged in terms of its ability to pay a good stipend to a professional minister is past. Some of us are doubtful about the faceless mass needed to form a church in our day. There is no reason except the financial one for a congregation to be so large that its members do not know and care intimately for one another. We foresee a time when in Botswana this necessity will pass, along with many other Western imports into Africa.

Grassroots No. 5

The last thing we want to suggest is still largely a dream for us. In our most recent development report to friends and donors this was said:

> ... BTTP does manage to meet the needs that the churches have demonstrated for training throughout the country despite the long distances and a very thinly distributed population in rural areas. This policy will continue with one major change, namely that persons who

have themselves trained with BTTP will be asked to act as group leaders in the more distant centres in time to come, so that the coverage can continue to meet the needs of people throughout the country.... It is anticipated that tutor travel to such distant places might in future be reduced to thrice a year "resourcing" of group leaders.

There are weaknesses inherent in a plan which would ask former students to be tutors for new students. In a rapidly changing society new students will not want to make the same decisions about what is good and what is useful as did the student of a decade before. But we have already seen how we as tutors have found that the students go before us, and if we can impart the skills of group leadership to our former students, who have in any case experienced this mode of learning, it may be possible for BTTP to become an organ of education to ever widening circles of the people of God throughout Botswana.

This "passing it on" plan is the logical extension of what we have been doing from the beginning. Why should not people who have experienced the joy of discovery with limited resources be the very people best qualified to bring the same skills and knowledge-in-context to others? Some may argue that for BTTP to take such a step would be to ask the blind to lead the blind. We would rather take the point of view that it would represent the next stage in the growth of grassroots leadership and initiative. We have tried it twice already, asking people who were fourth- or fifth-year students to help first-year people where they live. They have responded enthusiastically. We have asked pastors in some places to be group leaders, and they have done the job well, without any previous knowledge of the sort of educational process involved. Our course in teaching the Christian faith calls for people who, after themselves learning to teach, will teach others how to teach using the same methods they learned by.

Extension theology is not "theology on the cheap". The cost of transport is an increasing burden on a hard-pressed staff. To manage to produce and continue to update lesson materials while teaching is neither easy nor inexpensive. But built into the genius of extension theology is this grassroots option. There is no reason why, after some years of seeding, the plants cannot themselves do the re-seeding. It works very well for grass. "If God cares for the grass of the field which is alive today and burned tomorrow, will be not much more care for [us], people of little faith?"

Diocese of Mount Kenya East (Anglican)

Meeting community needs through theological education by extension

Part I: General survey and university certificate level

KEITH B. ANDERSON

Soon after the first Anglican TEE programme began in Kenya a student said to me: "We have been asking the church for ten years to set up a programme like this to train those of us who cannot go away to a college for theological education. Now it has happened." The speaker was a local primary school teacher. Three years later he completed the course. After two more years of in-service training he was ordained to serve in the diocese of Nakuru.

Church growth and the crisis of pastoral care

This desire for extension training came at first from Christians in the grassroot parishes where they could see that such training was desperately needed. It began to be articulated at higher church leadership levels in the Archbishop's Commission on Theological Training, which produced its final report in September 1973. It recommended that "extension training" should be adopted to meet the crisis in pastoral care throughout the Church of the Province of Kenya. It went on to say: "The Commission thinks that this might well become the main form of training in the future." It noted that all the Kenyan bishops claimed that they were understaffed and that for some of them this shortage had already reached crisis propor-

• CMS missionary Keith Anderson developed the TEE programme and materials for the University of Nairobi certificate in religious studies first in Nakuru diocese, then in the diocese of Mount Kenya East. N. Kiranga Gatimu directs the parish level TEE programme for the diocese of Mount Kenya East, P.O. Box 396, Kerugoya, Kenya, and is coordinator of the East African Association for Theological Education by Extension.

tions. In 1971 there were 234 Kenyan clergy of whom 204 were serving in the parish ministry. By 1980 the number had risen to 302, an increase of 48 per cent. In the same ten-year period, national population figures rose by 50 per cent from approximately ten million to over fifteen million people. So ordinations were only just keeping pace with the population growth.

More significant was the fact that the number of congregations being served had risen by 70 per cent from 1629 in 1970 to 2769 in 1980. In 1980 the Bishop of Nakuru reported an average of 50 new worshipping congregations starting each year, a growth rate of 4 per cent. In Mount Kenya East with a smaller total number of congregations, 20 new worship centres are started each year, a growth rate in 1980 of 9 per cent. This means that in 1970 the average Anglican pastor cared for eight congregations. In 1980 he cared for nine. So in the 1980s the Anglican community is receiving less pastoral care from its ordained ministry than in 1971. This trend seems likely to continue. In 1973 the Archbishop's Commission called for the number of clergy to double in 15 years. Their target was for at least 400 parochial clergy by 1988. Yet if the present annual growth rate in the number of congregations continues to remain constant at 7 per cent, these 400 clergy will be serving about 4,300 congregations, i. e. more than ten congregations for each ordained minister. A recent Partners in Mission consultation in the diocese of Mount Kenya East identified pastoral care as the number two diocesan priority after evangelism for the next five years. It is not hard to see why. If present growth rates continue, new Christians will be evangelized and then welcomed into a community which is only able to give a decreasing amount of pastoral care to its people.

The crisis in lay leadership training

Of course pastoral care is not restricted to ordained clergy. The Anglican Church in East Africa has always believed in lay ministry. Eight out of nine services every Sunday are led by lay men and women. Every local congregation is presided over by a lay chairperson who acts as pastor to the local community. This person knows the community intimately, is often called upon to intervene in local matrimonial and other social problems, and has to arrange pastoral care for the youth, teach the flock, visit the bereaved, and so on. All of this requires considerable pastoral expertise and the ability to apply biblical principles to all of these situations. A recent report on the need for extension training in the diocese of Maseno South comments on this fact that the lay men and women make up the stable pastoral component of every parish structure. The ordained clergy are transient figures constantly being moved from parish to parish and usually do not serve in the parishes where they grew up. The report goes on:

> With the exception of the actual celebration of the sacraments, effective ministry in the diocese will have to be in the hands of these lay leaders for the foreseeable future. This is no bad thing because it correctly focuses emphasis upon the local congregation as the basic unit of Christian life and so effectively counters any tendency to centralism in the diocesan structure.

It then refers to the lack of training received by these lay leaders:

> It is probable that a high percentage are functionally illiterate and so depend for so much of their teaching and preaching on a kind of oral tradition made up of acceptable doctrine and practice that has been handed down largely unquestioned for several generations of previous lay leaders in the area. Some courses have been held, but these have usually been for a period of only two weeks and only a few have been able to attend them.

This lack of training has been caused by the exclusive use of the institutional method inherited from the past. The urgent need to train clergy left them with little or no time to train the laity, even if there were money for such programmes. For these urgent reasons a lay leadership-by-extension programme was started in the diocese of Nakuru in September 1976. Within two years more than 600 lay leaders were being trained by extension throughout the diocese. Two other lay leadership programmes were started in 1980, one in Maseno South and the other in Mount Kenya East.

Community needs in education

Another important community need has been identified by David M. Gitari, Bishop of the diocese of Mount Kenya East. In January 1981 he wrote:

> Generally speaking it appears as if the churches have neglected their responsibilities not only to keep in touch with young believers in schools but also to uplift their spiritual life by pastoral care and the sacraments. To fulfill this task we need ordained men working as teachers in schools who will also serve as school chaplains. In this diocese we need 40 chaplains in our 40 secondary schools. If, during the next five years, we can produce at least ten such people, we will have achieved something.

After discussing the doubts expressed by many about TEE, the bishop continued:

> Today we have no doubt at all that TEE has opened a new important chapter in the life of the church. A good number of people who joined TEE without a clear idea of where it would lead them have gained a new vision of serving the Master. Some of the best candidates for full-time ministry we have interviewed are TEE students. In some of our schools religious education is being taught by teachers who have greatly benefited from TEE. At the present time I am convinced that there is no easy way in which we can meet the demands of our schools except by TEE.

The secondary schools to which the bishop refers are those sponsored directly by the diocese. They are "self-help" Harambee schools started by the efforts of each local community. Most of their pupils are those who fail to reach the high entry standards of the government secondary schools. Leaving on one side the issue as to whether these schools best serve the community and development needs of the country, the fact remains that these young people spend eight or nine months of the year away from home. They experience alienation from their local communities, from their peers and their parents, most of whom have had very little education even at primary level. These pupils need sympathetic pastoral care and teaching so that they can understand their rapidly changing society and be prepared to take their place in it. Many attempt the government examination in religious education after four years of secondary schooling. Many are not well taught. One TEE student who was himself a teacher in a Harambee secondary school once said to me: "When I was at secondary school I studied religious education but we never studied it as we do in TEE. I wish we could have done so. In TEE it is so much more interesting."

TEE at certificate level

It was to meet such community needs as these that the certificate level TEE programme was established first at Nakuru diocese and then in Mount Kenya East. I arrived in Nakuru less than a year after the Archbishop's Commission delivered its final report. The programme eventually started in May 1975 and still continues with more than 60 students and with two full-time tutors. I moved in 1978 to Mount Kenya East, where a similar programme was established with 30-40 students. Two other certificate-level programmes began in

1981 in Maseno South and Nairobi dioceses. There are about 150 students altogether in the four dioceses. Mombasa diocese is also keen to begin TEE.

To join the programme the students go through no selection process, although it is expected that they are involved in ministry in their local congregations or schools. Sex is not a barrier. Anyone who wishes may join who has had eleven years of formal education or its equivalent. Some students have had much more education up to diploma and degree level. Some have less: Nairobi University has established a special mature-age entrance examination for students with less than eleven years of education. Even students who fail this test can still continue with the programme. Some have chosen to do so. The approach is therefore not elitist, but heavy demands are laid upon the students through home study, local ministry in the community, and regular attendance at seminars on top of their normal work. This results in the course itself becoming self-selecting. In four years of the programme in Mount Kenya East 21 students completed one year of the three-year programme and then dropped out. A few of these may have been certificate seekers who were discouraged by the demands made upon them, particularly at weekend study conferences where they were required to lead services and to preach and then submit themselves to friendly criticism from fellow students in the subsequent worship and preaching seminars. All of the 23 who have so far completed the course are highly disciplined and mature people. Three were clergy who were upgrading their ability to minister to their congregations. Two have since been ordained, and seven more are currently undergoing further specific ordination training, two of them at degree level.

It will be apparent that in Kenya the Anglican Church has opted for the examination route in its certificate programme rather than the non-examination, ministerial-skills approach adopted by the lay leadership programmes in the parishes. The examination route, however, does not automatically exclude the learning of practical skills. One important skill gained by certificate students is the ability to extract information from written sources. In an oral society this skill is not easily acquired. The need to think biblically and to evaluate the "oral tradition" passed on by a previous Christian generation is another very necessary skill in a time of rapid social and economic change.

At the same time political and social awareness need to be developed. Hardly a seminar passes without the relevance of theology to politics becoming apparent. Recently we were grappling with the problem of propaganda posed by St Luke's gospel. How much of it is slanted theological propaganda, and how much is reliable reporting and justifiable theological interpretation of salvation history? We saw that Luke was drawing his theology from the history of Christ and that the value of his theology depends very much upon the integrity of the author. Students then began to see the difference between this and the political propaganda to which they are exposed every day. The need for integrity both in church life and political life became obvious to all. This was the crucial credibility factor in any situation. The students' own context is never far from any seminar discussion.

A contextual curriculum

The syllabus of the Nairobi University Certificate in Religious Studies, which is followed by the extension programme, was developed in 1972 specifically for the East African context. Five of the six papers of the curriculum are required. The sixth paper on research into the traditions of an African people is optional. The other papers cover the following subjects: introduction to the Bible and biblical theology; the study of four Old and four New Testament set texts; church history with special reference to East Africa; comparative religion with especial reference to the three major religions found in East Africa (Hinduism, Christianity and Islam) together with smaller groups like Jains, Sikhs, Baha'is and other movements such as evolutionary materialism, secularism, and Marxism. The final paper covers the study of African traditional religion and the need to make the preaching of the gospel relevant to this context.

Home study materials specifically related to this curriculum have been developed. Six and a half years of writing and rewriting have gone into them, and the process of revision in the light of criticisms from students and other tutors using them is still not complete. Five books have been written, one for each of the five parts of the syllabus. Two have reached the final revision stage, and money is currently being sought to print them. It is hoped that this will be done in such a way as to make it possible to revise individual units without necessarily having to reprint the whole book. The five books consist of 125 units. Five are concerned with general introduction including guidance on how to study the Bible and how to prepare a sermon. The books follow the approach adopted by the Open University in Britain. The questions inserted into the text are of two types. The first type is designed to help the student extract important information from the text. The second is the open-ended type of question where the student is invited to develop his own approach to the subject matter, which is then followed by some discussion in the text. When a student is invited to comment upon the relevance of the study to his own local context, the question is usually left completely "open" so that the tutor can make his own comments upon the student's written answer and enter into dialogue with him in private and in the weekly seminar.

One problem occasionally encountered by these contextual questions is the sense of frustration which the students experience as they begin to see the discrepancies between biblical teaching and local church practice in social and ecclesiastical affairs. As students they are not always in a position to do anything about these discrepancies because some of them are not the opinion leaders and decision-makers in their churches. Where they are able to do something, the exercise is very valuable. Where they are not, there is the danger that cynical indifference or angry defiance will result. A few are tempted to abandon their local church structure and set up their own new structural "utopia" elsewhere. In this way TEE can become the very opposite of the ecumenical instrument that it is sometimes claimed to be. Usually, however, students see positive ways in which the local situation can be altered.

Part II: TEE at parish level

N. KIRANGA GATIMU

In the diocese of Mount Kenya East TEE at parish level was started in October 1980 for those who do not meet the entry requirements for the certificate-level programme. At first the course was opened to everyone who was interested in TEE; later we held seminars for future local coordinators to equip them to lead TEE classes on their own.

The novelty of the course attracted 163 students in our first four centres! The statistical mean of their level of education was 4.6 years of schooling. Ten adults were completely illiterate and many more who indicated that they had been to school had, in fact, lapsed back into illiteracy or were semi-literate. About four of the first cohort had had 13 years of education. The youngest student was 19; the oldest was 75; the average was 36.7 years. Those who were over 40 complained of eye-sight problems, but this could also mean that they found reading difficult because they were not used to it. Two-thirds of those who enrolled were women, of whom most were illiterate or semi-literate. Some men did not want people to know that they too were in the same position. There was one clergyman, one nurse, one agricultural assistant, two adult education teachers, two primary school teachers, and one sales person. The rest were peasant farmers with no specific professional qualifications. The lay readers and evangelists of the church were less than ten in the first group of students.

The expectations of the first group of students

When I asked them what their expectations were from TEE, the response I got tended to be egocentric. Most of them said that they hoped that TEE would help them to "increase their faith in God". They also hoped that TEE would somehow help them in bringing up their children as Christians. Married people hoped that TEE would help them to lead happier married lives and/or win their marriage partners to Christ. Others vaguely thought that TEE would be instrumental in helping them to witness and to bring their otherwise unchurched friends into the church. TEE was also expected to help some to "get on" with others and generally improve their skills in social relationships. Surprisingly even those who said that they thought they had gifts in areas such as preaching, administration, counselling, teaching, etc. did not appear to expect this programme to help them in being more effective in their ministry. Even more surprising, few were prepared to be trained in order to train others. This could well be because the social expectation here is that it is only a graduate or someone well trained who can teach at all. In my first seminars it looked as if I was expected to "teach" the students. Some were clearly disappointed that the London graduate did not fill them with what they thought was the vast knowledge he had acquired overseas! Instead I appeared to insist that everybody should participate in what for them were merely "debates". At least this was true of the first month or so.

One advantage gained by the examination route in TEE is the opportunity it affords to compare results with residential institutions. In nearly every case the average results of TEE students are in no way inferior to those of residence programmes. In 1980 students from Mount Kenya East gained an average of 4-5 per cent higher marks in two papers when compared with the nearest residential programme where students had previously studied full-time for four years before sitting the examinations. Of course no one is suggesting that this is the only valid way of assessing the achievements of a TEE programme, but it does show that in terms of exams or examination results it is not true to say that TEE is an inferior or second class way of theological training. On the contrary it makes more demands of the students; it tests their motivation; it calls for a mature determination which enables them to achieve their goals by completing the course.

After six and a half years, certificate level TEE is being accepted as a viable form of theological education in the Anglican Church. It seems likely that the other three dioceses will want to adopt it as well as the parish lay training programme. Plans are already being formulated to set up a course for teachers who complete the certificate course to go on for further professional and pastoral training as school chaplains. It is hoped that the government will release teachers with pay to attend such courses. At the same time it is planned to direct certificate-level TEE more specifically towards secondary school teachers in an attempt to meet this community need. Methods of reaching the more remote areas of the diocese are being considered. These plans would require more staff and more funds. Such developments would be less cost-effective, but the need for TEE is probably greater there than anywhere else in the diocese.

TEE and the East African Revival fellowship

My apparent unfamiliarity with some of the local ways of doing things was attributed to my being "Westernized". Some were distressed that I claimed to be a Christian and yet I was not clean-shaven! This reaction to my beard can be explained by the fact that in our congregations there are often two identifiable groups of people. The first is the "inner group" composed of the "fellowship team", which owes its existence to the East African Revival movement which began in the 1930s. The second group is made up mainly of nominal Christians or, as they are described by members of the revival fellowship, "Christians who are not saved". This category broadly consists of the majority of the people in the church, that is, according to the standards of the revival team members. The revival group sees its role as "gukua murigo", that is, carrying the burden for the majority of the "less able Christians" by devoting themselves to prayer, Bible reading and encouraging one another on the "journey to heaven". Their theological stance is coloured by a strong eschatological tinge. They use well-worn patterns of speech and stereotyped phrases including the singing of the Luganda revival song "Tukutendereza Yesu", "We praise you Jesus". Deviation from their patterns of speech, dress, and hairstyles including my beard can be serious, casting doubt upon the sincerity of the individual's Christian commitment.

On the whole the revival "brethren" are over the age of 30 and suspicious of change. TEE, which seeks to work with both groups within the church, is viewed with suspicion. Some think that the TEE seminar is inferior to their own weekly fellowship meeting and so they cannot gain much by joining TEE. Their critics accuse them of a legalistic, holier-than-thou attitude which is dividing the church. Yet in spite of the obvious problems which their attitudes cause, especially among young people, they have a cathartic effect upon the spiritual and moral growth of the church. Their concern for a genuine spiritual life of holiness is sincere, and their willingness to witness openly and frequently to their faith in Jesus is one important reason for the growth of the church. It would be a pity if this group remained outside the TEE seminars. Their contribution would be valuable and perhaps, through TEE, some of their attitudes might change.

The importance of the mother tongue in parish level TEE

Most parish-level programmes in Kenya outside of the Church of the Province of Kenya use materials produced by the Association of Evangelicals of Africa and Madagascar. At first we used these materials, but almost immediately it became evident that there was a mismatch between the problems that developed out of our seminar discussions on the one hand and the issues covered by the AEAM materials on the other. Questions arose regarding social-ethical conflicts in such areas as polygamy, sexual immorality, trial marriages and the regulations established by the church governing weddings. As soon as we saw that existing materials did not deal with the questions that the community was asking, we began producing our own materials on an experimental basis.

The new materials had one very important advantage, namely in the choice of the language to be used as the medium of learning. I decided to ask the students what language they felt was most appropriate. They chose their mother tongue. Although Kiswahili is supposed to be the "lingua franca" of East Africa, very few people in Kenya outside the cities actually use Kiswahili for daily communication. Yet almost all theological material here is only available in English or Kiswahili. The people coming forward for enrolment in the parish-level courses have had little formal education. They are not competent in the use of English or Kiswahili. This "language failure" results in "failure" in theological education, although it is more of a failure in *access* to theological literature than an inability to reflect theologically. The use of the mother tongue has pedagogical advantages and also does full justice to the individual's ethno-cultural background.

Curriculum design and development

Inevitably the programme director influences the development of curriculum content. In an attempt to minimize this, however, I decided to involve the students in identifying the aspects of theology that they thought were important for them to learn. This has proved very difficult. The students expected me to "pour" all the knowledge I had into their "empty" heads. I was a disappointment to some as I tried to get them to identify the issues which touch them in their daily witness and the implications of their confessing Jesus Christ as Lord. Slowly, through trial and error, community needs began to emerge. First there was a question of defining who is a Christian. Immediately the question of the revival "team" members' understanding of Christianity largely in moral terms came up. We held discussions and studied the Bible together. The questions and the trend of the debate regarding the definition of a Christian led to a number of issues. These included:

— the mission of Jesus Christ and the preaching of the good news about the kingdom;
— the study of biblical passages on the coming of Jesus Christ to call people to repentance and salvation;

— the spiritual, social, and ecclesiastical implications of following Jesus.

These led to interesting discoveries in the seminars. For example, two men were coming to the seminars and then going home to beat up their wives! Apparently most of the class knew about this, but I did not. I was amazed to see an angry mother standing up in the seminar one afternoon demanding the expulsion of the two men from the seminar! After reading 1 Corinthians 5:1ff., a heated debate followed. The incident revealed an inadequate understanding of the implications of being a Christian in the context of marriage and family life. The vicar, the revival brethren "team" members and I helped to sort out the problem, and it had a happy ending when the couples were reconciled in the church.

Another issue was the authority of church leaders. There were numerous complaints regarding how church leaders were chosen. After listening to the questions that people were asking, I prepared study materials on spiritual gifts and the work of the Holy Spirit in the church. We studied how a church can discover spiritual and gifted leaders for ministry. Indeed the challenge to understand what ministry is led to the production and development of material on 1 Corinthians 12, Ephesians 4, and Romans 12.

Course methodology

We have already changed our methods. I now train seminar coordinators. These men and women are selected by their congregations as future tutors. I then run courses for them on basic pedagogical principles and the practical leading of a seminar group. From my first cohort of TEE students the parishes have chosen a number of key seminar leaders who have started new classes. The myth that one has to be a Bible school graduate in order to lead a seminar is slowly being broken down. These seminar leaders are now accepted as competent group leaders. The idea that we are all learners is also being accepted slowly. After the students have attended their first five seminars, they begin to see themselves as active participants in the learning process. The seminar coordinator more or less "chairs" the discussions. The Saturday practical preaching workshops have proved especially helpful to preachers and Sunday school teachers. At first it is difficult to get the students to accept positive criticism, but after the initial sessions they readily accept correction and even engage in self-criticism.

Some lessons learned so far

The programme started only just over a year ago. Already we have begun to learn a number of things.

1. The parish clergy are overworked, and it is almost impossible to involve them as seminar coordinators, yet their support of TEE is crucial. Where the parish priest has shown little interest, some of the key local leaders have often not taken TEE seriously.

2. The level of literacy is a significant factor in retaining the students who enroll. Although discussion occupies the greater part of a seminar, illiterate or semi-literate adults tend to get frustrated if they are unable to do their homework prior to seminar day. These form the majority of the two-thirds who tend to drop out after inital enrolment. In most centres few students drop out after attending five or six seminars.

3. Getting evangelists, lay preachers, Sunday school and other leaders enrolled as students helps the rest of the parishioners to see the value of TEE as they see improvement in preaching and teaching and positive changes in the ministry of lay people, whom they begin to see playing an important role in the church. Teaching on spiritual gifts has also helped people in the congregations to lessen the work of their vicar.

4. The training of key local seminar coordinators helps to cut down costs in travel. The charging of high fees beyond the purchasing power of the largely agrarian students could have crippling effects on the expansion of TEE.

5. While materials locally produced in the mother tongue help to attract students to TEE, they also have to relate to the spiritual, ecclesiastical and psycho-social predicaments of the students without which their needs cannot adequately be met. This requires the materials to be constantly evaluated. Listening to student feedback can help the tutor to identify areas which require revision. Students should participate in the process of evaluation of the materials.

6. It has also become clear that one course director acting alone cannot expect to start seminars in every one of the 35 parishes in the diocese and also train, supervise and encourage local coordinators, as well as write and revise study materials. Plans have been drawn up to employ two more full-time assistant directors to help in these tasks and also a full-time secretary.

Centre for Applied Religion and Education

Theological education and human development

ADEOLU ADEGBOLA

A renewal course

The Centre for Applied Religion and Education (CARE), Ibadan, Nigeria, has planned a Renewal Course for African Pastors (RECAP) and for other Christian men and women. In a number of senses, it is an alternative educational approach. First, it is deliberately a re-newal course. It is based upon the conviction that the educational system itself needs to be renewed. The individual student himself or herself needs a renewal from the pervading cynicism, indifference and fatalism which seem to turn many workers into human robots, and form the self-centredness, materialism and triumphalist belief in progress which turns service into social oppression in modern society. The renewal course affirms that the end of education is to enable the beneficiary to become an agent of change for church renewal and social transformation.

In most African countries, the traditional system of education in theological colleges caters mainly to the socially and economically privileged sections of society and can make those colleges to be termed "elite institutions". Students who come into them from the poorest background hope to pass out as part of the "educated elite" and expect to be regarded as belonging to that elite class even by the rural peasants among whom they may serve. We are in search of an alternative approach geared directly towards the interests of the less

---

• Dr Adegbola created CARE in 1979 after serving for many years as Principal of Immanuel Theological College and Director of the Institute for Church and Society in Ibadan. His current address is P.O. Box 9270, Ibadan, Nigeria.

privileged. For the sake of convenience we focus first on rural areas where about 80 per cent of our people live.

In Africa today we do not have many pastors who are able to transform the rural areas and make them a healthier, more enlightened and more comfortable place to live in. The training provided by the theological colleges does not make them capable to render such a service. Indeed, the rate of social change has been so rapid and its nature so complex as to make the churches' influence ever so limited in any case. It has been easy to concentrate on "saving souls" and to leave social change to the politicians. With political independence being just about 20 years old in the various countries the politican himself sometimes throws up his hands in horror and asks: Where on earth can we go from here? This is the background for the political dictatorships experienced in various African countries of late.

Our basic theological response to this situation starts from the Pauline concept that the Holy Spirit has given various gifts to all, for the building up of the church and of the social communities. The pastor has a role to "draw out" (educate) these gifts for the community to profit therefrom. The work of the ministry is to bring the members of the body unto "a perfect man, unto the measure of the stature of the fullness of Christ". God's purpose for the ministry, as for the coming of Christ, can be stated in human terms, "that they might have life and have it abundantly". This gives a focus to the development education emphasis in RECAP.

Principles of development education

We have had to clarify the operational assumptions of the development process and the educational implications of the same. A few of them may be stated here serially:

1. Development is primarily and finally the development of the people. National development planning has frequently devoted attention to economic growth, which has been denoted variously as gross national product, income per capita, industrialization, and so forth. Recent calls to change gears to providing basic human needs and raising the quality of life have no ready local advocates. Could churches see and bring out the correlation between "souls" and "quality of life" and help to identify and widen the practical categories of the latter?

2. As an extension of the independence movement, Africa needs to move towards people's control of the development goals and

methods on the village level. The alternative is to demand that the villagers, who in any case have controlled their own development until the recent whirlwind of change, should now fold their arms, to advocate that a new era of colonialism be swept in with the people's connivance or active cooperation.

3. The new emphasis of the churches in Africa on programmes of integral development will flounder unless it is related from the start to leadership training based on concepts of authentic participation, appropriate methodology, people's empowerment, requisite skills, and so forth. The principle of "The Bible and the Plough" formed the basis of the work of the earlier evangelical missionaries to Africa in the nineteenth century. Why was it abandoned? Has it any relevance today? How can it be revived? Is there any possibility of making new missionaries, this time from among African Christians themselves, for an appropriately modified "The Bible and the Plough"? What is the training response to Pope Paul VI's challenge: "Africans, be missionaries to yourselves"?

4. Churches, as national coalitions of voluntary development agents, need to mobilize and coordinate the disparate efforts of their younger members engaging in development projects of various kinds. Churches should consciously organize themselves and work as voluntary associations for the development of local initiatives.

5. Young people and the educated elite in African communities should play a redemptive role in development, but so far this has been subverted by a corrupt, exploitative, neo-colonial mentality. Their role can be fulfilled only by establishing a relationship more consciously between the young people and the peasants in the villages and the urban slums.

6. The educational system and the employment patterns of African youth need to be better correlated with the problems of urban and rural development. The pattern of village polytechnics in Kenya and the ongoing Tanzanian experimentation with schools for the communities need to be more widely known and tried. There are other experiments on this correlation all over Africa. Information about these perspectives and programmes can be passed on through a system of extension education, which at the same time might encourage replication.

7. The contribution of the churches to education today is to be seen, not so much as a transmission of accumulated knowledge to produce the cultured persons of the grammar school tradition, but

rather as a process of equipping persons as individuals and as groups to become agents of social change, active participants with God in the historic struggles of modern societies.

8. Our generation has at its disposal an accumulation of knowledge that can enable us to transform our societies, if only the knowledge is adequately passed on to those who require it for change in their own societies. As such, arrangements need to be made for a massive transfer of appropriate technology and scientific attitudes to rural people for the maintenance of primary health care, production of food, and improved water supply.

9. Non-formal methods in education now demand to be explored up through university level, combining work with study, enabling theory to grow out of practice, using the facilities of correspondence courses, programmed instruction, study guides, peer learning, and so forth. Experimental operation of the principles of a "university without walls" is needed for high level leadership development for both volunteer and career service in the Christian mission for a new society.

10. In connection with these there should be planned application of available research results and an intensification of high competency applied-research aimed at the solution of practical and concrete social problems in relation to church renewal, educational reform, and eventual social transformation.

In practice, our philosophy of education as stated above has itself become the curriculum of education. What is steadily emerging is massive development education, operating first on a non-residential basis, using the perspective of "another development" which has emerged in recent years and which has quickly accumulated its own literature, inter-relating economics, sociology, social anthropology, psychology, theology and biblical studies with the professional disciplines of agriculture, education, social services, town planning, and technological skills.

We have not had the time to write the appropriate textbooks. We simply hunt around for available texts, sort them out somehow, write appropriate study guides or study notes on them, and encourage discussion groups to be formed.

Among the resources available are documents from the World Council of Churches' Commission on the Churches' Participation in Development and Christian Medical Commission; the World Health Organization; departments of development education of "charitable" organizations in the first world; periodicals like *New Internationalist* and *Development Dialogue* (Dag Hammarskjold Foundation); Orbis Books; publications of university institutes for development studies, for example, Sussex, East Anglia, Nairobi, Dar Es Salaam; and the writings of individual authors like Presidents Nyerere and Kaunda, Professors Charles Elliott, Dennis Goulet and Samir Amin.

Categories of learners

Four categories of people engage our attention for the time being. First are *village men and women,* who are considered to be the primary agents for meaningful and lasting change in the rural areas. Next are *technology students* in polytechnics and universities; this reflects our understanding of the significance of science and technology in rural change today. Theological education in Africa today suffers from the lack of at least a modicum of science, and the whole church in Africa is the poorer because of blindness of pastors to scientific perspectives. While this can be corrected to a measure in the extension education of church workers, efforts are also being made to enable technology students to relate their faith and its moral challenges to their academic specialization.

The next category of people is that of the *working pastors.* The training or retraining of *church catechists* comes fourth, but definitely not because it is considered to be of the least importance. Since catechists who live in the village are closest to the villagers and enjoy their confidence, they are strategically important for the role of the church in rural development. But, since the work of the catechist is under the direction and supervision of the ordained pastors, the reorientation of the pastors needs to take some precedence.

Courses for pastors or other church-related workers are oriented towards motivating, mobilizing and sustaining those who carry primary responsibility for development, that is, the "grassroots people" themselves, the villagers, peasant farmers and slum-dwellers who need development most and who must personally and directly spearhead it. "Another development" means that the filter-down theory has not worked. The purpose of these courses is to re-educate those who have direct professional relationship with the people and convince them in the name of the gospel to "let my people grow".

Objectives

The development education of working pastors is specifically designed to meet the professional needs of persons ministering in a church facing the demands of a changing social order. The objectives of the course are clearly related to this. They are to investigate with others:

— how to develop one's pastoral sensitivity to the changes in contemporary African society;
— how to create a new sense of Christian mission;
— how to facilitate the witness of the church among people who are going through cultural change, political growth, and economic development accompanied by social stress;
— how to develop the necessary management skills by which the church may effectively bear its evangelistic and social witness in the spirit of self-reliance and international collaboration.

These objectives assume that the pastor is willing and anxious to do more than carry on a tradition. To be ordered by the bishop or synod to take the course is not good enough. Also, the number of participants is likely to be affected by how many pastors are preoccupied with the vision of studying for the recognized qualifications of the traditional educational system. This gives us a clue right from the start that we may not be able to play the numbers game for the periodic evaluation exercise.

So far, we are satisfied with those engaged in church work in rural areas, who have demonstrated an interest in rural development and who can afterwards influence the life and mission of the church in such areas. The trend of the course is closely related to the hope for a more massive result-oriented programme for church renewal and integrated rural development.

Process and methodology

Participants in each vicinity are encouraged to form themselves into a collegium learning group (CLG). Members of the collegium will evaluate one another's practical experience in rural ministry and work as a team to outline an appropriate plan to guide their future ministry for church renewal and social development in rural areas.

An early part of the course consists of a guided self-study programme within the work experience of the pastor in his home service context, assisted as may be possible by local colleagues or members of the congregation.

Another part, which follows soon after, is woven around a number of real life experiences towards personal renewal, church renewal and social awareness. The methodology consists of a judicious combination of formal and informal approaches on a participatory basis. Emphasis is laid on the new life-style essential for the church in Africa today. The results of the previous self-study programme are brought to bear on this. Course enablers are drawn from the community of the learner, including neighbouring theological colleges, the local university, specialist laymen and women, and others. A guide is provided for this process.

Through the use of case studies an effort is made to analyze the basic inter-relationship between the economic structures and the social forces active in Africa today, to identify the gospel for the liberation of the people, and to plan how to translate these insights into action. The participants are encouraged to take due account of the experience already available in church rural development practice and also through sensitive world organizations like the Christian Medical Commission and the World Health Organization.

The plan we have undertaken is an extension education which has various methodological and institutional components, including:

1. Periodic attendance at a local centre with a mentor and/or peers. Where possible, organized seminars led by specialists from different fields on theology for rural ministry, sociology of religion in rural areas, rural church growth, rural sociology, rural economics, new processes in agricultural development, methods of rural development will be arranged.

2. A correspondence course, study guide, or programmed instruction based on a learning contract, possibly congregation-related.

3. Educative study contacts with village projects related to congregations in the area and farther afield in selected communities. In some cases this will be operated as a supervized internship or professional attachment to a project.

4. Annual participation in a short residential course in a theological college or other centre. In some cases it may be necessary to spend a limited period in a research institution or any other place which has a facility relevant to the adult student's programme. The International Institute for Tropical Agriculture (Ibadan, Nigeria) is one such possibility. What the planners of this programme are slowly learning themselves is how to relate short courses taken at home or abroad (for example, at the Coady Institute in Canada or the

Ecumenical Institute, Bossey, Switzerland) to a systematic continuing education programme which combines formal and informal methods of education.

5. Workshop preparation of a basic step-by-step model plan for effective rural ministry in Africa.

6. Individual or team projects, *either* using available resource materials to produce written aids needed for implementing the model plan, *or* producing a "scientific" report on a home-base undertaking involving a wider circle of change-agents in evaluation, implementation and improvement of the methods and resource materials from the workshop in No. 5 above. This is to be undertaken as a practical project during the terminal period of the defined study programme.

At the time of writing, the course is in its early stages of growth. One thing is clear: our task is the promotion of continuing education for all, and its meaningful relation to national development and to desirable social change.

Organization of African Independent Churches
Spiritual revival Bible school

AGUSTÍN and ROSARIO BATLLE

History and description

The Organization of African Independent Churches (OAIC) was created in Cairo in 1978 during a meeting of leaders from representative African Independent Churches (AICs). Their aims were not to unite the AICs but rather to encourage fellowship and joint work on common programmes dealing with biblical teaching, leadership training and ministerial formation. Primate Adejobi of the Church of the Lord (Aladura) was elected chairman and Bishop Markos of the Coptic Orthodox Church, organizing secretary. The felt-need of theological training emerged, and since late 1980 the OAIC/TEE programme has been operating from an office in Nairobi under the leadership of Agustín and Rosario Batlle, who have had long experience in theological education by extension among independent churches in Latin America. The Advisory Committee is made up of heads of the following Kenyan AICs: African Christian Church and Schools, African Divine Church, Church of Christ in Africa, Episcopal Church of Africa, African Israel Church Ninevah, Holy Spirit Church of East Africa.

During its first year the OAIC/TEE programme has been going through three phases simultaneously.

• The writers developed and directed the extension programme of the Theological Community of Chile before going to Kenya in 1980 as consultants to the Organization of African Independent Churches, P.O. Box 21570, Nairobi, Kenya.

Phase I

The promotional part of the TEE work began with the circulation of the OAIC/TEE brochure under the name *Spiritual Revival Bible School* (in Swahili, *Maswali Na Juu Ya Elimu Ya Kiroho)* and through personal contacts and invitations to visit and talk to church groups about TEE principles and methods. The response from the very beginning has been very positive and hundreds of church members and spiritual leaders have said: "This is what we need, praise the Lord!"

Very early in the year AIC people who felt deeply the value of this programme for their own churches said to us: "I want to promote it in my church."

These persons were taken into consideration very early in the programme and have been acting as coordinator-promoters, key persons in any TEE programme. They arranged new contacts with their own church headquarters and officers; they themselves explained the TEE principles and methods to their people. Later on, some of these coordinator-promoters accompanied us on our trips and short TEE courses, introducing each study programme and functioning as translators from English to the local language and as seminar leaders in training also.

In Phase I, a total of 1,114 applicants were received: 860 from 26 Kenyan AICs, 124 from mission-founded churches, and 130 from women's groups.

Phase II

TEE studies were initiated using two correspondence courses of five lessons each. The first study subject, *Discovering the Bible,* was sent out 1 January 1981 in English and Swahili. The acceptance of this first course has been widespread; more than 1,200 copies have been prepared and distributed. Very early in the year some churches asked us to have a three-day discussion on the subject at the end of the five-lesson study (or period of five weeks) at their own church headquarters. The first course has been followed by course No. 2, *More about the Bible,* and course No. 3, *Women and Evangelism* at the request of some women's groups. Course 1 is for correspondence only, Courses 2 and 3 can be used in seminar meetings also. Other courses are being prepared for seminar meetings only (i.e. TEE proper).

Courses 2 and 3 were sent out in April (in English). The Swahili version of Course 2 was sent out in July, much later than needed, because we had no equipment of our own (IBM typewriter and duplicator) for such a large student community.

Phase III

The preparation of seminar leaders and TEE text writers began in March and June 1981 with a six-day workshop for TEE text writers. Two Kenyans and a South African attended. Four new TEE texts have been written as a result: *Every Christian an Evangelist* (course No. 4) and *The Pastor as Evangelist* (course No. 6) by the Rev. Daniel Oguso Obiero (African Independent); *Come to the Healer* (course No. 5) and *God's Guidance for You* (course No. 7) by Mr Joe R.W. Situma. Courses 1, 2, 3, 5 have already been tested in five AICs. The study subjects requested by different AICs make a list of twenty for the years 1981 and 1982, including *Church and Development* and *Primary Health Care*.

From the beginning of the year we enjoyed the cooperation of the NCCK Department of Theology under the leadership of Dr Hans Burgman (Church of Sweden) and Mr Stephen Githumbi (Presbyterian Church of East Africa). A ten-week extension course for Independent church leaders was held in Nairobi on Saturday afternoons at Church Army Headquarters. A ten-week course was held for two women's groups in Kibera and Kawangare (very poor neighbourhoods of Nairobi). A three-day programme was conducted at the African Christian Church and Schools Bible College with a joint budget (expenses shared between the College and TEE budget).

Four study centres were established in West Kenya at the head-quarters of the African Divine Church, African Israel Church Nineveh, Church of Christ in Africa, and Holy Spirit Church of East Africa. In each of these study centres the studies have been organized with attendance varying from 35 to 111 and with teaching responsibilities and expenses shared by local sponsors. Only one of the four study centres has electricity; the others use kerosene lighting. These joint adventures are a very encouraging and healthy factor because this kind of mutual endeavour does not damage the parties involved.

Analysis of context and goals of the programme: geo-social facts

A country that lies on the equator in Eastern Africa, Kenya became independent in 1963. The country covers an area of 224,959 square miles and is divided into seven provinces: Western, Nyanza, Rift Valley, Central, Eastern, North Eastern, Coast. It has a population of 15,700,000, whose chief occupation is agriculture; industry and trade have increased very rapidly during the last 35 years. Kenya is the largest tea producer in Africa. Per capita income is $350. Ninety-five per cent of the people are members of many different tribes, the names of the six largest being Kikuyu, Baluhya, Luo, Kamba, Kipsigis, and Kelenjim. Kenya also has about 200,000 Asians, mostly from India, 40,000 Arabs, and about 45,000 Europeans. Thirty-five per cent of the men and 45 per cent of the women cannot read and write in spite of the growing number of primary, intermediate, and secondary schools, and adult education programmes. Swahili and English are the official languages; tribal languages predominate in many areas. Thirty-five per cent of the people adhere to traditional African religions; 60 per cent are Christians; 5 per cent are Muslims.

There is a higher percentage of illiterate women than men, first of all because in any kind of educational programme men always have first preference. For instance, the new agricultural programmes brought to Kenya served the men, in spite of the fact that women do the agricultural work in the family plots ("shambas") because they are in charge of raising food for the family. Men do the odd jobs, take care of the animals, if any, and go to towns and cities looking for money. Women plant and harvest the food, using part of it for the family, and if there is any surplus they try to sell it at markets. Often the husband, in order to get money for himself, goes and sells it at any price. If he appears with a new woman to join the family, sometimes she is tolerated, but at other times a situation is created that forces the wife to leave her home because there is no law on her side. The law does not protect the woman; if a man gets tired of his wife, he can put her out without any possessions or children. The Christian religion has given a different viewpoint on male-female relationships, but women continue to be a very subordinated group, not of equal value as men, even in the church.

Church situation

There are over 6,000 Independent churches in Africa. The membership is around 26,000,000. These churches increase at a rate of 100 per year. The first one started in Ghana in 1868. About 4,000 are in Southern Africa. In some countries they are encouraged by the government; in other countries, where the head of the state belongs to one of the mainline churches, AICs are encouraged to join mainline churches. In Swaziland, the king is the head of the Independent churches, and he himself belongs to one of them.

In Kenya, the first separatist church movement began in 1914 when Johana Owalo, a Luo who broke from the Church Missionary Society, formed the Moniya Luo Mission. From that point and with an enormous impulse after 1963, the year of national independence, Independent churches in Kenya have mushroomed. There are now more than 160 with around 650,000 members. Most AICs isolate themselves from all other church denominations, having no relation with others. Preachers who belong to these separatist groups are all over the country. You will find them on Nairobi's street corners, men with evangelistic gifts who come with very strange doctrines. Some preach about the head of their church, not Christ. When it rains, they say that they have given the rain; the same thing in healing. Some of the AIC heads claim that they are Christ. One said: "I am Jesus Christ on earth and better than Jesus Christ, because Jesus Christ cannot show himself to people, and I can show myself to my people; people can see me, and they can touch me." They are in great need of relating to others, to learn and understand what is the church and what is the Christian ministry. On the other hand AICs have something to offer to the church in other parts of the world. They are not just an interesting novelty. Those who have been in contact with them often say that this is another type of Christianity that has enriched their Christian experience. We realize that each Independent church has a deep religious experience, but its Christian theology is still in formation.

Goals of the OAIC/TEE programme

The purposes of this programme are:

— to teach basic biblical theology to deepen the AIC's understanding of the church and of the Christian ministry;
— to enable everyone in the church to be a more concerned Christian in order to participate fully in the life and mission of the church "here" and "now", mobilizing the gifts God has given to his people;
— to prepare pastors and lay leaders and also to provide Bible teaching at the congregational level, from whence new leaders and better prepared laity will appear;

— to help Christians to understand that they are members of a worldwide Christian community without seeking to homogenize them or to rob them of their cultural identity.

The OAIC/TEE programme is an interdenominational organization concerned with:

— equipping the whole people of God for effective Christian ministry with a theology that is biblically based and also oriented to the African context;

— enabling theological thinking that will better equip and strengthen churches and their leaders to proclaim the truth which is salvation in Christ;

— developing attitudes of Christian citizens in their communities, helping them to overcome the evils of ignorance, sickness, poverty and other kinds of oppression;

— creating a universal, ecumenical spirit that has no barriers or discrimination.

Educational philosophy and methods

The TEE educational philosophy is based first on Christian values and second on a contemporary andragogical approach to education, in which the experience of adults is valued as a rich ingredient for learning (viz. the recommendations on the development of adult education adopted by the General Conference of UNESCO, Nairobi, 1976).

We started using correspondence courses due to the lack of resources (seminar leaders and money for travel) to respond to so many applicants and as an introduction to group experience and critical thinking. We moved from a behaviourist method and purely individual approach to the educational theory that gives freedom to each participant to share his/her own conclusions. The students move from passive reception to active participation and personal discovery with an emphasis on the community dimension.

The TEE texts are based on inquiries into the needs of the participants in order to begin with and speak to their experience. We seek to accomplish this task by: (a) organizing seminars and consultations on TEE principles and methods; (b) setting up study centres in the particular social situations in which the students are living (the study centres are provided with small libraries to reinforce learning); (c) training local leaders in TEE philosophy and the preparation of TEE texts; (d) providing workshops on the leadership of study groups and the use of dialogical methods.

Evaluation, results, problems, insights and future plans

Each course ends with an evaluation. The correspondence courses were highly appreciated by 95 per cent of the students. The participants almost invariably wanted to continue studying the next course. The courses were recommended to others, and they helped in a great way to make friends with the AICs and to introduce a more effective way of training. The three- and five-day seminars were also highly appreciated by all. The participants always asked when the next course would be given, and the courses were recommended to others.

Two study levels emerged during the first year, the general congregational level and the pastoral-lay leadership level. These are the ones most needed, as expressed by the heads of the AICs. In some cases pastors study beside their congregations.

A need emerged for some kind of recognition at the end of each course. A certificate has been used as a reinforcement and stimulus to continue studies. We believe that it is a way of beginning to establish study habits in people who, in many cases, do not even read the newspaper.

In some churches it has taken much longer than others to establish a study centre due to the structure of the church. If there was no one person to make decisions, such as a bishop, the board of the church would take longer than usual to reach an agreement.

Another problem is the limited Swahili of the students in western Kenya. Swahili and English have had to be translated into other vernaculars necessitating more than one interpreter in the seminar meetings. Further translations of the TEE texts from Swahili will be needed.

We have discovered within many AICs that most of the people have a call and a strong desire for developing the gifts that God has given to them, but the structure does not allow them to be educated theologically. Most of the people are not given importance within their own church; they seem to be there to justify the leaders. Seeing the way they participated in group discussion during the seminar meetings, the way they answered different questions, reflecting the way they think, we realized that they are "priests" and "priestesses". What is needed — and this is one of the main goals of this TEE programme — is help in discovering the value of each man and woman within their own church.

What gives meaning to this TEE work in Kenya is that one feels in tune with the aspirations of so many people. The majority of the participants are from the rural area, and they know many things of which the city-dweller is ignorant. The programme has helped these rural churches not to feel isolated or deserted.

Future plans call for reinforcement of the OAIC/TEE programme in Kenya due to the great needs and acceptance by the Independent churches. A TEE worker who has been undergoing training in TEE principles and methods will be located in western Kenya, where most of the students are.

Next year Phase IV will stress ecumenical seminar meetings with participants from different AICs in the area of a given study centre. Two seminar leaders-in-training have led studies this year in churches not their own.

Work with AICs in other parts of Africa will begin in 1982, starting with West Africa.

North America

Southern Baptist Seminary Extension
Increasing accessibility through inter-seminary cooperation

RAYMOND M. RIGDON and LEE HOLLAWAY

How to provide ministry education for those persons who need it most urgently has always been the central issue in theological education by extension. The six seminaries of the Southern Baptist Convention have confronted this issue out of the context of a free-church, congregational tradition. They have responded by creating a jointly-sponsored Seminary Extension Department. During its thirty-year history this department has developed some structures and approaches quite different from those commonly found in TEE. Most significant, perhaps, is the control and support which the seminaries of the Southern Baptist Convention have provided for Seminary Extension from its beginning — and continue to provide today.

In the years immediately following World War II, a floodtide of interest in adult education swept the United States. Theological seminaries felt its impact, just as did most colleges and universities. Many would-be students, however, either failed to qualify academically for a degree programme or were unable to move to a location where they could take advantage of a residential study programme. For these persons, correspondence study seemed to be an alternative which fit their needs. Two Southern Baptist seminaries responded by developing such courses. By the end of 1950 the

• Dr Rigdon is Executive Director of the Seminary External Education Division; the Rev. Lee Hollaway is Director of Communications. While the Division has granted only very limited permission for others to use their materials, the staff will respond to inquiries about any aspect of the programme. Questions should be addressed to Seminary Extension, Southern Baptist Convention Building, 460 James Robertson Parkway, Nashville, Tennessee 37219, USA.

seminaries had agreed that this kind of education could be done most effectively through a single office jointly sponsored by all of them.

Thus on 15 June 1951, the Seminary Extension Department began operation in Jackson, Mississippi, physically separated from the seminaries, yet under the administration of the seminary presidents through an elected executive director. Its first students were those it had inherited from the two seminary correspondence programmes. The department quickly took steps to expand this base. Within a year it had also begun the first of what was to become a far-flung network of extension centres. In 1963 the programme's offices were transferred to Nashville, Tennessee, where they are housed along with five other convention agencies in the Southern Baptist Convention Building.

Seminary Extension has continued to grow, with its most significant growth period coming in the five years beginning with 1973. During that time the number of students increased more than 100 per cent. At the conclusion of the 1980-81 reporting period, a total of 2,571 persons were enrolled in correspondence courses through the Seminary Extension Independent Study Institute. An additional 9,000 took one or more courses during the year at the 400 Seminary Extension centres. These students were scattered over virtually every part of the United States, and 160 of them lived in 18 other countries.

A full-time staff that has never been more than 15 persons coordinates the study programmes of those more than 11,000 students. This is possible because of a host of part-time paid and volunteer workers involved at many levels of the programme. The Independent Study Institute, for example, employs 17 highly competent staff members from other convention agencies to serve as part-time instructors. Fourteen of these have earned doctorates. Several of them have processed as many as 1,000 test papers in a year. The full-time personnel at the Institute spend much of their time responding to inquiries, receiving and mailing tests, recording grades, and advising current students.

The Seminary Extension centre system has a particularly indigenous character. Each centre has a local sponsor which controls the day-to-day operations. Most often this sponsor is an association of churches within a limited geographical area. Decisions about time, frequency, and location of class sessions, selection of teachers, and particular courses to be offered all are made by a local director, frequently in consultation with a committee. In order for a centre to qualify as a part of the Seminary Extension system, it must use curriculum materials developed by the Seminary Extension Department, submit final grades to the department for recording, and conform to the department's academic requirements. These requirements include scheduling at least 18 class hours per course, using standardized tests developed by the department, and enlisting teachers certified by the department. Most such teachers are local pastors who hold at least a master's degree. The Seminary Extension Department provides administrative assistance (including a notebook for use by the local director), maintains permanent student records, and makes available a varied curriculum based on those at its sponsoring seminaries.

Some viewpoints on learning

The Seminary Extension approach to learning is based generally on the following philosophical viewpoints:

1. Every minister needs to engage in purposeful, planned learning as long as he or she is in active service.

2. Learning produces changes in how persons think, feel and act.

3. Learning is facilitated when it is related to the problems and felt-needs of the learners.

4. Learning is facilitated when it takes place in the locale in which application is to be made.

5. Learning is facilitated when the learner is appropriately involved in setting goals, planning processes, and evaluating results.

6. Learning is facilitated when the methods used are consistent with the goals and abilities of learners.

7. Learning is facilitated when both course materials and the personal experiences of learners are used skilfully as resources in achieving the learning objectives.

8. Learning is facilitated when it is consistent with and improves the self-concept of the learner.

9. Learning is facilitated when the learner is encouraged and assisted in using what he or she has learned in real life situations.

10. Effective continuing education helps persons learn how to learn and commit themselves to life-long learning.

A pressing need

The Southern Baptist Convention itself has never had any educational requirements for its ministers. Individual churches set their own qualifications, which may place a higher priority on such factors as effectiveness of preaching, warmth of personality, familiarity with the Bible, or doctrinal stance. As recently as 1973, a survey revealed that 63.5 per cent of Southern Baptist pastors had not completed a seminary degree programme. About one-third of these have met the academic requirements for enrolling in a graduate theological programme at a seminary. More than four out of ten pastors, therefore, may be characterized as "non-degree pastors", whose only theological training likely will have to come from some source such as Seminary Extension.

Over the past ten years the Seminary Extension Department has placed a major emphasis upon the development of educationally sound and readable curriculum materials. The widely varying educational backgrounds of its students led the department to develop curriculum resources on three levels of difficulty. These include a basic (pre-college) series, a college-level series, and a CESA ("Continuing Education for Seminary Alumni") series.

Seventeen courses make up the basic series, organized under four content areas: biblical studies, pastoral ministries, ecclesiology, and applied Christianity. The chief distinguishing characteristic of this series is the simplified vocabulary used in its study guides. These courses have proved especially helpful to persons with limited formal education or for whom English is a second language. No textbook is used beyond the study guide, and no tests are required. Persons studying basic courses by correspondence also receive a cassette to help guide them in their study. Since college credit is not offered for those courses, requirements for those who teach them are less rigid. Permanent course completion records are maintained by the department, however, and a student may earn a Seminary Extension certificate for completing ten basic courses.

About half of the 45 courses in the college-level series are in the biblical area, with the remainder divided between theological-historical and practical subjects. Each of these courses was designed and written by a professor at one of the Southern Baptist seminaries. In addition to the study guide, each course uses one or more standard textbooks and a series of tests plus a final examination. Credit for these courses has been applied towards degree programmes at many colleges and universities in the United States. Correspondence students who desire college-level credit must take an officially supervised final examination.

The CESA series contains non-credit resources to help seminary alumni plan and engage in personal programmes of continuing education. One tool included is a booklet designed to help a pastor assess his or her own needs in ministry. A second booklet outlines procedures for setting up a "colleague study group", a small cluster of ministers brought together by their mutual concern for continuing education, such as projects offered by the various sponsoring seminaries. Also included in the CESA series are a limited selection of learning resources, such as cassette tapes, dealing with important areas in the work of the ministry and designed primarily for individual study.

A promising future

Early in 1981 the Seminary Extension Department experimented with a new approach to ministry training, using videotape as part of a telecourse. In a pilot course taught over a 12-week period, a seminary professor in Kentucky taught simultaneously two classes assembled in New York and Georgia. Each session opened with a 30-minute videotape or audiotape presentation by the professor, followed by an interaction period during which the professor was linked by a conference telephone connection with both classes. A learning facilitator at each site closed the session with a time of small-group discussion based on questions devised by the professor.

This model, which enables the seminary faculties to extend their teaching ministries to many new locations without over-extending their own time and energies, will make it much more feasible for graduate-level courses to be offered through extension. In May 1981 the six seminaries established a new Seminary Satellite Department to serve as a delivery vehicle for this higher level of study. It will function alongside the Seminary Extension Department in a new Seminary External Education Division. Raymond M. Rigdon was named to direct the division in addition to continuing to direct the two departments.

The development of this new approach, coupled with the continued growth of the well-established systems, promises even stronger days ahead for extension education in the Southern Baptist Convention. Other factors also should have a positive impact on this work: (1) a growing pressure within the denomination for easily accessible education opportunities; (2) an increasing awareness of the importance of the non-degree pastor and bi-vocational pastor, especially in serving the many small churches; (3) a rapidly growing number of ethnic/language congregations within the denomination, most without trained leaders; and (4) an increasing interest in Seminary Extension materials and models in other countries.

Doctrinal and missiological factors also will contribute to continued growth in Southern Baptists' off-campus approaches to theological education. One of the most ardently held doctrines among Baptists is that of the "priesthood of every believer". This doctrine affirms not only that every true believer has free access to God through Christ (Heb. 4:14-16), but also that each believer has a priestly responsibility to bring people to God (1 Pet. 2:5,9). Seminary Extension will continue to give its first priority to the equipping of those whom God has called into full-time ministry. As lay Southern Baptists increasingly see themselves in the role of minister, many of them will recognize their need for deeper theological training. Likewise as Southern Baptists establish new congregations in many non-Southern areas of the United States, there will be an enlarged need for training indigenous ministerial leadership to serve those churches. Thus, the more Southern Baptists remain true to their most cherished concepts and the more success they have in carrying out the commission of Christ to evangelize the world, the more they will need an extension programme in theological education.

San Francisco Theological Seminary

We heard the church
— towards a many-celled seminary

JOHN S. HADSELL

How did a seminary in a mainline Protestant church in the USA develop from a one-celled to a many-celled institution? This is the story of how it happened to San Francisco Theological Seminary (SFTS), San Anselmo, California, a seminary of the United Presbyterian Church in the USA.

Since 1871, SFTS has been preparing persons for the ministry. For most of the early years the candidates were young, male, white and unmarried; the underlying assumption was that their preparation would launch them into career trajectories that would persist through a lifetime, with little further learning needed. For certain, they had learned the basics of Bible, theology, church history, and preaching; the rest was practice and they would pick that up on the job. Fundamental changes in the culture and in the church were not expected; the world would go on pretty much as it was in the nineteenth century.

Then along came Karl Marx, Charles Darwin, Sigmund Freud and Albert Einstein. The intellectual world has been undergoing revolutions since, not to mention the political, social, and cultural revolutions that contributed to the shattering of the complacent view of nineteenth century educational and career assumptions.

In the years following the Second World War, SFTS educators began to hear the term "continuing education". It was, at first, something other vocations and professions undertook: law,

• Dr Hadsell is Director for Programme Development at San Francisco Theological Seminary, 2 Kensington Road, San Anselmo, California 94960, USA.

medicine, accounting. Who wants to face the tax agents of the state, represented by a lawyer whose education stopped ten years ago? Or who wants to roll into the operating room for a serious and delicate operation performed by a doctor who has not learned the latest techniques?

Not that SFTS and other seminaries in the USA and elsewhere were not somewhat engaged, on the side, with occasional seminars and conferences for pastors. They were. But the vast majority of time and energy and funding went into the degree programme for seminarians preparing for ministry — and these were the young people described above, yet untested, untried, inexperienced, potentials only. The church, both through its several bodies local, regional, and national, and through its individuals, invested large sums in these seminarians, in the hope that they somehow would prove competent as well as committed.

On a strictly investment basis, it was a poor risk, as the theorists of theological education by extension have proved. For every fifty of such students, perhaps twenty were gifted with the leadership skills necessary to bring a congregation into vital growth and mission; the rest either stumbled through careers, with minimal results, or left the ministry for other vocations. In no systematic, formal, educational way did the church continue to support the seminarians once they were ordained and called to the pastorate.

New questions: new developments

SFTS, through a president and faculty sensitive to the church, began in 1960 to ask the inevitable questions: Is it our responsibility to provide some formal type of continuing education for the clergy, as they face a world in intellectual, social, cultural, and political revolution, and a church demanding relevant discipleship? Again, on strict investment terms, is it not wise to protect and enhance the investment made in these clergy, to save them for the church, given the large sums we have spent preparing them for the ministry?

The culmination of this questioning came in 1961, when the faculty authorized and undertook an advanced degree programme for clergy. And, hearing the church, the programme was adapted, at least partially, to the personal and vocational lives of the clergy-now-students; it was part-time and non-residential, so it could be undertaken without leaving the scene of one's calling. Further, the curriculum was designed to incorporate one's practice of ministry; one's ministry became the laboratory for the academic components of the curriculum. For example, a study in homiletics demands not only a reading of books and the Book, but the preaching, and the evaluation by the congregation, of sermons shaped out of the reading. Thus preaching becomes informed by the people's evaluative responses, as the experience is reported and re-evaluated in an academic programme.

Despite these curricular innovations, the programme tended, in the first years, to feature a top-down, faculty-shaped, banking theory of education in most of its dimensions, certainly in curriculum building and faculty selection. Then, in the early 1960s, came a student revolt, leading by several years the same phenomenon in colleges and universities worldwide.

Young seminarians, and other young graduate students, may be patient with the banking theory of education, but the older clergy-now-students were not. They wanted a voice in the governance of the programme and a revision of certain policies. That voice was given, and now the programme is supervised by a committee consisting of four faculty, three clergy-at-large from the San Francisco Bay Area, and three clergy-now-students enrolled in the programme and living nearby. This committee oversees the work of the director of the programme and, responsible to the faculty, monitors and evaluates every aspect of the curriculum: admissions, faculty selections, dissertation/projects and other academic concerns.

The initial degree programme, "Doctor of the Science of Theology" (Sc.T.D.), was joined in 1970 by a second one built on the same premises: "Doctor of Ministry" (D.Min.). Together they currently enroll 600 students, and have graduated about 400, each of whom has undertaken and written, as the last phase of his or her curriculum, a "dissertation/project" on some phase of ministry and has reported the findings to a church agency, or has sought publication. For perhaps the first time in history a literature on ministry is developing that is being produced by the practitioners of ministry and not by theoreticians only.

These degree programmes, formal continuing education, worked a minor revolution within SFTS. First, the innovative curriculum and teaching methodologies, and the governance that includes students, began to inform the basic programme, Master of Divinity (M.Div.), for young people preparing for ministry. Second, it brought into the seminary's total student body a large number of practitioners, whose views and perspectives and questions began to alter the traditional concept of the nature and function of theological education. In the early years, the advanced programme functioned only marginally to the main task of preparing persons for ministry; gradually, as the number of clergy-now-students increased, faculty and administration and trustees began to realize that we had created, *de facto,* a parallel commitment to the renewal and re-education of the clergy. The step to *de jure* recognition of that realization came at a crucial, and somewhat painful, episode in the history of SFTS, in 1972, as the new reality took root and grew. Now it is agreed upon by all: SFTS is committed both to the preparation of persons for ministry and to the renewal of persons in ministry, and one major avenue for each is a degree programme, thus providing structure, coherence, logic, evaluation and certification.

The acceptance of advanced degree programmes for clergy led, by an irresistible logic, to non-degree programmes also. Not every pastor can afford additional formal education, and then probably only once in a career lifetime. But the necessity of continuing education remains and, if not degree, then non-degree. So the next step came naturally, and was then expanded to inlcude not only clergy but laity, again by a process of natural extension of a basic idea and commitment. A seminar on "The church and the alcoholic" is not intrinsically of interst to clergy only; many laity have professional and/or personal concerns with this theme.

Programmes of lay education

Once the logic of lay education had taken hold, we heard the church once again, this time in the form of the question addressed directly to us from church leaders: Can you undertake a degree programme for lay persons who are concerned with the integrity of their discipleship in their vocation, built on the model of your programme for clergy? Well, why not? Already the laity in our non-degree seminars and workshops were proving their competence and commitment.

The result came in 1974, after a committee of faculty and church persons had met over several months: a Master of Arts in Values (M.A.V.) for lay persons, conducted in extension up and down the West Coast from Seattle to Los Angeles. And the focus is something perhaps entirely new in theological education: ethical decision-making in one's vocational, or major avocational, arena. The common thread in the life of all persons is ethical decision-making, attempting to live out the value commitments one absorbs from the gospel without capitulating excessively to the values of the culture. Almost 200 lay persons are now enrolled in small, non-residential groups of ten or twelve; the instruction is given partially by SFTS faculty and partially by locally recruited visiting lecturers of equal competence. And all is overseen by a committee composed of three faculty, three church persons-at-large (clergy or lay) and three students in the programme.

Several years ago the national General Assembly of the denomination called for a renewal of theological and biblical literacy, across the church. And we at SFTS once again heard the church. Our response, first funded by the church nationally, and now by our own funds, is the current establishment of several "centres for theological reflection and renewal", in collaboration with regional church bodies in the western part of the US: southern California, northern California, and the states of Arizona, Oregon, and Washington/Alaska. These extension centres, with full- or part-time directors and local committees, collaborate with the regional church structures in providing non-degree continuing education on site, using both SFTS faculty and their peers locally as instructors.

One further dimension: "resource centres". Changing times and moods, revolutions both political and intellectual, demand an educational response of flexibility, allowing special emphases to emerge. So we are now developing several foci that will provide special resources to the seminary's several degree and non-degree programmes and extension centres. Five resource centres are operating or planned: Christian Spiritual Disciplines, Liturgy and Worship, Ministry with Senior Adults, World Ecumenism, the Human Prospect. Each centre will have a committee drawn from the constituency served; each will be served by a faculty/administrator director; each will offer courses and seminars and workshops in both degree and non-degree programmes. More listening to the church.

How did it happen?

Back to the question in the opening paragraph of this essay: How did we get from one stage to another, from a one-celled to a many-celled institution, from a seminary with a student body of young, white, unmarried males to one drawn from the whole church: young and old, male and female, married and single, lay and clergy, white and black and Hispanic and Asian? Several reasons coalesce:

— we heard the church; that is, we had the grace and good sense to respond to the needs of the church as the church perceived them;

— we had the grace at first gingerly to allow, and later boldly to encourage, the church — the people — to become partners with us in every phase of our life, from governance to teaching to selection of faculty to enrolling as students;

— we felt the impact of the revolutions of the twentieth century, Marxist, Darwinian, Freudian, Einsteinian, and the changes in ourselves, in the church, in the world, that they were bringing, and thus knew that we could not remain in the nineteenth century educational tradition in which we were born;

— we realized in proper capitalistic style that continuing education was a protection of a large investment already made; preparing persons for ministry is not enough; they must also be continually renewed in ministry if they are to remain effective;

— we were gifted with creative leadership in administration, faculty and trustees, perhaps due to the providence of God; anyway, as Presbyterians, we like to think so.

So San Francisco Theological Seminary has become a servant, a resource, a school of, for and by the whole church. The five educational programmes we offer (M.Div. for preparation for ministry; S.T.D. and D.Min. for renewal in ministry; Ph.D. towards teaching in the theological disciplines, done in collaboration with the Graduate Theological Union in Berkeley; non-degree education for clergy and laity; M.A.V. for equipping laity for discipleship) give us a full-orbed, many-celled structure; our extension centres enable us to be engaged closely with the church, and our resource centres keep us tracking with the times.

The change from one cell to many has not been without strain and struggle. Accrediting agencies have scrutinized us closely, making helpful suggestions as they have approved our progammes. Faculty have fretted, properly, over the issue of quality control of educational events conducted by adjunct faculty and visiting lecturers off campus. Trustees have sometimes longed nostalgically for the modes of earlier and simpler days. Administrators have been taxed to keep abreast of the increased complexities of record keeping, student housing, academic calendars, and church relations.

But these are the pains of a growing organism, signs of health. And the response from the church has made the pain of change worthwhile. We are becoming known as the church's seminary.

Was there an initial grand scheme that SFTS envisioned as it undertook this journey? One could wish there might have been, but the answer is no. Each step rather grew from those just before, with a logic only in hindsight. The critical factor in each step of change and growth, over these two decades, is the title of this article: We Heard the Church.

New York Theological Seminary
Seeking the shalom of the city

GEORGE W. WEBBER

New York Theological Seminary was founded in 1900 and almost from the beginning has been located in the heart of New York City. Until 1970 it functioned as a traditional seminary, training future clergy and teachers of religion for ministry in a variety of denominations. In 1970 a dramatic new area began. By decision of the Trustees the Seminary made a commitment to provide training for both clergy and laity in the New York area. This involves continuing education in a variety of forms meeting the needs of students at quite diverse educational levels.

The resulting diversity in the student body, faculty and trustees reflects the breadth of the religious community in the metropolitan area: black, Hispanic, white, and Asian; students from suburbs, satellite cities and inner-city neighbourhoods; Roman Catholic, more than fifty Protestant denominations, and even several Jewish rabbis; young and old, men and women, from all walks of life. The Seminary is a sign in the midst of the City that in Christ "there is neither Jew nor Greek, there is neither slave nor free, there is neither male nor female". Since most who study here are mature church leaders, we do not focus primarily on new knowledge, but on empowering them for greater competence in ministry, for better utilizing their leadership potential in church and community, and in developing coherence between theology and practice.

• Dr Webber is the President of New York Theological Seminary, 5 West 29th Street, New York, NY 10001, USA.

For several years now we have operated under the mandate of a passage in Jeremiah: "Seek the shalom of the City where I have sent you into exile, and pray to the Lord on its behalf, for in its shalom you will find your shalom." The resources of the religious community, brought to bear on the problems of God's world, can make a vital difference in the health and humaneness of the City. Our educational programmes seek to sensitize our students to injustice, to human need, to oppression in whatever form, and to the task of responsible love for our neighbours.

One of the remarkable discoveries that we have made is that only 10 per cent of New York's 2,500,000 Protestants are Anglos (white European stock), that most of the Protestant congregations are among the black and Hispanic and other ethnic groups who bear the brunt of poverty, unemployment, sub-standard housing, crime, and the other symptoms of urban blight. The flexibility of the Seminary makes it possible to respond to their varied educational needs and to shape programmes to meet their concerns rather than fitting them into programmes.

The enthusiastic response and serious dedication of these students have not only brought new life and a new sense of mission to the Seminary. They are a sign of hope for the City. Hundreds of indigenous leaders with great potential for spiritual and social change are being equipped for theological reflection and urban ministry without being uprooted or alienated from their people and context.

Brief history

The Seminary was founded in 1900 by a remarkable scholar-teacher, Wilbert Webster White, who had become thoroughly disillusioned about the adequacy of traditional theological schools. Trained as a biblical scholar at Yale under William Rainey Harper, he had then taught at Lane Seminary and also at Moody Bible Institute. The conviction gradually took root that theological seminaries, with their fourfold curricula, were not training men and women appropriately for Christian ministry. As White's skill as a teacher of the Bible grew, so also his determination to reorder patterns of seminary education. Thus in the fall of 1900, in Montclair, New Jersey, he developed plans for what became "The Bible Teachers' Training School". Actual classes began in January 1901. Within a semester, the base of operations was moved to the heart of New York City, meeting for classes in several different church settings until property at 541 Lexington Avenue became home from 1904 until 1927.

In 1925, the Seminary obtained new facilities in the heart of Manhattan, complete with dormitories, classrooms, chapel, library, gymnasium, and offices. This was home for 50 years. But the Seminary survived only with much struggle during the depression years, beginning in 1929 and thereafter. By the early 1960s the end seemed in sight. Only several large bequests kept the institution alive until 1969. At that point, drastic steps were taken. The hard decision was made to terminate the traditional Bachelor of Divinity degree programme, the primary purpose for the Seminary, and then to terminate the entire academic faculty.

During the years 1970-1979, New York Theological Seminary experienced a dramatic recovery from a long period of declining health. The decision made in March 1970 to terminate the basic programme leading to the Master of Divinity degree had been followed by a major reordering of Seminary staffing, financing, and programme emphases. Instead of giving primary attention to the training of future clergy and teachers of religion, as with all other seminaries, NYTS would concentrate on continuing education for clergy and laity serving churches in the greater New York metropolitan area. This took the Seminary out of competition with other theological schools and created a quite new range of programmes.

As one compares present programmes with the initial pattern that developed in the first academic year of the new era, 1970-71, it is quite obvious that a process of continuing evolution has been going on. At the beginning, there were three basic programmes in operation: an STM programme in either parish ministry or counselling for clergy with an M.Div. degree; a lay education division with a smorgasbord of courses each semester; and a one-year programme, called the "urban year", offering seminary students across the country an intensive, contextual year of study at the M.Div. level. During subsequent years these three rings have been drastically altered or disappeared altogether. The point to be stressed is that the evolutionary process did not result from substantial new planning or even from a careful evaluation programme. There was a unique reason for experimentation, for trial and error, success and failure. To a large extent the new shape evolved as the seminary administration was able to respond to clearly articulated needs from prospective students and to broker effective programmes. There has been a real sense of the leading of the Spirit that suggests that gratitude rather than pride is the proper stance for the Seminary personnel!

By the end of eight years — in the fall of 1978 — the Seminary had experienced a period of balanced budgets, moved to fine new rented quarters, following the sale of the property on 49th Street, and seen enrollments increase to around 500 part-time students. Now the three rings were shaped thus: a large Certificate Programme in Urban Ministry with black and Hispanic church leaders as the primary constituents; a college level programme, under the College of New Rochelle primarily for minority church leaders; and graduate degree programmes at four levels serving the educational needs of an incredibly wide range of metropolitan area clergy, and even some laity, seeking professional credentials. By the fall of 1981 the total enrolment had risen to 753.

Purpose and priorities

Several years ago, a statement of focus and purpose for the Seminary was drafted, after many revisions, and finally accepted as a basic statement of our self-understanding. Task Force II was asked to review this statement, revise and redraft as necessary, and thus provide us with a basis for evaluating the style, programmes and direction of the Seminary. The committee found this task to be less extensive than anticipated and for the most part affirmed the early statement with only modest revisions. It now reads as follows:

Statement of goals and priorities

New York Theological Seminary is an ecumenical centre for theological education and training where men and women, both ordained and unordained, are empowered to express their life commitment to Jesus Christ through ministry in the church and the world. In accordance with our history and tradition, the study of the Bible is put at the center of the curriculum where it informs and interacts with all other areas of study and practice.

The Seminary's primary student body are the women and men of this metropolitan area who have made a commitment to Jesus Christ and are engaged in some form of ministry through their church or secular work. The Seminary provides a style of education that is especially suited to people who wish to combine work and education. It seeks to remain flexible and innovative, being committed to an all-inclusive student body and taking seriously their diverse needs even to the extent of multilingual programmes. Our goal is to embody and witness to the kingdom of God in the lives of individuals and in the community as a whole, as we all seek to live out the claims of the gospel of Jesus Christ. Faculty and students together seek to relate educational programmes to different experiences of oppression, particularly those based on race, sex and class, and to support one another to work for the alleviation of injustice.

In seeking to fulfill these purposes, the Seminary is committed to:
— respond to unmet needs for theological education and training for both clergy and laity, and to design experimental programmes to meet their needs with a willingness to risk failure;
— carry out its programmes, wherever possible, in cooperation with other schools and institutions and with denominations, and to discontinue programmes when the need has passed or others can handle it better;
— support with sensitivity an untenured administrative faculty whose primary focus of ministry within the Seminary will be enhanced by participation in other forms of ministry in the life of parish or broader church;
— remain fully accredited by offering only programmes of quality and integrity regardless of educational level;
— maintain a continuous process of evaluation of all programmes, including a programme budget that provides for fiscal control and accountability, and for the assessment of any new programme proposals against major priorities;
— govern itself collegially through a partnership of a board of trustees, president, and administrative faculty who represent in their skills and membership the diversity of its constituents.

The Degree and Certificate Programmes at New York Theological Seminary in carrying out these purposes will:
— emphasize biblical competence as an essential in being equipped for ministry;
— encourage the development of specific skills for the particular tasks of ministry in which the student is engaged;
— provide education designed to help the participant grow in depth, breadth, and integrity of Christian faith, and in the skills of articulating it;
— instruct through action and reflection on the practice of ministry as it relates to the dialogue between faith and contemporary issues;
— endeavour to encourage interaction between clergy and laity in learning situations;
— utilize the greater New York metropolitan area as a training laboratory for Christian ministry and a base for theological reflection;
— encourage flexibility and innovation by designing its programmes, both curricular and financial, to meet the needs of its students;
— encourage ecumenical understanding and cooperation by the exposure of its students to the variety of Christian experience in the lives of other students;

— sensitize Christians to injustice and human need, search with them for ways to show responsible love of neighbour and to make the structures of our society more just.

In our cooperative programmes with other institutions we will encourage the implementation of the above goals.

The element of "uniqueness"

During the course of the discussions of the preceding statement, another question was raised: What makes NYTS unique? Or, put another way, what are the important traditions, patterns, style we have developed that need to be honoured and preserved for the future?

The Seminary is engaged in on-the-job training, as opposed to full-time, residential programmes. There is a heterogeneity and breadth among the students that is unparalleled in the seminary world: ethnic diversity (black, Hispanic, Asian, white), the whole spread of Christian traditions, all age levels, women and men. Commitment to a collegial style is symbolized in our rotating faculty chairperson, administrative faculty interaction with trustees and vice versa, and the use of first names. Commitment to the city is evident in the collegial style and multi-cultural constituency. Programme evaluation is continued. The use of rented space makes possible accessibility and convenience in location. The library is designed for practitioners, not for scholars; library facilities at nearby General Seminary and Union Theological Seminary are available for research. An efficient and functional support staff demonstrate a high level of commitment.

The confessional character of the Seminary is symbolized by the weekly faculty Bible study. Faculty share a commitment to biblical faith and to ministry, rather than primary loyalty to scholarly disciplines. The evangelical character of the Seminary is symbolized by the tradition that administrative faculty continue an active role in the life of the religious community outside the Seminary. The sense of mission is summarized by reference to Luke 4:17-18 and Jeremiah 29:1-7. The Seminary is student-centred. The programmes are designed to enhance their faith and competence in ministry, not primarily to teach them theological disciplines. The Seminary has become like a church or congregation with the president as the pastor and the students as parishioners. Relationships among administrative faculty, the style of operation and decision-making, and the delegation of authority all reflect the perspectives of a community of faith. Our primary concern is the welfare of the city.

Basic programme description
Programme I: Joint M.P.S./M.Div. offered in consultation with New Brunswick Theological Seminary
We have now completed the sixth year of this programme, which provides access to a fully accredited Master of Divinity degree to men and women for whom there is no other path to the degree. A student here is guaranteed courses each Monday and Wednesday evening, making it possible to take nine credit hours per semester. Six additional credits can be earned during two weeks of full-time residential study each summer. Thus, in four academic years the full programme can be completed.

This year the student body was even more diverse than in the past. The most striking fact was the increase in the number of women, numbering 16 out of 30 students in the first-year Integration Seminar. Mature and committed, they come with a strong sense of call and excitement over the fact that they have discovered a route that will qualify them for ordination, an option that a few years ago had seemed impossible.

The experience of the students in ministry and their maturity of faith provide for stimulating classes. This is on-the-job training at its best. Theory and practice, faith and life are in a process of continuous and creative interaction. The students fall into three basic categories in terms of their present situations in church leadership. Roughly one-third of the 80 or so who have begun the programme are mature and experienced clergy, black and Hispanic, who now want the legitimation and credential of the M.Div. degree, although it is not necessarily required in their career pattern. Another third are church leaders in their 30s and 40s who have decided they wish to seek ordination and are members of denominations that require the M.Div. They are teachers, social workers, several policemen, including a growing number of women who seek a second vocation. Many in this group are white. The final third are young Hispanic and black church leaders, both ordained and lay, whose commitment to their community religious traditions and families make it unacceptable for them to do graduate theological work outside of the City.

Programme II: M.P.S./S.T.M. in pastoral studies
Pastoral care and counselling are major elements in the job description of nearly all clergy. Increasing numbers of lay leaders are also engaging in counselling, both in parishes and institutions. These

groups seek educational opportunities that will increase their competence. We have, under the guidance of Dean Diana Lee Beach, spawned a growing number of programmes to train people for pastoral ministry. Briefly these include:

— programmes leading to the Master of Sacred Theology or Master of Professional Studies degree require one day per week over a two-year period and use, on a joint basis, the facilities of the Postgraduate Centre for Mental Health and the Institutes of Religion and Health, the Trinity Counselling Centre in Princeton, New Jersey, and with Guild for Spiritual Guidance at Wainwright House in Rye, New York;

— programmes designed for a hospital setting utilize Hospital Chaplaincies, Inc., Bellevue Medical Centre, Lutheran Medical Centre, and Brooklyn Methodist Hospital.

Programme III: M.P.S./S.T.M. in parish ministry

The parish ministry programmes are designed to equip and enable men and women in their various expressions of Christian witness and ministry. This is achieved through a biblically centred curriculum comprised of four workshops and various electives. In all, there is an adherence to the key concepts of collegiality, practicality and flexibility.

In small groups, candidates for the Master's degree begin to learn the meaning of *collegiality* in ministry. Morale is improved and supportive relationships are established as the participants begin to exercise the freedom to reveal how they really feel and then respond to each other's concerns and needs.

Practicality is emphasized in that the basic subject matter is the particular ministry of each student enrolled in the programme. The tools they acquire and the skills they sharpen are found in relation to specific problems facing them in their own ministry.

Flexibility is built into the process so that the projects, reading lists, and courses are designed to fit particular needs. Each semester participants in the programme help to shape the next semester's schedule of classes.

Programme IV: Doctor of Ministry programme

The D.Min. programme requires students to achieve a high level of competence in ministry. This must be demonstrated in actual practice and not simply reported upon in academic papers. Admission requirements are rigid, usually requiring the completion of an S.T.M. as well as a quarter of clinical training before entry.

Students in the programme are accountable to each other, to a mentor assigned by the Seminary, and above all to a site team (people to and with whom the candidate ministers). The site team involves the creation of a group of colleagues in one's ministry, a sense of shared responsibility, and a method for continuous feedback on one's competence. This is a unique feature of our D.Min. and clearly a very valuable aspect, one whose worth usually continues long after the degree has been awarded.

We have had an excellent regular Monday D.Min. programme this year with a group of nineteen. Keith Russell, team teaching with Bill Weisenbach, provided the basic faculty leadership. Dick Scaine, in his second year as mentor, devised a substantial and very disciplined process which has proven quite effective. It has now been drawn together in a workbook form.

The Washington, DC, group was exciting and successful from every standpoint. Dick Snyder and Bob Washington team-taught the seminar aspect of the programme. Bill Hayes, former vice-president of Inter-Met, served as the mentor in their local area. This group of eleven black Methodist pastors has been exceedingly rigorous and committed and shows substantial growth intellectually and practically.

We are well into our third executive D.Min. group, focused primarily around the issue of organizations and power. There are nine candidates. One of the most interesting aspects of this group's development has been their exploratory work on a theology of organization. Dick Snyder has been principally responsible for this group.

Two additional D.Min. groups have been formed in England as a joint project of the Seminary and the Urban Theology Unit of Sheffield. The total enrolment of D.Min. students in New York, Washington, and England is now 59.

Programme V: M.P.S. in religious education

The religious education programme leads to the M.P.S. degree and requires 20 credits in religious education and approximately 16 credits in theological and biblical studies. Two major emphases can be found in the courses and workshops offered:
— background courses with a philosophical and social science basis
   for relating religion to life, including world religions, philosophy

of religion, psychology of religion, etc. In these courses students are exposed to the broad nature of religion, the variety of beliefs, and the relationship of religion to culture;
— workshops and courses relating to the theories and practical methods of education and the practice of religious education in urban/metropolitan settings.

These courses are planned for professional workers (in parish, church-clusters, or community), pastors, and semi-professional workers in the church and community. In the cooperative programme with New York University, the student takes approximately 20 credits in religious education at the Seminary and/or New York University. Approximately 16 credits in theological and biblical studies are taken at the Seminary, which confers the degree.

Programme VI-A: English certificate programme

The certificate programme in Christian ministry is designed for ordained or lay persons who are actively involved in ministry and want to be more effective in their ministries.

The basic programme is a one-year course of study divided into two semesters, including at least 28 Saturday sessions meeting from 9:00 a.m. to 3:30 p.m. The advanced programme (second-year) meets on a similar schedule.

The goals of this programme include: competence achievement — to provide practical skills in areas of sermon outlining and manuscript preparation, pastoral counselling, leadership development, conflict management, church administration, the planning process, community organization, and group dynamics; knowledge — to offer and provide learning experiences in the Bible (exegesis, resources and techniques for research, Bible story-telling), church and Bible history, theology, Christian Education (curriculum development, teaching methods); personal growth — to offer new challenges that will provide opportunities for growth, e.g. courses on women and the Bible, the urban church, theology and contemporary social issues. The overall goal, to prepare persons to do ministry more effectively in the urban setting, is the same as for all programmes at NYTS.

Five years ago, we had 15 persons enrolled in our certificate programme. At our commencement on 17 May 1981, we awarded 66 certificates. Our students come to NYTS thirsting for knowledge. Many entered the ministry through the "apprenticeship system" and are eager to sharpen old skills and acquire new ones so that they may become more effective where they now minister.

The fact that more women are entering the ministry has been reflected in our student body. The student body is changing in other ways as well. More than one-half of our students have had at least one year of college, 20 per cent have earned baccalaureates, and six hold master's degrees.

The fellowship and support system in the programme are good, and the foundation is laid for further study. Certificate students buy books in great numbers — and read, assimilate, and use the information contained therein. The certificate programme continues to be the feeder for other Seminary programmes. Many have enrolled and will enroll in the College of New Rochelle because of the motivation they receive in the certificate programme.

Programme VI-B: Hispanic certificate programme

From the beginning this programme has been closely tied to the life and needs of the churches. Hispanic students from more than ten nationalities, representing twelve denominations and many Pentecostal churches, meet for 28 Saturdays during the academic year. Churches, professors and students engage in the formation of a solid, diversified programme, taking into account traditional curricula, ecclesial realities, and student concerns. The students are creative and active partners in the education and mission process. They are a young community, male and female, with a great dynamism and missionary enthusiasm.

Perceiving that the historic process through which the urban areas are going requires a more mature response from the churches, the Hispanic certificate programme has accepted the challenge of making a contribution, modest but significant, to the development of a pastoral/lay model which will exercise a more active role in the social sphere.

Programme VII: Clergy college programme

In conjunction with the College of New Rochelle's School of New Resources, New York Theological Seminary offers the opportunity for urban clergy involved in the practice of their ministries, as well as lay religious leaders, to work towards a baccalaureate degree. Courses are designed by students to meet their learning needs; credit may also be given for work done at other accredited institutions and

for an acceptable life experience portfolio. The programme is designed to fit into the busy schedule of people who normally carry full-
time jobs. Classes are held from 6:15 to 9:45 p.m. Monday through
Friday.

The School now offers each semester twenty courses or seminars in
such varied areas as college writing, sociology, psychology, religion,
urban affairs, literature and education. The content and assignments
for each class relate to the life experience, needs, and interests of the
students. The scheduling and philosophy of the programme respond
to the needs of adults, many of whom complete the degree requirements in four years. The courses are taught by the Seminary
faculty, the College staff, and able professors recruited with the
needs of the student constituency in mind.

Admission requirements include a high school diploma or the
equivalent and a personal interview. Students without the high
school diploma may enroll with special permission from the director
and upon successful completion of a language arts test. Students may
apply for financial aid through the federal Basic Education Opportunity Grant, the Tuition Assistance Programme (State of New
York), and the College of New Rochelle's Financial Aid Office.

Recently the Seminary expanded to eight classrooms and seven offices the space committed to this programme. This will permit an
enrolment capacity of approximately 300 students, a timely expansion considering the fact that 277 enrolled last semester. The State
Department of Education has approved branch campus status for the
programme, which means that all course work for the degree can be
taken at the Seminary.

Conclusion

New York Theological Seminary is no longer simply a school for
biblical and theological studies. It is a resource centre and a broker
for various educational programmes at the service of the people who
minister in New York City. It has not just added new appendages but
gone through radical institutional change in order to respond to the
realities of this context and the needs of these people. It has
developed a model of theological education that is not only
economically viable and educationally creative but also theologically
sound and missiologically primary.

Hartford Seminary

A doctor of ministry approach to continuing education — pastor and laity learning and growing together

DOUGLASS LEWIS

Since the 1950s in the United States there has been increased interest and participation in continuing education by clergy. This phenomenon combines with a growing emphasis on professional competency in ministry by church leaders. As evidence, the Association of Theological Schools in coordination with major denominations developed an instrument called Readiness for Ministry to measure a person's readiness or competency for performing ministry upon graduating from a seminary. This concern for professional competency has led many denominations not only to encourage, but require some form of regular continuing education for its clergy.

A variety of programmes have emerged. Some are run by the denominational agencies. Others give free reign to individual pastors to select among a variety of educational offerings ranging from courses in universities, to independent centres specializing in certain aspects of pastoral training, to programmes developed by theological seminaries. Some church leaders, however, are still concerned that many clergy do not continue to grow personally and professionally throughout their ministry. They recognize that continuing education programmes for clergy are not regular enough, do not have enough structure and discipline to make an impact upon a person's practice

• Dr Lewis, the former Director of the Doctor of Ministry Programme at Hartford Seminary, has been appointed President of Wesley Theological Seminary in Washington, DC. An extensive description of the Hartford programme and also the papers from the National Symposium on Issues and Models of Doctor of Ministry Programmes may be requested from Hartford Seminary, 77 Sherman Street, Hartford, Connecticut 06105, USA.

of ministry, and involve only a small percentage of all the ordained clergy.

Almost as if it were a response to these concerns, a new model of continuing education emerged in North America and capitalized on the growing interest and emphasis on continuing education for clergy. Its name: the Doctor of Ministry degree programme (D.Min.). The D.Min. degree first emerged in the 1960s. It was offered as the first degree by a few seminaries who extended their basic degree programme to four years instead of the traditional three and thus offered a D.Min. degree. Despite the fear of many of the US and Canadian seminaries, the programme never caught on as a first degree. What did catch on was an extra year on a continuing education model. This additional year was spread out over two to four years while a pastor remained in his or her parish. The growth of such programmes has been phenomenal. In 1969 there were seven schools offering D.Min. degrees with 325 students. Ten years later, 84 seminaries enrolled 5,327 students in D.Min. programmes, with the number continuing to increase annually.

The programmes varied, but most were designed to: allow a pastor to continue in full-time ministry; provide educational experiences in a flexible time and location setting; focus the curriculum around the needs of a practising pastor; and offer the tangible reward of a doctor's degree upon completion of the programme. D.Min. programmes seemed to be an answer to the church's need for a competent clergy that continued to grow personally and professionally. They attracted large numbers of clergy. They provided structure and indepth educational experiences. They were usually practical and relevant to the practising pastor. They offered a tangible reward as an extra motivation for pastors to enter and complete the programme. In addition, the programmes had an important impact on the seminaries themselves. They brought seminary faculty in contact with practising pastors who demanded a different style of education that was more relevant to parish ministry. As one official from the Association of Theological Schools stated: "The D.Min. is probably the most significant development in theological education in North America during this century."

Concerns about the educational model

Without question, D.Min. programmes have been a very successful model of continuing education for pastors in North America.

Nevertheless, their very success raises concerns about the educational model. Some of these concerns are:

1. The focus continues to be on professional competency of clergy. While few in the church, lay or clergy, would deny the need for well-trained and competent clergy, the tendency is to focus on the professionalism of clergy. This focus in turn subtly but inevitably leads to the assumption that the primary ministers of the church are clergy. It undermines the understanding of ministry as the calling of all the people of God. Its positive side is to recognize certain gifts and roles that need to be performed in the church. These have been assigned to clergy. On the other hand, if these become the primary understanding of ministry, it ignores or misuses the gifts of the largest body of ministers in the church, the laity.

2. The church has at various times in its history emphasized education of the laity. Within this century there have been a variety of movements which have stressed lay education. Too often, however, these educational events or programmes have been separated from clergy. In an effort to stress lay education, they have isolated laity. The tendency has been to stress lay ministry as different and separate from the ministry of clergy. The danger clearly is to regard the ministry of laity as secondary. Stressing the professionalism of clergy only increases this possibility.

3. Continuing education for clergy, particularly degree-oriented programmes of extended length, which take clergy away from the parish and which focus on increasing professional competency, tend to alienate or distance a pastor from his or her present ministry setting. That is certainly not the intention of the programmes, the pastor, or parish, but it has been a frequent result among pastors in D.Min. programmes.

The laity feel the pastor is being pulled away from them, that his or her education is of little assistance to the parish, or that once finished, the pastor will want to move on to bigger and better things. On the other side, the pastor becomes excited and stimulated by the educational programme. He or she tries to apply some of these learnings in the parish setting but without working them through with the laity first. He or she is disappointed when the laity seem to reject or fail to respond enthusiastically to the new ideas.

4. The focus of most Doctor of Ministry programmes has been on knowledge and skills for clergy and not on the development of con-

gregations. The stress, again, is on professionalism and not on parish life and development.

5. Because the D.Min. programmes are located in and run by theological seminaries, many of the seminaries' traditional academic norms and assumptions influence the design of the programmes. Some of these assumptions are:

— a residential education is better than non-residential;
— access to a major library is essential to a quality education;
— writing and research skills are stressed over oral and relational skills;
— quality is understood hierarchically;
— significant in-depth learning for ministry requires the proper background and preparation by the student.

In 1974 Hartford Seminary made a radical shift from a traditional seminary offering a first degree (M.Div.) for those preparing for ordination and a Ph.D. for those preparing to teach, and became a centre for continuing education for clergy and laity, parish development, and research on ministry. The intent was to become a non-degree resource centre for those already in the practice of ministry.

The staff, however, soon became aware of the strengths and possibilities of a Doctor of Ministry programme, as well as its liabilities. In keeping with its new mission, the staff designed a D.Min. programme which would combine continuing education and professional development for clergy, education in ministry for laity, development of the life and ministry of a parish, and the use of an extension education model.

The intent of the education model was to shift the focus away from professional development of a pastor to the quality of life and ministry of the parish church. Pastors and their congregations were enrolled together in a D.Min. programme. The intent of the design, however, was primarily to have impact upon the parish church. The model did not exclude personal and professional growth for the pastor. It assumed that such would result. But the crucial presupposition of the model was that the primary focus would be the congregation, not the pastor.

Immediately, this approach posed a problem. Seminaries normally focus on the pastor and his or her professional competency, not the congregation. Even the Hartford Seminary faculty, which made this commitment, often found it difficult to remember the target of its educational efforts. Pastors were more readily accessible than the congregations. Doing traditional education was easier and more natural. It required an enormous psychological and theological leap to redirect the programme goals and designs.

Other barriers quickly surfaced in the pastors and the laity themselves. Both assumed, despite the programme's rhetoric, that the real target in the end was the pastor. Many congregations felt that they were participating in the programme in order that their pastor might get a Doctor of Ministry degree. The idea that the congregation in its setting was the primary educational target appeared too radical and unorthodox. Seminaries are not interested in developing parish churches. They educate ministers whose task it is then to translate that knowledge into parish ministry.

The seminary and its faculty also struggled with the uncertainty of how to perform the task. Nevertheless, it committed itself to join in a partnership with pastors and parishes to develop the life and ministry of that parish through an educational model.

The model as conceived had four principal partners — the seminary faculty, the pastor, the laity, and the congregation as an organizational entity. Theologically the key descriptive phrase was mutual ministry. It presupposed several things.

1. God calls all of these entities to be instruments of ministry. God bestows particular gifts and responsibilities to each.

2. No one of the partners is more vital, important or expert than the others. Each has something unique to contribute without which the body cannot be whole.

3. The arena for ministry is the parish church, not the seminary. The type of education employed in the model became known as "experiential education". It meant three things:

— It presumed that all parties in the educational setting brought their previous experiences in ministry with them and were expected to share and build on this experience.

— Each educational module normally had an experiential component which required interaction on the part of the participants. They were not passive observers or recipients of information, but they shared and interacted with each other. Various educational methods were used such as lectures, role play, case studies, group discussion, simulation games, etc.

— Each educational module required the participants to apply their learning in their life and ministry setting. Sometimes there was a formal project and other times it was personal goals for the purpose of applying the learning. Occasionally, members of a class contracted to act together in ministry.

Components of the model

The model had some educational experiences designed specifically for pastors and some for laity and pastors together in the congregational context. Not all of these were of a traditional classroom type in which a teacher primarily shared information with students. The model adopted a more dynamic form which focused on growth and change. New information and ideas were part of that process, but not necessarily the focus of the process. This approach can best be understood by examining the five components around which the design was constructed. Each component had a pastoral and parish part.

Assessment

Learning, growing and changing begin by assessing or examining where one is in the present. For each pastor, it meant taking some diagnostic tests, some self-reflection and evaluation, and some analysis and feedback from other pastors, laity, and faculty in the programme. The purpose was to assist the pastor in identifying his or her strengths, interests, and areas of needed growth. For each parish, it meant a parish survey which attempted to gather information from a large number of parishioners about their perceptions, satisfactions and hopes for that parish and its ministry. The process attempted to hold up a mirror, so to speak, in which the parish and the pastor could look at themselves and ask: "How do we like the way we are? Where do we need to change? In what areas do we want to grow or place more emphasis?"

Setting goals

It sounds easy, but it proved difficult for pastor and parish alike. To identify precisely what they want to learn, where they want to grow, how they want to change, what they want to accomplish through a particular programme proved to be a difficult and exacting task. The Seminary faculty resisted telling a pastor or a parish what they should learn or what they should become. The faculty, of course, did have some input in the form of a basic model of the church and ministry. The model was defined in terms of functions of ministry that every church needs to perform if it is to be the church.

The programme was not designed to produce specialists in any area, but was to provide resources for pastors and parishes to become more effective and faithful in ministry as they understood it.

There were tensions in this area. Some faculty felt that the Seminary had an obligation to prescribe for pastors what they needed to learn, that the Seminary should advocate, push, promote, even require certain things of pastors and parishes. Pastors and parishes on the other side wanted to be told what to learn and how to learn it. On the other hand, they wanted responsibility and freedom to decide their own goals, seek their own directions, and understand for themselves what faithful ministry meant. The tension even went beyond the scope of the project. The Association of Theological Schools and its accrediting process raised some serious questions. Should not the Seminary take more control and direction of what learning should take place?

Resources for learning and growing

Once the pastors and parishes identified goals or areas on which they wanted to focus, the Seminary tried to share its resources in the form of teaching, consulting, library resources, curriculum materials and educational designs for the use of the participants in moving towards and achieving their goals. Formal courses were offered for pastors, and specific courses were designed and taught in the parishes for laity and clergy together. Again there were tensions. The Seminary could not always deliver precisely what every pastor and parish wanted and needed at the time they desired to have it. The Seminary did have the flexibility to bring in outside teachers and resource persons for particular courses. The courses and consultations were scheduled at times and in locations that were convenient to pastors and parishes.

Support and accountability

For persons and organizations to change and grow, they need support that affirms and sustains them in the effort. They also need accountability that reminds them and calls them to account for what they said they wanted to accomplish. The model attempted to provide sustaining support and loving critique for pastors and parishes.

For pastors there was a colleague group with other pastors in the programme that met monthly to share concerns and seek advice, counsel and feedback from one another, to plan their own educational programme, and also to define the role they would play in the leadership of the parishes. In the parish setting each pastor had a group of lay persons that became his or her support and accountability group within that parish context.

Among the lay leaders, the programme attempted to build a community of support and accountability. Each parish had a steering committee that was responsible for developing and directing a programme in the parish in coordination with the seminary faculty.

As with the other components, tensions and problems developed. It was threatening for pastors and laity alike to admit they needed support and care from each other and to make themselves open and vulnerable to each other. Some pastors felt that they had to remain in the authority role. For some laity it was difficult to criticize their pastor. Overall, the experience enriched both. Through it they came to know in a more concrete way what it means to be the body of Christ with all its tensions and possibilities in ministry.

Evaluation

Growth and change require knowing whether one has changed. The programme attempted to build in, at various stages, means of evaluation, so that the Seminary, pastor, and congregations could continually evaluate their progress and determine what alterations needed to be made. For the Seminary faculty it meant receiving feedback on all their courses from pastors and laity. For pastors it meant having regular criticism from laity and fellow pastors as well as faculty.

The model attempted to build new forms of accountability which were untraditional. Normally accountability in an educational institution goes only from student to faculty. In this model the pastor became accountable in his or her growth not only to the faculty but to pastoral colleagues and the laity of the parish as well. In each parish, regular means of evaluation were instituted. At the end of the two-year programme the parish survey was repeated to see what areas of change had occurred in the parish's ministry.

Lessons

This model, which combined continuing education of pastors and laity, parish development and research, produced some interesting results and lessons. Some of the major ones were:

1. The model began to bridge the gulf between seminaries and churches. Pastors, laity, and faculty grew in appreciation of each

other as colleagues in ministry. They also experienced the joy of learning and growing together for their mutual benefit and for the sake of the church's ministry.

2. Many pastors and laity remarked that for the first time they felt valued by a seminary. The project created a positive climate for learning and opened up pastors and congregations to change in ways that surprised even themselves. The design embodied one of the key educational principles of the programme — that persons and organizations are most open to change and growth when they are feeling positive about themselves.

3. The programme had a tremendous impact upon the Seminary faculty, giving them new insights into parish ministry and the skills and knowledge needed by pastors and laity for the practice of ministry. This experience of faculty, in turn, influenced and shaped the total programme of the Seminary.

4. At the same time, the programme made great demands on the Seminary faculty. They had to teach in new ways and in new contexts. One could not merely offer a prepared course without also taking into account the ministry context and the hopes and concerns of the learners in that setting. Teaching became "teaching/consulting". Both had to occur for learning and change to take place.

5. Laity and clergy experienced being in ministry together in new ways. For many of the parishes, mutual ministry became not just a slogan, but a reality.

Questions and the future

The kingdom of God did not arrive because of this project. The high hopes and expectations of all the parties at the beginning would lead one to think it might. There were modest achievements, some growth, some changed lives and renewed churches, but also many unfulfilled expectations. One of the dangers of such a new venture, in fact, is that all the parties invest in it such high hopes and expectations. This "kingdom wish" inevitably led to some disappointments, even anger and frustration. The programme did raise important questions with which theological education should continue to struggle:

1. What is the best context for education for ministry? Education does require some distancing from experience in order to reflect, renew, consolidate lessons and plan new actions. Education, however, too distant from practice becomes abstract and irrelevant.

This programme moved education into the arena of ministry practice. It increased the risks for students and faculty alike. In some cases it created unrealistic expectations and usually left people a little disappointed. It was messier and less able to be organized cleanly than traditional education for ministry. Thus, some accused it of not being rigorous enough or of being of a lower quality.

2. This charge led to questions of how to measure effectiveness in education — a perennial question for all education, but one that seminaries have often avoided. First, what criteria should be used in such evaluation? Second, is the primary focus of evaluation the programme itself and its internal quality and consistency or is it the end product? How do you measure the product? Is it the effectiveness in ministry of those who were a part of the educational programme? How then is effectiveness in ministry measured?

The Hartford programme struggled with each of these questions with varying degrees of success. One thing became clear. It is a mistake to isolate evaluation at only one level of the system. Too often seminaries have operated in isolation from the church's ministry at the parish level. If they are going to take seriously their educational task for ministry and to evaluate its effectiveness, they must struggle over and over again with the questions: What is ministry? How is it done effectively and faithfully? How does the training and educational process influence pastors? How and where should that education take place?

A final word: Hartford Seminary's own programme has moved away from this direct integration of continuing education of pastor, laity, and congregation. It has moved away from direct attempts to change congregations and has focused its continuing education in a more traditional mode. As an institution Hartford Seminary is committed to experimentation and change of its own programmes. Such flexibility has advantages. However, the development and testing of new models, particularly in dealing with complex issues such as parish development and contextual education, demand trial and error, willingness to risk failure, and a sustained effort over an extended time period.

Cook Christian Training School

New directions for Native American theological education

CECIL CORBETT and GARY KUSH

Within ten years there will be no ordained Native American clergy: that was the probable conclusion in 1974 of research on the leadership crisis confronting Indian and Eskimo congregations in seven denominations with significant Native American ministries. While the Native American churches faced a crisis, Cook Christian Training School was confronted with declining enrolment and financial problems.

This leadership crisis was addressed by Cook School by adding an extension programme, by helping to form a consortium of seminaries and colleges, and by providing a variety of technical assistance services to judicatories.

The leadership crisis

Only 68 ordained Indian or Eskimo clergy could be identified in the 499 Native American churches and chapels of the United Church of Christ, the United Presbyterian Church, the United Methodist Church, the Episcopal Church, the Reformed Church of America, the Christian Reformed Church, and the American Baptist Church. With only four Native American students in seminary out of 28,000 in 1974, and with an average age of 52 for clergy, the crisis was apparent. In five of the seven denominations there were fewer Indian or Eskimo clergy than 25 years previously despite the fact that self-

• Dr Corbett, a member of the Nez Perce tribe, is the Executive Director, and the Rev. Gary Kush is Director of Educational Services at Cook School, 708 South Lindon Lane, Tempe, Arizona 85281, USA.

development and self-determination were major emphases in denominations during this period.

Clergy, of course, are not the only leaders in the church. A part of the leadership crisis was that laity who were the backbone of Indian and Eskimo congregations were often not seen as leaders or adequately supported in their ministries.

What were the seminaries doing about the crisis, we asked? We found that none of the 202 accredited seminaries in the United States offered any special training for Indian or Eskimo ministries. Only one Indian seminary staff member could be found, and he had left the seminary in part because he was denied faculty status.

We approached several seminaries and accrediting agencies trying to enlist their help, but were greeted with polite yawns. To make matters worse, we calculated that it would cost $26 million to solve the leadership crisis if existing ordination and school requirements were maintained.

From the beginning we felt that the base of leadership in parishes had to be broadened. Systemic change was needed in the parishes, judicatories and seminaries. Theological education by extension became a renewal movement, not just an education method.

Environmental factors

President Nixon said: "The first Americans are the most deprived and the most isolated minority group in our nation. On virtually every scale of measurement — employment, income, education, health — the condition of the Indian people ranks at the bottom."

With a median income of $1,500 per year, unemployment at above 50 per cent on many reservations, a 70 per cent drop-out rate from high school, and an average educational level of eighth grade, it was no wonder that Cook School had to find an alternative approach to theological education. For Native Americans to have reached an equal proportion of enrolment in higher education with non-Indians would have required a 650 per cent increase in 1971.

Indian and Eskimo people were thought to be "good with their hands". In 1970 the government's Indian education budget for vocational education was $47 million as compared to $6.6 million for college studies.

Many tribes began to reassert their tribal sovereignty in the 1970s. By law and treaty, tribes in the United States are sovereign nations rather than cities or states. Treaties can only be signed between sovereign nations. The United States government has signed over 420 treaties with tribes. Indians also became citizens of the United States, without their permission, by law in 1924. For this reason, Indian and Eskimo people have dual citizenship. Relationships with Native American people, therefore, are more legal than racial.

The competent Indian or Eskimo pastor today needs to understand something about treaties, tribal sovereignty, tribal jurisdiction and relations between the United States government and the tribe. These subjects are vehicles for a ministry of liberation and reconciliation.

Working with the Institute for the Development of Indian Law in Washington, DC, Cook School helped to develop 28 filmstrips on the subjects of treaty rights, tribal sovereignty, tribal jurisdiction, and other related matters. These resources were used by the Institute to instruct over 3,000 tribal council members and tribal employees. The same materials are being used in the Cook School extension and residency programmes.

An interesting result of these workshops occurred when church members saw parallels between the tribe and the church on the one hand and the tribe and the United States government on the other. This awareness caused us to develop denominational polity courses on the assumption that one cannot improve a system unless one understands it. Our polity courses have been very popular, something that often astounds non-Indian church leaders.

The energy crisis also occurred at the same time that the Native American church leadership crisis was being discussed in 1973-1974. Under tribal lands lie approximately 50 per cent of the nation's radium, 15 per cent of the coal reserves, 30 per cent of the West's low sulphur strippable coals, 4 per cent of all oil and gas reserves, and a substantial portion of the country's oil-shale and geothermal reserves. The energy crisis has created new pressures on tribes to change by using more of their natural resources. Given the close relationship of the land to Native American spirituality, the energy crisis has caused serious pressure on Native American culture. Spiritual leadership was greatly needed to help people face these times of transition.

Tribal sovereignty and the renewed interest in tribal resources created new incentives for higher education, created tribal jobs, and renewed tribal interest in extending their land base. Some of the tribes even began to question the churches' use of land and asked how they got their land on reservations.

The relationship among church, state and tribe must be understood in order to comprehend our programme. Many authors have concluded that the churches and federal government cooperated to civilize and Christianize the Indian people. In 1819, Congress established a civilization fund to support churches and their mission schools.

After the Civil War, President Grant in his Peace Policy appointed a board of Indian Commissioners composed of church members. In 1870 army officers were replaced by reservation agents recommended by denominations. Indian nations, therefore, literally were divided among the various religious groups. The government had established Christianity as the state-supported religion on reservations and determined what denomination people should belong to. These comity agreements are still influential today. While in 1978 there were only about 320,000 Christian Indian and Eskimo people, about 43 per cent of the total population, the churches were responsible for the reservations assigned in the comity agreements.

During the Peace Policy a move was begun by the government to make Native Americans into farmers in order that they might become more "civilized". Many denominations actively supported this goal which led to the Dawes Act of 1887. This Act caused Indian people to lose over 90,000,000 acres of land. Many churches received their property at this time. Today churches may own as much as 52,000 acres of Indian land.

These acts and policies have caused the church to seem like an enemy to many Indian and Eskimo people. It is no wonder, then, that in the 1960s during the war on poverty a number of Native American pastors left their pulpits for tribal jobs because they saw this as a way to help their people. These factors also partially explain why many of the Native American youth felt a call to other careers than the ministry.

Theological consultations with seminaries and Native American religious leaders also began about this time. These dialogues planted the seeds of a Native American theology and produced several books and seminary study units. The process is continuing.

Another movement occurred in the 1970s that gave us direction and support as a school. For the first time some of the mainline denominations hired Indian executives and gave their national Native American committees more authority about policy. When these leaders and groups became increasingly aware and concerned about the leadership crisis, the partnership between Cook School and them was strengthened.

Our strategy for making the leadership-crisis study was to be supportive of the Native American church executives who were faced with denominational budget meetings without sufficient data to build their cases. We felt that we could help by calling attention to the crisis, and by securing the facts.

Cook School

In 1974 Cook School faced an internal crisis. The school was begun by Charles Cook over seventy years ago as a mission among the Pima Indians who live south of Phoenix, Arizona. The school was Presbyterian in its beginning but became ecumenical in the 1940s. Like other mission schools, it had been supported substantially by denominational giving. Between 1970 and 1973, denominational support dropped from 31 per cent to 12 per cent of the income. Without endowments, without a fund-development office because we were not allowed to have one by the denominations, and with student tuition only 3 per cent of the income, decisions had to be made. Staff were also concerned about the amount of time being spent dealing with problems of alcohol, drugs and family turmoil among students who were expected to be ordained pastors in a few short years. We also learned that between 1968 and 1971 only 15 per cent of the graduates were ordained. Fifty per cent of the graduates just went home and were not employed nor did they continue their education.

We found that we had been admitting students who had hoped to prove themselves at Cook School to their community in order to become leaders. But our research showed that the leadership identification and development process operates in a different way in many Native American communities. Churches' leaders tend to be older and more mature. The average entry age into an employed church career was 34. When the young students at Cook School were not accepted by their community or denomination, they were frustrated and the school felt as if it had failed. We therefore changed our admission policies to become compatible with the leadership development processes in the Native American churches.

One of the bright spots in the Cook School curriculum was an Individualized Learning Centre begun with a foundation grant to help students improve their basic skills. This Centre, with its use of educational technology, taught us much about programmed texts, video tapes, audiovisual equipment, and computers. These lessons helped us launch our extension programme. We were pleased to be recognized by the United States Office of Education for this project.

The Cook School Board decided, in 1975, that "theological education by extension shall be the emphasis of the school in the immediate future". What to do about the residency programme and other related matters was up to the staff to decide.

The extension programme

The Navajo Episcopal Mission was the first to ask for an extension course. One of our instructors went to his first seminar with 15 copies of a Bible course and was greeted by over 150 students!

Over 1,200 students to date have enrolled from 11 denominations, twenty-four states or Canadian provinces, representing 27 tribes plus some non-Indians. These students have studied in 108 different locations and have been taught by 95 teachers. Some of these students are in the Marshall Islands, a trust territory of the United States, in the Arctic regions of Alaska and Canada, and some within a short driving distance of Cook School.

We define extension as non-residential programmes which do not disrupt the learner's productive relationship to his or her family, community, tribe or church. The educational forms include seminars, workshops, independent study, and internships, although seminars have been emphasized.

The programme operates on three levels. Level 1 leads to a degree and ordination. Level 2 leads to a diploma for those such as lay pastors and parish teachers. Level 3 leads to a certificate and is general theological education for laity based on the assumption that all Christians have gifts and ministries. Credits transfer from Level 2 to Level 1 and these credits transfer to our consortium member colleges and seminaries.

Cook School relates to extension sites and centres. A site is a place where a group meets for about two hours a week in a seminar with a seminar leader. An extension centre is a group of extension sites supervised by a full or part-time director who recruits and supervises the extension sites.

The extension students reflect our research about leadership in Native American communities. Over 60 per cent of the students are married; a majority are between the ages of 30 and 50; most are high school graduates; most are employed; and nearly all of the students hold responsible positions in their churches and communities. The course completion rate last year was 73 per cent.

The teachers, whom we call seminar leaders, are mostly pastors who serve as teachers without salary. We are working to start a "second generation" of teachers of laity who have taken extension courses. Some of the pastors, however, are reluctant to let their laity teach.

In addition to courses that one would expect in the area of Bible, theology and ministry, there are others unique to Native American ministry. Some of these include *Federal and Church Indian Policies,* the *Indian Bill of Rights, Introduction to Native American Church History, Introduction to Proposal Writing,* and *Currrent Indian Issues.* Other courses have lessons specifically written for the Native American church, such as "How to Do Paperwork for the White Man's Church", a lesson in *Introduction to Parish Administration.* Presently being written are *Helping Others as Christians* (a course in pastoral care for laity), *Introduction to Christian Worship,* and *Discovering Our Gifts for Ministry.* Many others are in the planning stage.

Our courses begin with a needs assessment that usually requires computer analysis. Try-out of materials is done on campus and in the field after consultants have reviewed the materials. Test results are carefully analyzed and related to student characteristics. We especially watch the reading level of the materials and students. Most of our courses have at least two learning levels and some of them include audio tapes in addition to printed materials.

We have learned in writing courses to limit the number of true-false questions in tests. We have an objective test for each lesson. Students often did poorly on our true-false questions. They could not believe that we would make a false statement even in the form of a test item. Multiple choice questions have proved to be the most reliable form.

Writing has been done in a variety of ways to combine knowledge of materials, students and methodology. Seldom have we been able to find a person who knows all three and has sufficient time to prepare a course. One Native American pastor, for example, spent a year at Cook School studying to become a course writer. When he returned home his bishop assigned him to a parish with responsibility for seventeen churches and chapels. He has not even had time to look for his typewriter, let alone use it. Partnerships have worked best, involving seminary professors, Cook School staff, and consultants.

The Native American Theological Association

A consortium was formed in 1976 in order to tap the resources of several colleges and seminaries and to utilize their credibility so that Native American graduates could be full partners in mission. We have found that ordination is not always sufficient status for Native American clergy to serve as equals in the church. In one denomination, which took over 75 years to ordain the first Indian person, the person was never asked to be on a committee in his judicatory.

The Native American Theological Association (NATA) includes the University of Dubuque Theological Seminary (Presbyterian), the United Theological Seminary in Minneapolis (ecumenical), Luther-Northwestern Theological Seminary in St Paul, Minnesota (Lutheran), Northland College in Wisconsin (United Church of Christ), the Dakota Leadership Programme in South Dakota (Episcopal), and Cook Christian Training School in Tempe, Arizona. Other schools and denominations are in the process of joining.

The consortium is administered by an Executive Director with an office in Minneapolis, Minnesota, an Indian Executive Committee, and representatives of the member schools. Cook School did the conceptual and developmental work of NATA as a contract. Our present relationship includes a contract to manage the extension programmes of the consortium. About 8 per cent of the present NATA students have come through Cook School programmes.

The successes of NATA have been many. Whereas in 1974 there were only four Native Americans in seminary, there are now 33 students studying by extension or residency for ordination. Ten others have graduated including eight who are ordained.

Evaluation of results

Increases in the number of clergy have occurred in three of the denominations that participated in our leadership crisis research. The situation has worsened in one denomination and the results are undecided in three others.

The effect of Cook School's extension programme on congregations and teachers was carefully evaluated in 1980. We learned that 65 per cent of the lay students now see themselves as ministers, as compared to 37 per cent before they began their courses. We also discovered that 77 per cent of the pastors felt that a significant number of their parishioners had assumed additional responsibility in the congregation. The extension programme had its least effect in the area of evangelism. No new chapels or churches were started during the programme.

Pastors have also been influenced by extension. One of those interviewed said that he now has to preach better sermons since so many people in his congregation know what he is talking about. Seventy-five per cent of the seminar leaders interviewed said that they now see themselves as trainers of laity for ministry, which is one of our major goals.

The effects of the extension programme upon Cook School and our related associations are more difficult to measure. Enrolment in our winter term workshops increased significantly, partially because of extension, but enrolment in the residency classes has not increased proportionately.

Challenges

It is difficult to administer an extension programme by "remote control". Nearly all of our teachers and students remain in their local communities rather than travel to Cook School. In some communities there are no telephones, and mail is delivered only once a week. The typical Indian and Eskimo pastor is without office equipment and a secretary; therefore nearly all the paperwork must be done at our end. We use the telephone rather than mail where possible.

The training of seminar leaders and our programmed texts have served as the means of quality control. Seminar leaders who use materials are required to complete a 22-hour training programme taught by Cook School staff. One of the unique features of this programme is that we have defined in behavioural terms the competencies of the seminar leader. These definitions help us in training and evaluating effective teaching.

Teacher turnover is a major problem. Of the ninety-five persons who have taught so far, 41 per cent have left Indian ministries, and many of these are yet to be replaced. At the same time we have experienced resistance from some pastors to let laity teach with or instead of them.

Relating the extension programme to our residential programme has been a major source of tension among some staff and an important question for our board of trustees. Our board gave us the freedom to eliminate the residential programme, but we chose to make campus classes, even though small in number, like extension seminars, and to use the same materials. Thus we hope to train residential students to become, among other things, extension teachers.

We continue to encounter hesitancy about extension from some judicatory executives, seminary staff, and national church executives. The Association of Theological Schools, the accrediting agency for seminaries in the United States and Canada, adopted a statement about TEE which says that seminary extension programmes for credit must be similar to residential programmes including the use of the same teachers, administrative procedures, and resources. Given the isolation of reservations, the level of poverty, and the educational background of many students, the ATS policy could become a significant barrier if enforced. We hope our graduates are doing well enough in their ministries to demonstrate that extension is an alternative rather than an exception to an adequate training programme.

Ordination standards and candidacy procedures are still a problem for many Native Americans. All of the denominations with which we work have a clause in their "rule book" which allows for an alternative route to ordination, but we find confusion about these standards. Cook School has expended considerable time and energy doing research, providing facilitation, and disseminating information to help judicatories develop culturally fair ordination standards and practices. Two working models are now in place in the Episcopal Church in Alaska and in the Grand Canyon Presbytery of the United Presbyterian Church in Arizona.

Plans, concerns and dreams

We plan to encourage the development of more extension centres where there will be a full- or part-time person to train and supervise seminar leaders. To accomplish this we are experimenting with a training and certification process to train trainers of seminar leaders.

Record-keeping has become a nightmare as the programme has grown, so we are planning to computerize records.

We are increasing the number of our seminary-level and non-credit courses, and we are counting heavily upon seminary professors to help us as writers.

Extension will be broadened to include more workshops. Our winter term workshops have grown beyond capacity enrolment and have attracted students from several nations.

The residential programme has grown some in numbers with an improved financial picture. We are trying to enhance this programme and relate it to extension. Our relations with a community college have improved the curriculum, increased scholarships, and attracted some students.

We continue to see the need for a national training and information centre about extension in the United States and would like to play some role in its development. Continuing to stay in touch with other third world people, especially tribal people, is important for us, so we dream about faculty and student exchanges. Educational technology such as the use of micro-computers, satellite and cable television, hold fascinating possibilities for extension.

School of Theology, University of the South

Theological reflection
— a necessary skill in lay ministry

DAVID P. KILLEN

Education and the kingdom

Education done by the church is justified as a long-run commitment to the promotion of the reign of God proclaimed by Jesus. Such parables as those of Matthew 25 give stark testimony to the virtues required of those taking part in this endeavour. In the ancient world — and no less today — the development of critical skills of assessment was needed if the work of the kingdom was to be well done.

Doing this work requires of us that we take into account the environment of our local world. This environment is made up of all those forces, social and personal, which must be considered as we attempt to move effectively towards the coming of God's kingdom, here and now.

The church's responsibility, both universally and locally, is to be the intentional and effective instrument of the emergence of God's role. This is the work which Jesus does, to which we, as his followers, are called. Yet it is not enough to do these works of faith simply out of good will. The work of the kingdom of God must reflect both his compassion and his commitment to the welfare of his creation and its fulfilment. We need to to these works, whether quietly and unobtrusively or in public and manifestly, with a clear understanding of our intentionality and that of the works themselves. These must

• Dr Killen, a Roman Catholic of the Latin rite, is the Executive Director of the Bairnwick Extension and Continuing Education Centre of the School of Theology, University of the South, Sewanee, Tennessee 37375, USA.

merge and speak as clearly as possible the word of the gospel of Jesus.

It is this Christian need to deal in effective and meaningful acts that gives rise to the theological enterprise. Our commitment to God's kingdom is at least two-fold. While it is *God's* kingdom as manifest in Jesus' life, death and resurrection that claims our energy and ourselves, it is at the same time *our* commitment that we are asked to make. The fact that our intentional acts require meaning does not do violence to, nor impede, our participation in the coming of God's kingdom. Rather, it is this meaning*ful*ness that makes them specifically the acts of God's sons and daughters, sisters and brothers of Jesus the Christ. As responsible siblings of Christ, we are to know what we are about and whether it is supportive of the goals which have been laid before us. It is at this point that the theological enterprise comes to the fore. It is not only necessary but pervasive. It not only needs to be done so that meaning is grasped and generated; it is being done anyway, every time any Christian attempts to do the Lord's will in a new and potentially pregnant situation.

The quality of theologizing is not to be judged primarily by the immediate output it generates but by the appropriateness of its address to the issue at hand and its illumination of Christians' lives with the values inhering in God's rule. Studied and disciplined theological reflection is key to our churches' putting into practice their values.

Theology will be done by non-professionals. It will be done, if for no other reason, because secularization, modernity, and pluralism cannot be stopped. This is as true of the third world cultures as it is of second and first. People faced with religious choices will make them on the bases of their understanding of their religious traditions, their experiences and their convictions. Unless they have developed a process of integrating tradition, experiences and convictions, their theologizing will be largely responsive to the variety of disconnected and inevitably dissonant values which impinge upon their consciousness. Such theologizing cannot help but be ineffective. For the church's mission, it may be downright disastrous. People are not going to be effective in, or reflective of, God's kingdom unless they are able to discern, own and implement the processes by which it is being manifested in their lives, and that of their local world.

Theology vs religious education

Some attention must be given to the difference between religious education and theology. Unless it is well grasped one may think that both do the same task. This results in a misalignment within the system of reflection whereby the individual Christian, attempting to understand the word of God and apply it in his or her local world, is frustrated and, even more seriously, is unable to understand the reason for failure.

It is not an unfair generalization to say that more often than not religious education bears the connotation of an activity whose learning subjects are at the introductory levels of religious knowledge, that is, children and adolescents and adults whose background lacks extensive information and formation in the religious tradition to which they actively adhere. Thus the content of religious education is usually thought of as being elementary or appropriate to the life state or vocation of the learning subjects. Its purpose is to help these subjects be intellectually (and perhaps emotionally) symmetrical with their role in their particular religious community. Without doubt, the motives of those who do religious education are nearly always benevolent. Yet such education's impact on the religious community is largely supportive of the status quo. The extensive work done in the field of sociology of knowledge as it applies to religious knowledge certainly makes such a minimal assertion tenable.

Theology is probably most often perceived by the laity as the specialized knowledge of the clerical or professional religious class, a class which may include some few people whose formal religious assemblies designate as laity. Theology also functions in a very different modality. While committed to the values of the community, it also tends towards the reformulation of the meanings which by being shared within the community enhance its vitality. This is especially so when the religious community is embroiled in a world of competing and dissonant values.

One of the major determining structures of Christian theology is its commitment to enhance the probability of the coming of God's kingdom. This requires that it deal with the meanings of the world on its own terms, not just within the Christian field of allegiance and commitment. Facing into the a-Christian world by Christians doing theology results in change within the social knowledge order of Christianity itself, whether slowly or rapidly. It is this aspect of stepping into the "other" world that most clearly distinguishes theology from religious education. Functionally, the distinction is greater the more thoroughly theologizing is engaged with the "other" world on its own terms. However, it needs to be realized that only rarely is this distinction positioned along clear lines of demarcation. Almost all modern catechisms and even some of the classical ones are theological to the extent that they are produced for persons whose formally a-Christian social knowledge is diverse. All religious education has theological aspects and all theologizing springs from and returns to religious educational concerns.

Christians inhabiting local worlds where there is wide and diverse knowledge combined with rapid changes in social values will, if they are to carry onward their commitment to furthering God's kingdom, need to be adept at a kind of theological reflection and action which allows and encourages effective hearing of and seeing in place the word of God.

Educational model

The School of Theology at the University of the South, located at Sewanee, Tennessee, has long been a force in the life of the Episcopal Church, especially in the south-eastern United States. The theological graduates expect help in developing the vitality of their congregations as they struggle with the issues of religious education appropriate to adults in Episcopal parishes.

The Sewanee programme, Education for Ministry, comprises a vast intra-continental system of indigenous, adult education in theological reflection. Its four-year duration allows the necessary time to read the 24 basic volumes of text produced specifically for the programme and simultaneously to be formed in the process of reflection which makes possible adequate theologizing.

At this writing there are approximately 4,000 students in the United States and Canada. These are gathered in about 500 groups led by 430 mentors (the individual seminar group's facilitator/administrator). There are another 750 students in Australia and New Zealand,and approximately 100 in the Caribbean area. These non-North American groups have their own administrative and training systems which, while linked to Sewanee through contracts and training events, function on their own.

The North American programme is largely (but not exclusively) linked to dioceses of the Episcopal Church in the United States and of the Anglican Church of Canada. These participating dioceses have sponsoring contracts with the Bairnwick Centre of the School of Theology at the University of the South. The contracts provide for the ongoing in-service training of mentors, the local coordination of the programme for the individual diocese, and reduced tuition rates for students.

The programme's academic level is postgraduate but non-professional. The programme is not offered for credit through the University of the South, although continuing education units are available to students.

All administrative support is located at the Sewanee, Tennessee, headquarters. Communications with students are through the individual mentor and a quarterly newsletter. Communication with the mentors occurs in a variety of ways: annual in-service training events (approximately 200 per year) held largely in the field and under the direction of some 30 trainers who are located in areas relatively accessible by mentors; regular reports initiated by Sewanee and responded to by the mentors; tuition billing processes initiated by Sewanee and mediated by the mentors; payment to the mentors by Sewanee of a monthly honorarium; thrice annual distribution of textbook material to the students by Sewanee through the mentors; departure surveys returned to Sewanee by all students leaving at any point in the programme for whatever reason; biennial surveys of students in the programme initiated by Bairnwick.

Bairnwick's staff is 12 full-time persons and three others part-time. Four of these are primarily responsible for programme management and training. Five are occupied primarily in administrative support, which utilizes a number of computer terminals and has access to an HP3000 computer. The remainder of Bairnwick's staff is involved in specialized editorial, educational design, and executive functions. All of this system has as its reason for existing the individual education for ministry seminar groups and the students who are in the process of learning the skills of theological reflection indigenously.

The impetus for the programme came out of a concern to equip local Episcopalians with an extension of the seminary's curriculum which would meet them in their natural environment (their local world), while retaining its traditional content as well as its analytical edge. As this worked out in practice, a system of non-traditional, at-a-distance, extension education developed which had its theoretical base in a simple, but inclusive concept of education described by

Prof. Ted Ward, Director of the Learning Systems Institute, Michigan State University.

Ward uses the analogy of a two-railed fence to describe an effective model for any educational system. One rail of the fence stands for all the ways by which the learner is provided with *knowledge* about the subject being studied. The second rail stands for the learner's *experience* in the matter being studied.

Ward's major point is that neither rail by itself provides an adequate educational experience. A person who has no theoretical knowledge of the effects of gear ratios will have difficulty working on a car's transmission; on the other hand, someone whose familiarity with automobiles is limited to reading about them does not have sufficient "hands-on" skills to repair them.

In Christian theological education the goal is to enable persons to be more faithful and effective ministers of the gospel. This requires knowledge of the gospel — its roots in the life of the people of Israel and its substance as revealed in the person of Jesus and the life of the church. Also necessary is experience in the Christian life and the practice of ministry. But the two-rail fence analogy involves more than just the two rails. Knowledge and experience must be interrelated, so that each sheds light on the other. The two rails must be joined together by *fence posts*.

In the Education for Ministry programme the knowledge rail of the fence is provided by the specially composed textbooks. The experiential rail is the participant's total life as a Christian. Every Christian inescapably affects the lives of others. This experience involves action a Christian takes in day-to-day living and in one way or another brings the church to bear on the lives of others.

The fence posts which tie together the knowledge acquired from the textbooks with the experience of Christian ministry are the seminar sessions. It is important that mentors and students alike understand the purpose of the seminar sessions. As *fence posts,* the seminars link the *knowledge rail* and the *experience rail.* In these sessions, students examine experiences of ministry in each other's lives in the light of the tradition as learned through their study. The mentor is instrumental in seeing that the seminar sessions provide this link.

As the regularly occurring connecting event between the knowledge learned by the students and their life experiences, the seminars and their ongoing life are crucial to the theological formation of the student participants. No two seminar groups function in exactly the same way. The communal life of the group and the styles of the persons involved vary within each group. Nonetheless, there are three kinds of activities in all Education for Ministry seminar groups: discussion, reflection and worship.

The lesson for the week raises some issue which is important to one or more members of the group, perhaps a challenge to a long-cherished position. Such issues can be profitably addressed by the group as a whole even if the group is composed of people at different points in the programme.

Reflection involves the process of using the themes and disciplines discovered in the textbooks in interpreting and criticizing one's own life and ministry. This is a highly disciplined process and not easy to do. It is, however, the most rewarding aspect of the programme and its principal goal. The most fruitful form of reflection uses experiences in the lives of the students — specific events which a student reports to the seminar group and offers as material for reflection.

The length of time it takes to establish a trust level sufficient to permit personal event reports varies among groups. The same reflection process used for such an event can be used with other data as well. Case studies, perhaps from the experience of the mentor, can be drawn upon. Events in novels or plays are often rich in possibilities for reflection. Current issues of controversy in the local community, the congregation, or the group's own life may also be used.

Education for Ministry needs to be done in the context of a worshipping community. The seminar group is a Christian community. It is small, and its members may be members of several congregations. But the seminar group is itself an assembly of the people of God. Worship of some kind is a regular part of its life.

The three seminar activities — discussion of issues, reflection on life and ministry, and worship — need to be kept in a creative balance. The maintenance of this balance is the mentor's task, using those kinds of group facilitation skills which are taught by Bairnwick's training staff.

The whole programme comes to fruition in the skills being learned in these seminar groups. Many could be learned equally well in other groups. The Education for Ministry programme intends specifically to train Christian laity in the single skill of theological reflection. Such a skill can be learned only if it is grounded in the ministering experiences of these lay people. It is the skill which underpins all other ministries of whatever kind whether performed by laity or clergy.

Education in theologizing must *not* be the private or professional preserve of the clergy, not if the churches take seriously their mission to pray and work for God's coming kingdom. A world less and less conscious of the gospel of Jesus and its cucial impact is far more the habitat of the laity than it is of the clergy. The skill of theological reflection is essential for those who would communicate with that world.

Theological reflection

Reflection is looking back on life to see and understand what has happened. A simple outline of one such discipline process is:

Experience: *Do* something.
Identify: *Look* at that something which happened.
Analyze: *Think* about the meanings, interpretations, and positions implicit and perhaps explicit in that which has happened.
Generalize: *Change* understandings and/or actions based upon the first three steps above.

This process is not, in itself, theological. It can, however, become such when specific reference to a religious tradition is included in the reflection process. Education for ministry uses a triangular model of theological reflection which draws on three sources: experience, tradition and personal positions (convictions). This triangular model may be diagrammed as follows:

THE THREE SOURCES FOR REFLECTION:
TRADITION, EXPERIENCE, POSITIONS

Salvation-history:
— Bible
— Church history and doctrine

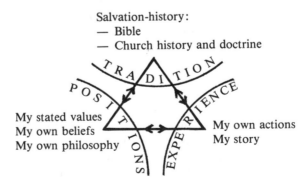

My stated values
My own beliefs
My own philosophy

My own actions
My story

While theological reflection may occur spontaneously, the seminar group provides a context for intentional theological reflection. Its method of teaching theological reflection starts from the experience of the students.

It is important to distinguish group theological reflection from two other group activities, problem-solving and therapy. The purpose of therapy and problem-solving is to provide help for the person whose experience is under discussion, and the strategy of the group members is to give support, challenge and advice. The basic purpose of doing theological reflection is:

> To enable the participants to become more faithful and effective ministers of the gospel by examining their own experience of ministry in the light of an increasing knowledge of the meaning of the Christian tradition.

The strategy of the group members is to identify with the person whose experience is under discussion and together to discover a bridge between this experience and the religious tradition.

One way to become more faithful and effective as Christian ministers is to look at personal convictions and how the individual's life is lived. This indicates that actions are governed by perspectives on life of which one is not always conscious. By examining thoughts and feelings in particular experiences these perspectives which are shaping vision and directing actions can begin to be identified. It is a little like taking off one's glasses and examining the lenses. Perspectives, like the lenses, shape what is seen and done. Each of us has these perspectives which, if examined over a period of time, can help clarify the meaning of our actions. These perspectives refer to the "experience" corner of the triangular model of theological reflection.

At the "positions" corner of the triangle are those values, beliefs, and convictions we would state as our own, if asked. The perspectives which form these positions come generally from the culture and sub-cultures to which we belong.

At the "tradition" corner of the triangle are the various bodies of material and lore which the student has received in his or her community as its heritage. This will be very extensive and include such things as the following: the Bible, church teachings, popular piety, lives of "the saints" and the major figures in the community's memory, etc. In the Education for Ministry programme the students encounter "tradition" and its perspectives in the texts. They gain an increasing understanding of what has directed the people of God in their continuous journey.

The model used here defines theological reflection as the creative interplay of the three sources: experience, tradition, positions. The *perspectives* inherent in each source are identified to give bases for comparison and contrast among these sources.

The following outline highlights the major points in the theological reflection model most frequently used in the programme, i.e. the "microscope method":

1. One of the group members shares an act of ministry.

2. Decision points contained in the presented event are listed, and one of these decision points is chosen for reflection.

3. The presenter reports his or her feelings and thoughts experienced in the event presented.

4. Individual group members identify and describe events which elicited similar feelings and thoughts; their events are expected to be different than the one presented.

5. The group brainstorms images and metaphors which characterize both the feelings and the thoughts of the presenter and those of similar nature offered by the group members.

6. The perspectives implicit in the presented experience are explored.

7. The perspectives in the world of the tradition are explored.

8. The perspectives implicit in the group's positions are explored.

9. The integrative process occurs by comparing different perspectives found in experience, tradition and position. Insights will generally occur at this stage.

10. Implications for action are identified. Decisions to act *are not* elicited. They may be volunteered but not encouraged or discouraged.

Involvement in this programme has been far greater than the School of Theology ever imagined. In less than seven years it has become the largest single programme of the University of the South. In full-time equivalent students (1,136) it is greater than that of the College of Arts and Sciences (1,049). It is more than 16 times greater than the residential seminary programme of the School of Theology. Impact on parishes from which students enroll has not been fully assessed at this writing. Such studies are being formulated. Personal testimonials reveal that people's lives have been radically altered in directions which they find both satisfying and productive of their vision of God's rule.

The fruit of our work is just beginning to manifest itself. In another two or three years we will know whether we are doing the Lord's work as effectively as we hope to.

Asia and Australia

The Association for Theological Education by Extension

An Indian approach to training for ministry

VINAY SAMUEL and CHRIS SUGDEN

The Indian context is twenty per cent urban and eighty per cent rural. Sixty per cent of the people live below the poverty line due to religiously sanctioned injustice and exploitation. The Indian church has emerged largely among poor people, and in rural areas it is still mainly composed of the poor. In the urban setting it is increasingly a middle-class church with a growing number of competent middle-class professional people. These people, along with able leaders in rural areas, have a deep commitment to being involved in Christian ministry, but they have no opportunity to become suitably equipped. To help the churches meet this need for training leadership, TAFTEE was formed.*

The Indian church is marked by the following characteristics. First, it is almost entirely dependent on professional leadership. Paid pastors are expected to do all the work of the ministry. They are required to be experts in everything from counselling to chairing committees, from preaching to keeping accounts. They also have to act as

---

• Dr Samuel is pastor of St John's Church of South India in Bangalore. He and his assistant pastor, the Rev. Chris Sugden from England, work as a team with others in Partnership in Mission-Asia. They are respectively Chairman and Assistant Director of TAFTEE, P.O. Box 544, Bangalore 560 005, India.

* The Association for Theological Education by Extension (TAFTEE) was formed in January 1971. It was established as the official extension work of six Bible colleges backed by fifteen church and mission groups and now includes the Church of South India and the Church of North India. TAFTEE is a member of the Board of Theological Education of Serampore University, which coordinates training for full-time ministry in most of the Protestant churches.

private chaplains to families in the congregations. Their attendance is obligatory at births, deaths, festivals and even minor bouts of sickness. In addition, they have the major task of keeping numerous church institutions such as schools, hostels, clinics, hospitals and orphanages going, in the midst of pressure from government and other outside bodies.

Secondly, the professional leadership is grossly understaffed to meet escalating needs. One diocese of the Church of South India has almost no clergy between the ages of 40 and 60. One Methodist conference is finding it impossible to fill key pastorates. In north-east India one church has 300 congregations but no theologically trained pastor; yet in 1979 it reported 1,000 baptisms. A survey published in 1974 found that only 2 per cent of pastors and church teachers in India had seminary training. This 2 per cent was largely involved in the cities in administering church properties and taking communion services to the many congregations in their charge.

Thirdly, there is tremendous freedom for Christian witness. This has encouraged the growth of indigenous movements with a strong emphasis on reaching the unreached and an influx of para-church organizations which are branches of large multinational Christian agencies. Such organizations come with the intention of reaching the seventy per cent of the population who have never encountered Christ, and they seek support from the churches. Active support for these indigenous movements and multinational agencies comes not from the overburdened pastors, but from committed lay people who are eager to be trained for and active in reaching the unreached.

The freedom for Christian involvement in India's democratic society has also encouraged the growth of Christian agencies for promoting social justice, largely staffed and supported by lay people.

All these organizations bypass the local churches and cream off the best lay leaders, not because of theological differences but because the local churches and their leadership are tied to keeping their structures going and have no time to embrace new initiatives and opportunities. TAFTEE sees as its role the important task of training committed lay people to exercise ministries for evangelism, mission and justice through the work of the local congregations.

A fourth characteristic of the Indian church is that there has been a steady decline in the participation of women in the church's ministry since Independence in 1947. With the passing of missions and women missionaries, women's work and ministry have been progressively downgraded in the church's priorities. Seminaries and training institutions cannot redress this imbalance since the churches have reduced the avenues through which trained women can serve.

The seminaries struggle to provide respectable degrees with adequate academic content incorporating the best in theological scholarship around the world; to meet the requirement of churches for ordinands to have recognized degrees; and also to provide proper ministerial formation, which can only take place in a context of action and reflection. In our estimation, the current seminary programmes are in the end forced to opt for high academic content and degree orientation. Ministerial formation is expected to be a by-product.

The poignancy of the situation is not lost on pastors and bishops in the institutional churches. A gathering of pastors in one diocese who all had bachelor of divinity degrees complained that they did not have the skills to open up biblical resources for enabling and motivating their church members to apply their Christian faith to the whole of life in society. In 1978 20 bishops of the Church of South India complained that seminary graduates were not able to act as facilitators for their congregations in Christian mission. The vast majority of church people want to know how to address the current social context with biblical faith. They are very open to change, to grappling with issues, and to involvement in mission.

The graduates who arrive in pastorates find that to fulfill the current expectations they must be technical experts on all aspects of ministry and on running the church's institutions. As a result a number of creative young leaders abandon leadership of local churches and participation in their denominations out of sheer frustration. They join para-church justice movements or mission agencies.

Churches and training institutions have been struggling with these problems and developing plans for extension education for lay leadership based on the seminaries. But the solution does not lie in new methods of training alone. The need is also for a proper understanding of mission and ministry and an appropriate methodology to disseminate it.

Theology of mission and ministry

TAFTEE's programme developed out of its underlying understanding of mission and ministry. Its understanding is that the whole church must be equipped for mission to address the whole gospel to the whole of life. The whole church must be equipped; all its members must be enabled to develop and use their gifts for ministry. The church must hold forth the whole gospel of the kingdom, i.e. of right relationships between God and humankind, between people in society, and between people and their environment. The gospel must address individuals and peoples in all the structures which express and shape their distorted and redeemable humanity. The whole gospel must address the total social, economic, political, religious and personal context of men and women.

TAFTEE programmes are based on the conviction that every member of the body of Christ has gifts to be developed and used in ministry. In the Indian context the local church will only take its central place in Christian mission when training in Christian ministry is focused as much on the members of local churches in their setting as on young future leaders being trained out of their contexts. Ninety-eight per cent of church members have a devout attitude towards the authority and place of the Bible in the Christian life. TAFTEE is convinced that when the Bible is central in Christian lives, people are open to being moved in the direction of holistic mission. TAFTEE studies are also based on the conviction that the role of the vocational, ordained ministry is to enable others to develop their gifts for ministry. TAFTEE seeks to provide a framework to enable pastors to facilitate the ministry of others.

TAFTEE courses are not patterned after residential degree programmes. They are designed to enable students to grapple with their total context and to be involved in creative activity and practical ministry. We are convinced that such a process will bring about a change in the balance of power in the church and a true democratization of the people of God. In Indian society access to information and knowledge is restricted, which confers power on those authority figures and experts who have such access. Once people in the churches are given information, knowledge, awareness and expertise, they will no longer accept oppressive power structures in the church or in society without question. They will gain confidence that they also can do the job of ministry and provide alternative leadership if necessary. This process will also enable pastors to fulfill their true role as enablers of others.

There is clear evidence that this change is happening in the lives of TAFTEE students and graduates. Some TAFTEE graduates are giving significant leadership in city-wide organizations working with local churches. They are undertaking important aspects of Christian ministry which the monolithic denominational leadership has avoided or neglected. TAFTEE has given them the skill and the confidence that they can do Christian ministry. Others are gaining new insights and awareness beyond the narrow limits of their own traditions. They are forming a reservoir of articulate, questioning and committed lay people. They are giving significant support to new initiatives as they emerge. A new initiative for national missionary work in Bombay churches was supported mainly by TAFTEE students and graduates.

Originally the four goals of the TAFTEE programme were approached separately: that each student would be (1) effectively engaged in evangelism, (2) an able Bible student and teacher, (3) an ongoing participant in spiritual growth, personal and corporate, and (4) a responsible member of society, in the family and the nation. To achieve these goals primary emphasis was placed on the study of biblical books, with the addition of some more "general" courses on, for example, the family and society. As the studies progressed, writers, tutors and students came to realize that studying biblical books separately from real social issues was not real Bible study. These four goals are now approached in a more integrated fashion so that students are truly able to exercise relevant Christian obedience in the total context. A survey of some course objectives shows what students are expected to be able to do through studying the courses: evaluate and plan orders of worship, relate the principles of Jesus' ministry to the context of poverty, oppression and injustice; understand astrology; compose and deliver a sermon; visit poor people in slums; organize a house group; through personal interaction with Hindus and Muslims, to understand the role of religion in their lives.

An important mid-course correction was made in 1978. The degree-level courses were not getting to the grassroots of the churches: people who did not speak English, had little schooling, and lived in rural areas. So the certificate-level programme was introduced, adapting and translating the SEAN materials from South America.

Educational philosophy

TAFTEE's target group are men and women, aged between 25 and 55, engaged in secular employment. They have been trained in an educational system which by and large does not encourage analysis, individual research or reflection. School and university students live off a diet of fast-food answer guides.

Programmed instruction, one of the main methods of instruction, is designed to enable the students to study on their own. It provides a checking system so that they can evaluate their own learning as they interact with the material. Though initially a number of courses were based on the behavioural philosophy of B.F. Skinner, we are increasingly modifying the approach of programmed instruction to provide a basis for interaction, analysis and questioning of ideas, and case studies. Thus many of the questions in our courses are open-ended with no specific answers given. Students must defend their own answers at the bar of the tutorial, which adds a social dimension to their learning.

Tutorial groups in the degree-level programme often comprise students from a number of churches and cultural backgrounds. They are important ecumenical meeting places where students and tutors are exposed to alternative Christian insights and traditions. Ninety-seven per cent of students value the tutorial, which TAFTEE insists on as an essential part of its programme.

The courses also involve practical learning activities. Many courses contain compulsory practical exposures and assignments: to survey community health facilities, to discover the reasons for church growth (or lack of it) in one's own church, to plan a stewardship campaign, to produce communication material, to prepare study guides for Bible study groups, to reflect on situations of pastoral counselling. All the courses have therefore been specially written to train people in practical Christian living and ministry. They are not packaged seminary courses for non-residential students. The result is a very real and growing involvement of the students in ministry. A survey made by an institution that runs TAFTEE courses and its own programme of a packaged seminary course for non-residential study showed that the TAFTEE students increased their church involvement by 100 per cent, while the other students gradually shelved involvement in ministry through the pressure of book study.

Such a level of involvement in ministry results in a type of programme that cannot be evaluated by the existing criteria of the present degree-awarding institutions. At present the lack of any agreed parity hampers those TAFTEE graduates who want to undertake recognized ministry in the denominations, and it encourages extension students who want courses recognized by the churches to opt for non-residential, academic seminary programmes merely to gain recognition.

Self-study materials and tutorials are reinforced in a number of ways. Enrichment reading is suggested in many courses as a voluntary component. Experience shows that where students have access to books, they take this up; however, the dearth of accessible, relevant theological literature eliminates this possibility for many TAFTEE students. In-seminary programmes have also been held for two-week periods to provide experience in residential fellowship and learning. Lack of staff has hindered this from growing as it should. Tutors' workshops on local and national levels develop tutors' skills and sense of pastoral responsibility for growth in ministry.

Evaluation

Throughout its ten years of existence TAFTEE has been seeking to learn from its context and experience. The first courses included a number of international TEE texts. Now 85 per cent of the courses have been written by people living and working in India. Ten per cent have so far been written by Indian staff writers. There is a great shortage of theological literature relevant to Christian life and ministry in the Indian context. TAFTEE courses are providing an important source of relevant material. Students particularly value the opportunity to discuss issues of integrity, corruption, strikes, trade unions and family life which are rarely discussed in Christian meetings. The courses provide a library of material that students draw on long after their courses are completed.

The writing process has been maturing. Originally by force of circumstance, when most of the executive and writing staff were expatriate, the Western model of one person writing a book alone prevailed. Now a more contextual model of a writing team has emerged. Five national staff and two expatriates develop writing projects, draw on local experts in the various theological disciplines, and feed material and support to one course coordinator.

Pastors and laity are the focus of TAFTEE studies. But in a recent survey we discovered that only five per cent of students had been encouraged to take up TAFTEE studies by their pastor. Nevertheless, every one of our graduates is involved in a church-related ministry in some way. The ripples are beginning to be felt all around. One graduate who was appointed to the leadership of an evangelistic organization turned it in the direction of a holistic ministry to the whole person in society. A number of graduates in one denomination have been providing leadership for cell groups, thus facilitating face-to-face fellowship and ministry in local neighbourhoods. One graduate has used the resources of his studies to train Bible study groups through writing study notes. He is now training others to write them. Students in a preaching course provided preachers for a series of Lenten sermons. A salesman and a senior officer in the Indian Administrative Service provided insights on the meaning of the cross in their professional lives.

The significant percentage of women among TAFTEE students (30 per cent) is a clear indication of the potential among women for ministry. TAFTEE helps them to be equipped and trained.

In future planning TAFTEE proposes to translate its degree-level courses into the national languages, to produce courses for specialist groups, and to develop post-graduate courses to enable people to pursue ministerial studies in a particular field to a greater depth.

TAFTEE has shared its experience and materials with groups outside India. It facilitated the start of a similar programme in Sri Lanka in 1979. Its degree level materials are used as training manuals and Bible study guides in Pakistan, Malaysia, Indonesia, Lebanon, Papua New Guinea, Nepal, the Philippines, England and Australia.

So far we have only been able to conduct a scientific evaluation of the ten-year-old degree-level programme in which 1,275 middle-class and professional people have registered; it appears to be meeting its target goals. The three-year-old certificate programme is too new to be able to evaluate it properly. But the 1,500 students who enrolled in three language areas in three years demonstrate that it is very attractive to lay people in rural areas. It has every prospect of escalating when it becomes widely available in ten languages or more. It places in the hands of village elders a tool for ministry which they have never had before. It has the potential for producing a true church of the people.

Many movements have arisen throughout history to promote people's participation and to devolve power to the people. Often these end tragically in new tyrannies. The church should be the resource centre for renewing the vision that every person has a gift which is vital for the wellbeing of the whole community. TAFTEE sees its certificate-level programme as a major contribution towards enabling the church in this generation to be such a movement. The movements in urban and rural churches should reinforce each other and demonstrate a true partnership between the "strong" and the "weak" in the life of the church and of the nation.

Building theological education networks among the Batak churches

WARNER W. LUOMA

Theological Education by Extension (TEE) in North Sumatra had its origins in the 1860s when the Rhenish Mission of Germany sent missionaries to the Bataks. Dr I. L. Nommensen became the recognized head of this group. Under his tutelage individuals who displayed qualities of leadership and ministerial potential were chosen to become elders. These men were prepared to accept responsibility for instilling spiritual life in local congregations. The rapid establishment of new congregations necessitated the opening of a school to prepare candidates who would serve as preacher-teachers; they would become ministers of local congregations and head the village schools under mission supervision.

By the early 1880s the burgeoning church outgrew the available pastoral and leadership care from missionaries. A seminary was opened to prepare Batak preacher-teachers — who had already demonstrated ability to serve, teach and lead — to become ordained pastors.

The denominations that resulted from this early work still rely heavily on local lay leaders whose ministry is overseen and guided by ordained pastors. In 1974 two of these denominations, the Christian Church of Indonesia (HKI) and the Simalungun Protestant Christian

• The Rev. Warner Luoma, a US missionary in Indonesia since 1972, is an advisor to the TEE programme of the Christian Church of Indonesia (HKI), the Simalungun Protestant Christian Church (GKPS), and the Indonesian Protestant Christian Church (GKPI), which have a combined membership of 590,000. His address is Box 33, Pematang Siantar, Sumut, Indonesia.

Church (GKPS), decided to work together to build a theological education network to provide in-service education opportunities for lay and ordained ministers.

The primary objective of the programme is to provide educational opportunities on a regular basis for preacher-teachers and elders. Development of the programme was complicated by the fact that at the beginning there were almost 900 preacher-teachers and about 4,000 elders but no materials or teachers. It was necessary to design a TEE programme by stages, utilizing the historic structure of the churches. The first stage would offer courses to the 90 pastors of the HKI and GKPS in order to help them upgrade their ministries and to prepare them to be teachers in TEE courses for the preacher-teachers in their parishes. Following the completion of this first stage, there would be a sufficient number of trained people to begin TEE at the parish level. To achieve these goals it was necessary to train a core group who would be able to carry out the task of writing materials, of developing a network of course centres and — particularly in the first stage — of leading these courses.

Research and development

In the development of this TEE programme we first thought we would be able to use traditional materials. But initial efforts proved they were too theoretical and irrelevant.

Few of the congregational lay leaders had had a residential, formal education to prepare them specifically for the work they were doing. Most of them had learned by experience and had been called to their present work because they were capable persons. They had little academic preparation, but they were steeped in the life and context of the congregations. We were working with people who had a concrete idea of what it meant to minister to a congregation.

Many of the pastors had not had college-level training. Quite a few had been prepared for their ministries under the old theological education programme where they served first as preacher-teachers for five to ten years. Then they entered pastor's school. All pastors supervised an average of ten congregations and much of their time was taken up in administrative and sacramental work. The pastors were, in general, highly committed and functioned well in the traditional setting, but they were having many difficulties adapting to new situations and problems. Part of this, we discovered, was because they lacked needed skills to upgrade preacher-teachers and elders.

Since this latter group really carried the day-to-day ministry of the local congregation, it was they who of necessity had to learn how to deal with new situations if ministry was to be effective. Thus the pastors needed to learn new pedagogical skills to give the necessary guidance to their lay assistants. As long as the social and economic milieu had remained unchanged, the pastors did not have to give much attention to helping experienced lay leaders deal with local problems. It was when new problems came on the scene that difficulties arose.

The people who were to participate in the TEE programme all had full-time responsibilites. The curriculum would have to identify precisely what they needed in order to serve effectively. They would not have time initially to indulge in studies that were not closely related to what they perceived as real life problems.

Because of this we scrapped our original approach and began to research the actual problems as understood by our students. We also wanted them to participate actively in analyzing their situations and problems in order that they and the core group assigned to develop materials could come to deeper understanding about causes and possible solutions. If we were to develop a curriculum that was to be relevant, we felt the future students must have a dominant voice in shaping it.

Issues

We began by opening a dialogue with the pastors who were to be students in the first stage. Based upon the process outlined by Paulo Freire in his book *Pedagogy of the Oppressed,* our object of study was the world of the pastors, how they understood it and responded to it. In the process some of the underlying problems and contradictions of the society served by the pastors were identified and clarified. These were used as the basis for designing practical experiences and tasks which would help the pastors engage in wrestling with significant cultural matters as a part of the learning programme.

From our initial research we began to understand several important problems that had to be overcome if the pastors were to provide adequate ministry and leadership for lay leaders and others. Skills of community building and stewardship development were not adequate to meet contemporary needs. Knowledge and ability to help congregations utilize the limited resources available to deal with economic and social problems needed upgrading. Skills in teaching basics of Christian faith and in guiding congregation members to understand and apply the Bible to their daily life were antiquated. The relationship of Christian teachings with the rules and customs set down by the ancestors needed much attention. Too much of the traditional teaching content dealt largely with European problems and questions and had little relation to the issues of faith that were challenging the church in North Sumatra. The concept of the church as a community or a family of God's people with a mission and ministry for others was overshadowed by the concept of church as a hierarchical organization. This organization was centred in building a nice "church" building and paying the pastor and lay ministers for duties performed. The concept of vocation in terms of ministerial offices was in danger of being degraded to a system of status and honour for the office holder who looked upon the office as a privilege which granted honour and favour rather than being a calling.

An underlying problem was the distance between the clergy and the members of the church. The problems that were being faced seemed to require a style of ministry that would bring the pastor very close to the people. He would have to venture more into public places where people traditionally gathered but which were deemed "sinful" for a pastor. The people, however, have a great respect for the pastor and their image of this person precludes involvement in worldly matters. The old concepts of education were reinforcing this underlying problem. Education was seen as the transferral by an expert of something called knowledge to students who were assumed to know little. Knowledge had an existence apart from daily life. The expert — such as the pastor, in the perception of church members — was expected to know everything. Not to know was considered a weakness. A story told to me once concerned the response to two different teachers. One gave a lecture which was obviously over the heads of the listeners. Foreign words and strange concepts were freely tossed out. The second teacher built upon what the listeners already knew. He involved them actively in his class and had them work together to share ideas and thoughts related to what he was sharing. The first teacher was admired by the students. He obviously was a learned person since he knew foreign words and what he was saying was far beyond comprehension. The second teacher was thought to be incompetent because he had to ask many things from the students. Since his presentation was clear and understandable it was obvious that the students' knowledge was on a par. In other words the second teacher was no better than the students.

This same view of reality was present in the understanding of ministry. Church members were to be passive; the pastor had the answers. One needed only to wait for truth to be revealed. The pastors were afraid that if they did not respond to the role they were cast in, they would no longer be respected. The people did not act, since they felt incompetent and unable. A vicious circle was created. Pastors, lay ministers and congregations were locked in a dependency situation where no one was free to cooperate, to act and reflect together. We needed to try to find ways they could free themselves to discover how to live in their culture in accordance with God's word.

As the TEE group began to understand this issue, we looked for ways to avoid creating just another dependency-generating educational programme. We felt that one way to do this was to involve students and teachers in working together to develop educational goals and to define problems and priorities. If we did not do this, the core group of the TEE programme would fall into the trap of becoming a new elite of experts who would tell passive listeners how they should think and act. This would reinforce attitudes that were at the heart of the underlying problem discovered in our dialogue with the pastors.

We decided to take the risk of approaching education in a new manner, since the core group had no face or status to lose. At worst, in case of failure, the Western missionary could be made the scapegoat for bringing in another one of those "half-baked" ideas.

We went back to the dialogical research programme we had started and began to have the pastors assist in looking in more detail at the problems. We wished to find causes, areas where knowledge and facts were lacking, skills that needed to be mastered, and what the solution of a problem might mean to the life of the congregation. In doing this we involved the pastors in an active way with the objective of establishing an educational process where the role of learner would include teaching and that of a teacher would include learning.

Courses

Through this process the core group was able to develop goals, objectives, and priorities with the active assistance of the pastors. Having these in hand, we sought to design materials and experiences which would help the pastors achieve what they felt was important to them in their ministry. Because the core group wished to continue this dialogical process, it was decided to involve a wide group in the preparation of materials. We asked people who had experience and competence related to the goals of a course to sit down with us and suggest what kinds of knowledge, skills and practice might be helpful to the students if the goals were to be achieved. For example, we wished to design a course on the Bible and Adat — Adat is the customary law of the Batak peoples of North Sumatra which is rooted in the traditions of the ancestors. We obtained the services of four people: the late Ephorus of the Batak Protestant Christian Church (HKBP), who at 87 years of age was able to share much with us; the retired president of the HKI, whose family was converted to the Christian faith when he was a youngster; a Roman Catholic professor whose field is church and culture; and a GKPS lay person who has devoted many years relating Christian faith to the traditions of his people. These persons each prepared a paper on a particular aspect of the subject and spent three days in consultation with the core group. From this exchange we designed the course material which was presented to the pastors as a continuation of the dialogue that had begun during the initial research period. The pastors in turn were asked to relate what they were studying by engaging their congregational lay leaders in reflecting upon key problems in the relation of Christian faith to traditional beliefs and in trying to develop concrete action in the parishes. This helped the pastors learn to bring lay leaders and church members into the educative process.

As we turn our attention to courses for preacher-teachers, we are striving to bring them actively into this process. The pastors are active participants in carrying out this dialogue in their own parishes. Thus we have been attempting to deal with the basic underlying problem by slowly introducing a new understanding of education. We have tried to do this step by step and in non-threatening situations. In this way people can not only accept changes, but can make those changes themselves.

In addition we have discovered that this approach involves the students and teachers in a very practical kind of social analysis. The gospel is encountered in the centre of the social, cultural, and economic realities that make up the world of the student and the teacher. Our understanding of God's word has been enriched and expanded. We in the core group have been challenged because we feel we too are learning as much as our students. All of us are participating in an exciting adventure.

We also discovered the importance of training Indonesians to prepare the course materials. Too often the tendency has been to supply missionaries as writers or to translate materials prepared in other regions of the world. From our experience we found that the period of four years it took to prepare people to write was well worth it. We have been able to develop a more effective training programme and now need only two years to bring people to this point.

I tried my hand at writing in the first course we developed. Before our field tests of the materials I was disappointed because my co-workers had seemingly not learned well how to write a programmed text. I felt myself a failure as a teacher because their material was not as logical and informative as mine. Yet the results of the testing showed conclusively that my "well-written" lessons did not work nearly as well as theirs. It became apparent that differences between cultures in such matters as logic and the ways in which people learn mean that it is very difficult for an outsider to present material as effectively as someone from that culture.

Evaluation

Evaluation has been an important part of our TEE programme. Because elements of the educational philosophy, methods, and materials we are using are new to the participants, we have had to strike out into uncharted regions. This has meant a constant need to examine closely where we have been, where we are, and what this means to where we want to go. We have attempted to avoid merely using forms and structures that have worked elsewhere. Our objective has been to adapt ideas and concepts in ways that are relevant to the life of the Batak people and their churches.

We have been looking very closely at the materials we use. A major problem is lack of interest in reading. Though Bataks are generally literate, reading has not become a habit. Thus we are continually striving to encourage reading by preparing material that is interesting and useful. Also, since we are using programmed materials, we have had to introduce people to a new type of study material and help them learn how to use it most effectively. Recently we have begun to present material in a study guide format and are still evaluating its effectiveness. We are also trying to determine appropriate lesson length and to give homework assignments that are realistic. We are attempting to overcome a weakness in the evaluation of homework by having each student keep a notebook in which are written notes from each seminar meeting, homework activities, comments on what is being studied, and insights and ideas that have come from the course. At each centre a person is assigned to collect, evaluate, and comment on this material.

We are facing problems due to schooling and age differences. For some people study materials seem too easy and for others too difficult. As we gain more experience and train part-time personnel, we hope to be able to give more attention to this problem. In the first place we are becoming more competent at determining the different groups and their characteristics, and perhaps we can prepare additional materials as an adjunct to core study lessons and assignments.

Since we have determined concrete goals for the courses, we have been learning how to measure what the student has achieved in comparison with what was hoped. We have discovered that too often our goals have not been as measurable as we had assumed and need rewriting. We have also discovered weaknesses in testing. We haven't given enough post-seminar tests to study student progress. Because of this we have started holding an evaluation session following each seminar.

An area that is taking much of our time at present is the evaluation of TEE's contribution to the sponsoring churches. Our hope has been that TEE would:
— supplement and reinforce other educational activities;
— help lay and ordained ministers overcome problems;
— strengthen leadership.

Results so far are encouraging, though they also indicate that we cannot afford to rest on our laurels.

We are continuing with our dialogical research programme. New problems continue to appear as the people of North Sumatra face new problems brought about by continuing changes in their social, economic and political environment. Old problems need to be restated and clarified as we learn more about them. As students progress, their priorities change, and the courses need to reflect this.

Our main challenge now is to expand the programme to include the preacher-teachers. We are now conducting research concerning their problems and needs. We are training new people to assist in doing the necessary research and writing. Pastors in the present stage of TEE are finishing preparation enabling them to be course leaders in their own parishes.

In 1979 the Indonesian Protestant Christian Church (GKPI) was accepted as a full member of the TEE programme. Courses for their pastors began in February 1981. To accomplish this, four new centres have been opened to serve the 75 pastors of that church.

The churches in North Sumatra have come a long way since the 1860s. On the foundations laid by Dr Nommensen and his colleagues, they have grown and are continuing to develop. Building on the tradition of continued training for church ministers, we are trying to make our contribution to build the church envisioned by the leaders of our day.

Union Seminary

Alternative education for church workers in the Philippines

JOSÉ GAMBOA, Jr

After eight decades of evangelical work in the Philippines, the two major Protestant denominations — the United Methodist Church and the United Church of Christ in the Philippines — have expanded the scope of their work to cover the whole country. The jurisdictional limitations agreed upon by the denominations were abrogated after the war as various circumstances, such as polity development of some churches, post-war migration of population to sparsely populated areas, economic development and rapid growth of transportation, made geographical boundaries for denominations untenable. Thus the churches found themselves serving vast territories and needing to increase the number of pastoral leadership. The post-war years also opened new vistas for the ministry, such as specialized leadership in rural life ministry, in community development, urban industrial mission, mission to cultural communities, teaching ministry in church-related educational institutions, ministry in the armed forces, hospitals, ecumenical agencies, and many others.

The demands for pastoral leadership grew, but opportunities for theological education did not expand as much as the recruitment programme of the churches. In 1976 the United Methodist Church (UMC), for example, had 612 pastors, 255 of whom are seminary graduates; 357 or 58.3 per cent of the total number had no seminary

• Dr Gamboa, Jr, is Director of the extension programme of Union Seminary, P.O. Box 841, Manila, Philippines. He has also served as President of the Commission on Non-Traditional Studies of the Association of Theological Schools of South East Asia.

education. During that year only 29 students were enrolled in the traditional seminary programme. The traditional theological education programme is therefore creating an elitist group in the church while failing to meet the needs of the majority of the clergy population. Seminary-educated ordained clergy receive higher salaries and better church assignments, get elected to top positions in the church, have the vote in the conferences and other privileges, while most church workers, the lay preachers and local pastors, do not vote, are assigned to "hardship" parishes, and receive low salaries.

The need to supplement the traditional seminary programme with an alternative model for theological education was discussed from a quantitative view. Equally important was the need to gird the church for her emerging role in the Philippine context.

Philippine society is characterized by a wide base of poverty-stricken, deprived, and underdeveloped people who in the present struggle of the country for development are most susceptible to exploitation, manipulation and oppression. They participate in the development programme from a position of weakness compared with the resources of the rich, powerful political leaders, the educated and the technocrats. The poor, with mere labour to offer and with many restrictions imposed by the government, participate at a disadvantage.

In the context of martial law and an accelerated programme of national development, with wealth in the hands of a very few, controls on the products of farmers, and restrictions imposed on labour, the church needs to assume leadership for justice, liberation, and development of the majority population.

Alternative theological education must therefore facilitate the development of leadership in the church to carry out the ministry of liberation, justice, and development in the context of Philippine society.

Objectives for an alternative model

The two objectives in developing an alternative model for ministerial formation of parish leaders of Protestant churches are:

— first, to provide theological education for the many church workers who are already serving in the field, and for the ever-increasing recruits to the ministry;

— second, to design appropriate theological education for church workers for leadership in the ministry of liberation, justice, and development in the context of Philippine society.

The first concern must take into account certain conditions:

1. The model must accommodate a large number of students, more than the traditional seminary programmes accept.
2. It must make use of available resources or structures, without necessarily creating new institutions which may entail large-scale expenditures.
3. The new model must be economically viable, with the church able to support the cost.
4. The model must accommodate students from all over the country without requiring them to leave their places or work, so that local church leadership will not be dislocated and so that students do not leave their large families.

The second concern, which is to form leadership for the ministry of liberation, justice, and development, must take into account the following conditions:

1. The new model must de-emphasize regimentation, conformity to authority, patterns which prescribe or limit student response.
2. It should expose students to issues, problems, needs, and concerns of people (communities and congregations) and allow a wide range of response.
3. As the model elicits creativity among the students, it should encourage them to make use of available resources in the church and in the community and particularly to make use of their own experiences. The students must learn how to educate themselves, to become self-reliant.

As a result of these concerns, the United Methodist Church, through its Division of the Ministry, and the United Church of Christ in the Philippines, through the Office of the General Secretary, worked with the Union Theological Seminary faculty in developing the programme for theological education by extension, which later developed two modules, namely, the self-directed study module and the self-propelled group module. The TEE programme admitted 180 students in the initial year of operation. Six years later, 1980-81, 701 students are enrolled in the programme. Seventy per cent of non-seminary-educated clergy of the United Methodist Church are now participating in this alternative programme; in the United Church of Christ more are being prepared and qualified for their ordained ministry. The students who complete the requirements receive the bachelor of ministry degree and qualify for ministerial membership and ordination in these two churches.

Self-directed study module

The self-directed study module makes possible the admission and participation of as many church workers as desire to take part in the theological education programme. It enables students to carry out an autonomous individual study programme. Through the use of various components, efficient education processes, and selection of pertinent educational philosophies, students can capably work through a block of five to seven subjects in a period of 6 to 12 months and finish a degree programme in a minimum of four years. Each module has several components which contribute towards the operation of the educative system, such as:

1. *The individual learning kit:* This kit is composed of a study guide, study materials (textbooks and references) for the subjects being studied, and several rating scales so that the students can evaluate their progress in the study programme.

2. *Experience input from the students:* The student must learn to use resources in and from oneself, such as the wealth of experiences one has accumulated in working and living in the community, one's observation and exposure to the resources in the church and community, also one's knowledge of issues, problems, needs and concerns in the community. The educative system helps the student to become aware of this wealth of resources to use for one's own development.

3. *The church and community:* This component is the laboratory for learning of the students, who immediately apply all learning in the context, in actual situations.

4. *The log book:* Students must have time to reflect on the results of their application of learning in their work in the church and the community. The log book gives them opportunities to articulate their insights, impressions, and evaluation or assessment of what they have done in their parish. The log book also serves as a record of the students' progress in their study programme.

5. *Seminary and adjunct faculty:* The seminary faculty, with the assistance of regional faculties, provides the orientation seminar to start off students in the self-directed study programme. A supervisor

works as a consultant for every TEE study group; he is also a member of the adjunct faculty.

Every year the churches recruit students to study in the TEE programme. The seminary faculty, with the assistance of adjunct faculty in the region, go to the various regions to hold orientation seminars to start the students in the self-directed study programme. They are given study guides, the study materials, and evaluation guides; they are oriented on how to use these materials, to identify and make use of the various components of the self-study module.

The students must study at least two hours a day with the use of the individual learning kit. They organize their learning experiences so that they can apply them in their work. They must make the learning and application relevant to the needs of the church and the community. In doing so, they must criticize, analyze, and assess the ideas or knowledge they obtain from the kit with their experiences and with the issues obtaining in the church and the community. They must reject, accept, modify, and synthesize. They must try out and verify what they have learned. They must learn by working with people, as a doer and/or as a facilitator, as the situation may call for.

Students must learn to transcend themselves, look at themselves from the outside, and reflect on what they have done, forming a total view of the educative processes. They must articulate all important insights, impressions, even the reactions or responses from the people in the context. As they do this, the students also make use of several evaluation guides to evaluate themselves and the study programme. They may reward themselves for achievements, but they must correct and improve where they find weaknesses.

Once a month, as a rule, students who live in a particular geographic area gather for sharing and evaluation. They share in order to enrich others and to benefit from the work of others. The TEE study group also makes use of evaluation guides to assess one another's work.

Self-propelled study group module

This module reinforces the work done in the individual study programme. The students must obtain a clear perspective of their progress through sharing their work with others; they share the results of their reflection upon their studies and application of learning, their insights, discoveries, impressions. They gain access to various approaches, interpretations, insights, criticisms, and learning tools other members bring to the group. They can avail themselves of the services of a consultant, the supervisor, for their problems or concerns. The group serves as a learning laboratory for group processes and management, for gaining a clear self-image, and as a source of strength and determination in carrying out the study programme by mutual support of one another.

The educative processes involved in this module can be traced through the activities of the TEE study group. The first hour is spent in the opening devotions. One student is assigned to preach and another to be the liturgist. During the next hour the group discusses their work in homiletics, first by evaluating the sermons presented at the devotions. They make this the starting point for sharing. In the third hour the group evaluates the liturgy and makes use of this to start their discussion of liturgy. Doctrine comes next. The doctrinal context of the sermon is evaluated, and this starts off the discussion of basic Christian beliefs. The group then asks: How did the preacher interpret the text? Exegesis, exposition, and so on. The discussion of the biblical area is on.

A student is assigned to observe the group process as the members participate in the discussion. Then the functions in the group may be discussed. How did communication take place? At the concluding hour, the group evaluates the work done by the members and the group as a whole. Planning for the next meeting is part of the business session. Problems encountered are discussed also. How can the group improve its work?

Some current and widely accepted philosophies of education were adapted for the alternative model, such as those taught by Ivan Illich, Freire, Montessori, Piaget and Dewey. Illich emphasizes that individuals have the right to determine their destiny, to educate themselves in the direction they choose. Society has regimented the educational system, encouraged conformity; people have lost their right to creativity, to develop themselves in the way they want to be. Montessori saw that individuals can learn by themselves with the least interference from their teachers. Children are like plants in a garden; they will bloom with beauty whether there is a gardener or not, although the gardener can help the plants to bloom beautifully. Piaget says that we are always ready to learn at some points in our lives, when some maturity or development takes place in our bodies. We must sense that readiness to help individuals venture to new learning experience. The fault of parents and adults is that they frustrate or stamp out the readiness for learning in children; adults insist that children conform with their interests or norms.

The self-directed study module and the self-propelled study group module used in the TEE programme recognize the capacity of individuals to learn by themselves, to learn how to educate themselves, and their right to develop according to their convictions as God has called them to serve in his vineyard. By working in groups, individuals can help each other through socialized activities. Individual differences can contribute to the enrichment of learning through mutual sharing of different views, approaches, tools, and learning.

Education for liberation and development

The second main concern in alternative theological education is to develop leadership for the church's ministry of liberation. The preceding paragraphs demonstrate how individuals can go through the liberating process of becoming creative and self-reliant, becoming aware of and learning to make use of the resources in themselves and in their contexts. Church workers must go through the experience of liberation, experiencing the gifts of their humanity in God's creation. The theme of the TEE programme, as annunciated at the initial stage by an ad hoc committee composed of representatives from the seminary faculty, the UCCP and the UMC was "The Christian Community in Today's World". Its purpose is to gear the workers of the church towards the mission of the church in the world.

Area 1 of the curriculum is called "The Contemporary World". It provides learning experiences to familiarize the students with the conditions of the context in which they work and live. They are provided with tools of research and social analysis to study the world in microcosm, the community, and in macrocosm, the country and the world. They are led to discover the conditions in which people live and the Philippines as a developing country in relation to other countries.

The second curriculum area, "The Christian Tradition", helps them to reflect on the conditions of people in their communities and country, to reflect on the will of God, and to consider what the Christian community can do in bringing about his will. They are led to make use of the resources of our faith, the Bible, the doctrines of the church, the social creeds of the churches, and lessons from history. What can we do as a people to bring out God's will, to liberate people from ignorance, disease, poverty, oppression, exploitation, to lead them to freedom, to fulfilment of their humanity, to be saved from the harshness and bondage of sin?

The third curriculum area, "The Christian Vocation", provides learning experiences for church workers to gain skills and deeper commitment to Christian service, so that, knowing God's will for the world, they may go into action in the world.

The minimum requirement for admission into the degree programme is a high school diploma. Students must be endorsed by their proper church agencies and, whether church workers or lay people, students must serve a local church for the immediate practice required by the studies. Students without a high school diploma may be admitted as certificate students, who do not earn a degree but receive a certificate to qualify them for ministerial membership or ordination. Students without high school diplomas may also be admitted as probationary degree students after passing satisfactorily the first block, and they may be admitted as regular students after the faculty has reviewed its second block studies. Students may complete studies in the bachelor of ministry programme in four years. The programme is composed of six blocks of courses, a block of which may be completed in eight months, with exception of the sixth block, which may be completed in three months.

Curriculum

The curricular programme of the bachelor of ministry degree in the TEE programme is organized into a system of six blocks of courses. Each block is composed of five to seven subjects. Studies in the block are arranged to make the subjects inter-related or integrated. Studies in one subject contribute to the learning of other subjects. One subject may deal with methods or procedures, while another may deal with the content. The preaching course deals with sermon preparation, while doctrine provides the contents of the sermon. Students must complete one block before they can proceed to the next block. They proceed at their own pace, but they try to maintain the pace of the other members of their TEE study group.

Nanking Union Theological Seminary

Theological education in New China

Part I: New beginnings

K.H. TING

Theological education is a subject on which we would particularly like to learn from the experiences of our Asian fellow-Christians. We are only trying to find our way. During the years before the Cultural Revolution we maintained the theological seminary in Nanking, which was and is a union theological seminary. The range of cooperation within the seminary is very wide. We have evangelicals — strong evangelical groups — as well as colleagues from theological seminaries run by many mainline churches. During the years of the Cultural Revolution, this seminary was closed down following an announcement to that effect made by a group of Red Guards. During the early days of the Cultural Revolution the Red Guards came to the seminary to search out what was called the "Four Olds" in those days, and many of the books in our library were burned or taken away. We stopped working. Most of our faculty members had to go to work on a farm near Nanking and some of us were allowed to stay in our homes awaiting the assignment of new work, although this assignment never came. Since the downfall of the Gang of Four, we have again formed ourselves into the Nanking Union Theological Seminary.

• Bishop K. H. Ting is chairman of the Chinese National Christian Three-Self Patriotic Movement Committee, President of the China Christian Council, and Principal of Nanking Union Theological Seminary. His exposition is adapted from the report of the historic CCA consultation with church leaders from China at Hong Kong, 23-26 March 1981, and is used by permission. Raymond Fung is Secretary for Evangelism, Commission on World Mission and Evangelism, WCC, and former Secretary for Mission, Hong Kong Christian Council. His remarks are dated July 1982.

At present we are really two things; we have two existences. In the first place we are a theological seminary of the Protestant churches in China, and at the same time we are also the Centre of Religious Studies at Nanking University. It is very interesting work which we try to do in Nanking University.

As for theological education, the goal we set ourselves is the producing of Chinese people's Christian intellectuals. We in China need intellectuals of all sorts. Among them we need Christian intellectuals. It is a special characteristic of Chinese Protestantism that it has emphasized the work amongst the intellectuals; there has been a large number of intellectual converts to Christianity in the course of the history of Protestantism in China. We need to produce more of these Christian intellectuals. We say these intellectuals have to be Chinese; they need to be concerned with the problems of China. In old China our theological seminary seemed to be interested in problems which China had not raised. The problems dealt with in our classrooms appeared to be problems raised by Christians in other countries.

We also say these intellectuals must be the people's intellectuals. That is, politically and culturally our graduates have to identify themselves with the common people of China. These Christian intellectuals ought to be those who have dedicated themselves to the work of the church and to the work of evangelism in China. They can be pastors and evangelists in local parishes. They can be teachers. They can serve on the staff of Christian organizations — national or provincial. We need writers, translators and artists. We need experts in technology with theological training and teachers with theological training. Since the end of the Cultural Revolution we have a new group of people in academic circles who devote themselves to the study of religions. We hope our theological seminary will produce some of these people too. And of course we need to train more teachers for our theological seminary.

At present, we try to do two things at the same time. One is to elevate the theological level of our membership, and the other is to popularize theological knowledge. We feel that the work of popularization and elevation could go together. For the time being we emphasize popularization more than elevation, but if we take a longer period into consideration, then elevation of the level of theological education will be even more important. As far as popularization is concerned, our seminary is at present producing a syllabus by the correspondence department. This is a booklet published monthly and sent out once in three months. At first we thought a few hundred copies would be sufficient, and that we could do it as a correspondence course. But the need is so great that this little publication now has a circulation of 30,000 copies. So you should not think we can keep up correspondence with 30,000 people in China. This is now really a magazine. We call it a syllabus. It is sent to those "naturally evolved" leaders of Christian groups all over China.

Although we have reopened a number of churches since the end of the Cultural Revolution, the number of Christians worshipping in churches is still smaller than those who worship in homes. These home meetings are under the direction of leaders who are "naturally evolved", who are better qualified and more enthusiastic. Participants find these home gatherings very fulfilling and spiritually uplifting. But because of the lack of leadership, deviations of all kinds could happen, and we hope that through this syllabus the quality and content of these meetings can be improved. We are now able to link ourselves with 30,000 of these non-traditional, "naturally evolved" group leaders.

As to direct theological instruction, we now have for the first time 48 students of Nanking Theological Seminary. They should be of two types. The majority, we thought, should be graduates of senior middle schools and a smaller number university graduates. At present we have not divided the students into two groups, but have put them together at least for the first term. Probably we could differentiate by the end of the term.

Theological curriculum

The subjects of our theological education are more or less the same as those in theological seminaries outside China. I think the content will be found to be different and may well become increasingly so. We think our theological education should be centred on problems that we face as Christians within China. At least two of our colleagues in Nanking who are experts in Chinese church history will probably say that the main problem with some Chinese thinkers was that they were entirely oblivious of the most important reality in China in the 1940s and 1950s — the existence of the people's liberation movement, the movement for national salvation in areas of Kuomintang and the existence of the liberated area under communist leadership in north China and the northwest.

These theological thinkers usually write things without any knowledge of the existence of the most important political and cultural realities. If they were living today, they would probably acknowledge that this was true, and they might tell us they would like that chapter of their writings to be closed. So the study of Chinese church history will result in something quite different, and we hope before very long we can present this history to Christians in Asia for criticism and for comment. I think a large part of the content of our theological education has to be related to the many new currents of thinking in Chinese intellectual circles today. Since the downfall of the Gang of Four many magazines have appeared to which social scientists and philosophers contribute. In our Nanking Theological Seminary we subscribe to 60 or 70 of them. As we turn the pages of these magazines, we find very many articles dealing with subjects that do not seem to interest academic people abroad but which we think are extremely important to Christian witness in China.

Evangelistic approaches
Now, among us Christians there are two approaches to the question of evangelism. There are those who think that the only sharp line to be drawn is between belief and unbelief or between believers and non-believers. On both sides people are more or less the same type. There should be no differentiation among the believers. They form one bloc. The non-believers are also a bloc by themselves. There is no change or difference in view among the non-believers. In other words all in the camp of non-believers, no matter what point of view they hold, are equally distant, and equally unhelpful in our preaching of the gospel of evangelism. Therefore, the inner development within the camp of the materialist is of no interest to us. We say in Chinese: "Within that camp everything is just black." I think when this idea was a ruling force directing us in our work of evangelism, then there was a tremendous amount of blindness and haphazardness in our work of evangelism. Sometimes we succeed, but sometimes we fail, but we would not know why we fail.

There is another kind of thinking about our evangelist task, and that is to realize that there are many different currents of thinking among our intellectuals, and certain developments among the intellectuals would make them entirely non-believers. There are certain developments which are beneficial to the introduction of the gospel or the Christian message. To evangelize is not just to tell people of

Jesus Christ; it also includes our attempt to seek a common ground with certain emphases that have evolved in the intellectual field, to seek a common language, and to make use of certain things which we have in common within the intellectual sphere. The discussion of whether idealism has a certain progressive role to play in history seems to be a very important one from the evangelistic point of view. Our theological students must not be trained as if such a discussion is not going on around them.

We may consider the role of some of the classical philosophers in Western history, like Hegel, Kant, Schiller — how they in their own philosophical manner prepared for the bourgeois revolution in Germany. This has met with affirmation in many articles in Chinese magazines. I think, as evangelists, our theological students and our pastors and theological teachers cannot afford not to pay attention to these developments, especially because religion has always been considered an extreme form of idealism, of objective idealism. To affirm the progressive and political role under certain circumstances of idealism opens the gate, as it were, for the affirmation of the role of Christianity in society. During the Cultural Revolution no difference was made between our philosophical, ideological and theological assumptions on the one hand and the political standpoint on the other. I think it is a healthy development today in China to make a very clear distinction between people's religion and philosophical convictions, which ought to be respected, and their political stance. Many articles have appeared in our newspapers telling readers that such a distinction is important. In religious and philosophical matters we have to respect one another. And in politics, as long as we have a common basis of patriotism, we ought to be united.

Another very important development among Chinese intellectuals today, which we Christian intellectuals cannot afford to ignore, is the description of truth, of goodness, and of beauty. We feel that an atmosphere of cynicism is the worst climate for Christian evangelism. In such an atmosphere you will find no seriousness in your audience. Young people talk about truth, beauty and goodness even though they are far away from the Christian gospel. We have good reason to welcome that discussion. In the past two years, many articles have appeared especially on what is the test of truth. There are two answers. The first is that truth is what Marx said, truth is what Engels said and Lenin said, truth is what Chairman Mao said. This school of thought can be called the "whateverist". This group seems to be less and less popular in intellectual circles in China today. More and more intellectuals still show very high respect for the teachings of Marx, Engels and Chairman Mao. They say it is practice (praxis) which gives validity to the truth — the ultimate test. In other words the "whateverists" are actually advocating the infallibility of these classical Marxist teachings. Those who advocate practice as a test of truth claim a more scientific attitude. Because they want to establish truth from facts.

Another very important subject of discussion is the meaning of life. I know of no other country in the world where the subject of the meaning of life — what is the good life — receives such tremendous attention as in China, although I am ready to be corrected. In just one single magazine in China, called the *Youth of China,* in six months the editorial office received over 60,000 letters discussing the very question of the meaning of life and of what is good. Now I think we as evangelists will find it very difficult to communicate with an audience if it is an audience of cynics who have no interest in what is good. If their only question is, why should I be good, why should I not be selfish, it is very difficult for Christian communication to happen. But today a very large number of young people, workers and educated youth in rural people's communes and students, would like to know what is a good life. The girl who started the whole discussion with a very pessimistic letter was herself very greatly moved by the whole discussion. She received many gifts sent from sympathizers — books and money and other things. She thought it was very important that all the gifts she got should be sent to an orphanage for those boys and girls whose parents were killed in an earthquake near Peking a few years back. So in spite of all her pessimism, I feel she has not lost her conviction about the meaning of life and the place of service to others. And in all this discussion Christians would find a common language with these non-Christians.

I can say more about beauty. There is lot of discussion on beauty. Recently we founded the national association of philosophers of ethics and another association of aesthetics. Recently our newspapers have been advocating five emphases in life: civilized life, good manners, hygienic living, order and morality. Besides these, there are four beauties: spiritual beauty, the beauty in the use of language, beauty in conduct and beauty in our environment. These are not promoted by Christians, but we feel that these emphases provide the Christians with a good environment for Christian communication.

Theological agenda

Our theological education should not be detached from what is happening around us. We can make use of all of these things as a common starting point. There are so many currents of non-Christian thought going on all around us, and our theological education should not be detached from all these. And there is of course a lot of discussion on religion itself, on the religion of Christianity, on the role of religion, on whether religion as an opiate is a sufficient description for religion. We should relate our theological education to these problems. Then there are many problems within our churches. We call ourselves the China Christian Council because the China Christian Council is not a church. They have many problems that we have not solved yet, and we need students to study all of these.

Quite a number of our friends here have discussed with me the question of liberation theology. We do not know very much about liberation theology. We know we are for liberation and we are for theology and we are also for liberating theology from its bondage to Western history, to colonialism, and so on. From what we gather from books on liberation theology we are very sympathetic with its emphasis on the necessity for a change in social systems, with its opposition to reformism, with its criticism of social developmentism, with its stand for liberation and for revolution, and with its relating theology not only to philosophy but even more to social sciences. Of all these we really are very appreciative and sympathetic. Its emphasis that theology should not only be responsible to our church traditions but should have an accountability for the reconstruction of human history — we think that is great. But many of my Christian colleagues would hesitate to say that they themselves are liberation theologians because we somehow feel that we must not relativize the absolute or absolutize the relative. We sympathize with the liberation theologians' support of the poor and concern for material uplift. But we feel that Christian theology must deal first of all with the relationship between human beings and God. That is a much more ultimate question which theology must not shy away from. We in China needed liberation. We do not want to return to our pre-liberation days. Yet we do not think that political liberation is a solution to that much more ultimate problem: the problem between human beings and the ultimate ground on which the whole universe is structured. The question of life in Jesus Christ — that, somehow, we feel that liberation theologians have not dealt with adequately.

New China has definitely produced better men and women, but these better men and better women are not the same as the "new man" St Paul speaks of. St Augustine wrote: "Thou hast put a restlessness in our heart so that we would find no rest until we rest in thee." This restlessness is something that we experience even after our political liberation. As to sympathies for the poor, while we are in agreement with liberation theologians, we from our own experience think that it is not something to absolutize. In post-liberation China we still have poor people. We haven't achieved complete egalitarianism. There are some people who leave the poverty line earlier than the rest. There are people who get a little richer before the others. I think it is the law of social change that if our policy is to identify ourselves always with the poor, to fight against the more wealthy, then society would be chaotic. There can't be any national reconstruction to speak of. The very suffering that we experienced during the days of the Cultural Revolution was due precisely to the doctrine of perpetual revolution of the poor against the wealthy, and that is why we would hesitate to idealize the poor — not to say that the poor can sometimes be exploited by certain deceivers.

As to the many problems which Western theologians seem to be interested in just now, we would only select those that are of immediate interest to us. Homosexuality, we do not seem to be aware of that problem so acutely in China. Feminism, to the extent of changing the language of the Bible and liturgy, we haven't felt that to be a very pressing problem, nor the ordination of women. Our question at present is the question of ordination itself. As to women's ordination, I do not think it is an acute problem with us. Nor is the question of church unity. Our perspective is quite different, and I do not think we are going to use all the Western material. The question of atheism is a very interesting one to many of our colleagues in China because here atheism is a very open and legitimate ideology. We know that atheism is a universal problem but in other societies it is not so noticeable. In the US only six per cent of the population would declare themselves to be non-believers in God. For us to exclude God from the concerns of the world is also to exclude the world from all our religious experiences. In China we would come across atheistic articles quite often in our magazines. You will find many Chinese Christians not so angry with the atheist for various reasons. We hope in our theological seminary in Nanking we can have a special centre of some sort for the scientific and theological study of atheism.

These are some of our thoughts about theological education. We are way behind all our Asian colleagues in theological education. I would be very grateful if those who are theological educators and other church leaders in Christian churches in other countries could enlighten us with their experiences.

Part II : A current report

RAYMOND FUNG

The church in China is young. But its leadership is old. A whole generation went by without the benefit of any theological education, and for almost ten years public worship and Bible reading were effectively banned. Religious fervour, however, did not die. Christians have been meeting wherever and whenever possible. But superstitious and heretical teaching is also widespread. The training of Christians for pastoral work thus has become the foremost priority of the church in China.

Much has been written about the Nanking Theological Seminary which, until now, has been the only institution providing theological training in China. But the picture is fast changing.

With the coming into being of provincial-level Christian councils, the formation of provincial centres of Christian training is rapidly becoming a reality. As of September 1982, a Bible school is scheduled to open in Shenyang, in the north-east. The Associate General Secretary of the China Christian Council described it as a "mid-level" institute. Similar schools are being prepared for opening in Szechuan and Chekiang under provincial auspices. In the former, the site will either be Chungching or Chengtu. The town of Iwu near Hang-chow will probably be chosen to host the Chekiang seminary. It was understood that negotiations among churches and with the authorities will begin soon for similar ventures in the city of Peking and the provinces of Fukien and Honan.

In the process, there will be many problems such as the securing of physical facilities and the installation of faculties which reflect the theological balance of the churches. What will certainly not be problematic is the availability of students. There will be plenty of applicants. Over 1,000 were turned down a year ago by Nanking for lack of places, and many formally untrained church workers have attended the short-term courses which have gone on for some time in many cities throughout China.

This dynamic process is important in the development of theological education in China. It is part and parcel of the growth in number, maturity and unity of the Christian community. The emerging institutions should not be seen as providers of theological training, but as the logical development of what is happening at the grassroots.

The emphasis on the grassroots or the people, as the Chinese put it, can best be seen in the importance Nanking Theological Seminary has been putting on its correspondence course. Of the 32,290 paid subscriptions, 85 per cent go to church workers in rural areas, most of whom are unordained Christians engaging full-time or otherwise in pastoral work in rural churches or "meeting points". Just as some of the most effective public churches are developing into a form of a cluster relationship with nearby "house churches" in terms of sharing pastoral work and resources, Nanking and the new schools seem to be embarking on a similar journey in terms of sharing theological knowledge. The correspondence students meet in local groups where they discuss the study materials and their work in the house churches and newly opened public congregations.

What is being taught and how is it taught? The short-term two-to-three-month residential courses deal with theological basics such as the Apostles' Creed. The correspondence course from Nanking is very largely biblical. The Collection of Sermons, two or three editions per year with 60,000 in circulation, mainly concerns itself with Christian behaviour. The Nanking curriculum carries a large amount of biblical studies. There is an interesting entry called "politics" which actually means "public affairs". From what I can gather, the theological pedagogy of Chinese theological education is one of studying the scriptures in the midst of living in China's reality, trying to find God's will for the church and the Chinese people. I earnestly hope they succeed.

New England TEE

A rural Australian experiment in training church leaders

Australia is a dry continent. In those inland areas where farming is possible, incomes depend heavily on adequate rainfall, and at this time much of the country is just emerging from one to three years of serious drought.

An earlier drought in 1972 had given rise to rural economic recession. One region as hard hit as any was that spanned by the Anglican diocese of Armidale in northeast to north-central New South Wales, Australia's most populous state. The 45,000 square miles of the diocese extend from the state border in the north to the town of Quirindi in the south, from the rugged New England ranges and the tablelands in the east to Walgett and Baradine on the central western plains.

The population is essentially rural and, by world standards, sparse. There are numerous small towns and one or two larger centres, such as Tamworth and Armidale, with between 20,000 and 33,000 inhabitants. Local primary industries include sheep grazing — some of the world's finest merino wool is grown on the western slopes and plains. Farmers also raise cattle, chickens and pigs, and grow various grains. Cotton is the major crop in one area.

Members of the largest Protestant communion, the Anglican Church, are therefore mainly farmers or residents of rurally-oriented

• The writer was formerly TEE coordinator for the Asia Theological Association and later the Secretary for Theological Education in the Theological Commission of the World Evangelical Fellowship and a member of the TEE committee of Armidale diocese, P.O. Box 40, South Tamworth 2340, Australia.

towns. Life in the region is generally comfortable, and the standards of living and education are comparable to those in rural areas of other Western nations. Prolonged drought, however, can bring severe hardship.

In the early seventies, as again more recently, life was difficult for the average family on the land. Farmers began selling out or taking second jobs. Retraining and rural adjustment schemes along with financial aid from the government helped but were never sufficient. Towns heavily dependent on wool or wheat cheques suffered economically too. Young people, prone anyway to leave the country for the attractions of the city, left in still larger numbers, seeking work in metropolitan areas.

Predictably, the church also suffered. More and more small parishes found they could no longer afford the services of a resident minister. Some clergy were already responsible for more congregations than they could adequately handle. In a number of cases the choice was between closing churches or training lay people to carry on between the infrequent visits of ordained clergy.

Within the broad theological spectrum of Anglicanism, it happened that the diocese of Armidale had for some years been predominantly evangelical or "low church" in orientation. Within this framework there had grown a widespread acceptance of the doctrine of the universal priesthood of believers. Many ministers de-emphasized the clergy-lay distinction and encouraged lay participation in numerous aspects of ministry and worship. Not surprisingly, the decision was made to concentrate on training local leaders and to close churches only as a last resort.

A prime mover in lay training in various parts of the diocese had been the Rev. Ray Smith, to whom I am indebted for much assistance in preparing this article. He had used a number of training methods, such as short seminars and correspondence courses, but was looking for something more comprehensive and better suited to the needs that had arisen. Providentially I had returned not long before from some years of study abroad, during which I had learned in the United States about theological education by extension and had visited the Presbyterian programme in Guatemala.

As we conferred, the pieces began to fit together. It seemed that TEE would meet our needs better than other kinds of training we had looked at. Under the capable leadership of Ray Smith and with some help from others, New England TEE was born. We had the blessing of the diocese, but they were in no position to offer us much help at that time. A small sum was contributed, and the plan was to depend, at least for the time being, on voluntary labour and student fees which, because of the situation, could not be high.

Programme

The new programme certainly provided a challenge. Our mandate was to train lay leaders and potential leaders. Although the needs of struggling parishes were very much to the fore, these were not our only concern; all interested churches could benefit. We had no mandate to prepare candidates for ordination.

An ecumenical dimension was included, though not strongly pursued. Persons from other denominations would be welcome to participate, and a number have done so, including at least one clergyman and his wife, who wanted to develop further their preaching skills.

Our main target group includes lay readers and preachers, parish councillors, Sunday school teachers and those who conduct the voluntary religious instruction permitted in state schools, and group facilitators of various kinds.

A tentative curriculum was drawn up and courses were prepared as personnel and funding allowed. Our small staff used spare time for the project, and we were all heavily committed elsewhere. No salaries were paid, and only out-of-pocket expenses were covered. It was remarkable and encouraging to see how much was accomplished under these conditions.

Today we still have no full-time worker, although Ray Smith is currently diocesan Director of Christian Education and devotes a high proportion of his time to TEE. We also have some part-time paid office assistance. Otherwise, course writers and tutors receive only expenses.

New England TEE is responsible to the Diocesan Board of Christian Education through the Director, who in practice makes most of the day-to-day decisions. Unlike many extension programmes, we have no central theological college to use as a headquarters. We work from an office in a church school in Tamworth, and this houses our offset press, stock and workers.

The nascent programme commenced with felt-needs. The courses we wrote first were those practical ones that parishes requested, such as homiletics and Christian education of children. New courses were added at the rate of one or two a year, and include biblical and theological subjects classified as core courses and various practical electives. Today Bible surveys such as Old and New Testament and a hermeneutics course are among the most popular. A short course in counselling and mutual ministry has created much interest outside as well as within the diocese, and such subjects as local church principles, Christian beliefs, and study on sharing one's faith have continued to be popular. A number of important courses remain to be written.

New England TEE has chosen to use the workbook format rather than programmed instruction. Our courses are frequently geared to textbooks.

General policy has been to open centres only when requested to do so, to offer those courses parishes want, so far as possible, and to ensure that participation at all levels is entirely voluntary. We have seen elsewhere the problems which can result when some are "conscripted" as writers, tutors, or students!

Initially, after parishes had been informed of the new project, we introduced subjects by conducting a short, self-contained seminar, usually on a Saturday afternoon, in centres that had expressed interest. A little of the subject matter was presented along with extension methodology. The idea was to whet appetites, and also to make sure folk were aware of the time and work involved. Numbers were not our main goal; we wanted serious students who would not pull out after a few lessons because they had not realized how much work was involved.

The number of people who enroll varies from centre to centre. Eighty enrolled in the Christian education course in Tamworth, but more usual numbers range from 3 or 4 to 30. We have currently about 12 centres in the diocese, some of which are classed as key centres and which offer courses more regularly than others. Only one subject is offered in a centre at a time and usually the maximum is two per year. Each course lasts 10 to 12 weeks, since we have found this best for interest retention.

We have not worked according to strict dates or terms, preferring to adjust to local seasons and needs. This flexibility helps account for the good interest shown; several hundred students in all have studied with us, and in 1981 the enrolments were just over 200, of whom six were isolated students studying by correspondence. The vast diocese of Northwest Australia has also begun using our courses in the outback situation, and it now has over 100 students in several parishes. Other dioceses have shown interest in our materials, as have other denominations, and books are sold to interested parties. The Anglican Church Army College in Sydney sends all its second year students each year to our TEE tutors' training workshop, and at times we conduct similar workshops for other groups on request.

We learned quite early that the bigger towns are not necessarily the most responsive to extension training; there may be too many competing activities, Christian and secular. Some of our best centres have been tiny hamlets with keen, warm-hearted parishioners delighted that the programme extends to where they live.

Academics are not stressd in our programme, and progressive assessment is used instead of examinations. All subjects, however, are offered at two levels, ordinary and advanced, and students are free to choose their preferred level in each subject. The overall level is roughly equivalent to high school standard.

A small certificate is issued on completion of each subject, and two more comprehensive awards are offered at present, the preliminary certificate of ministry and the certificate of ministry. These awards do not, however, generate much interest. Various factors account for this. We are not always able to offer the needed subjects frequently enough in each centre, and the awards are not recognized beyond the diocese. Nor is their attainment required at present for any specific church office or function, a condition which, if introduced, would probably encourage more students to complete them.

Our students seem to be more interested in learning and applying what is learned than in receiving paper awards, an attitude that we have encouraged by emphasizing the setting and fulfilment of the student's own learning and ministry goals. In this spirit, we do not regard as a "drop-out" someone who chooses to take only one or two subjects and completes these successfully. The whole atmosphere of our programme is considerably more relaxed than that of many extension programmes in other places. This is in part due to different goals.

Initially, most seminars were led by two of us, and this involved considerable travel by car, bus, train and light aircraft. Since more tutors have been trained, many of them local clergy, most seminars are now led locally, and less travel and cost are involved. Many rectors have found leading an extension class a rewarding experience which has added depth to their teaching ministry. Larger groups sometimes need team teaching. Localization ensures greater relevance but may occasion some loss of the interest which a visiting tutor can generate. Thus it helps to arrange where possible the visit of the Director or another person at the beginning or end of a course. This also helps learners feel they are part of a wider study body.

Extension programmes that need to cover vast distances may profit from our handling of this problem in the early years. It was impossible for a tiny travelling faculty to visit distant centres more often than once a month, yet we felt students needed to meet at least fortnightly. We developed a system of major and minor seminars. Major seminars involved visits from the tutor, while minor seminars, between our visits, were led by the local rector or some other person. In the minor seminars, students met for discussion, prayer, and mutual encouragement. Often they used "canned seminars" we had left with them — cassettes, filmstrips, activities, instructions for a field trip, discussion questions and the like. Those who led these "in-between" sessions often went on to become full tutors in the programme.

In addition, students were actively encouraged to meet together on their own in small local groups for mutual help and learning whenever they wished. Thus there was considerably more interaction at the local level than would have been possible if we had relied solely on the monthly visits.

Evaluation

The introduction of TEE to the Armidale diocese has undoubtedly made a substantial contribution to the quality of parish life and ministry. Of course there have been problems, some administrative, some deeper in nature. An enumeration of some of the administrative difficulties may assist others:

1. Despite planning, our programme often grew "like Topsy". Its flexibility is both its strength and its weakness, and we have not always been able to offer sufficient courses in sufficient centres when the need was there.

2. It has not been easy to procure the amount of clergy involvement needed, nor sufficient cooperation from theologically-educated lay people. While many of these people serve as tutors, we still have too few, as well as too few course designers and other helpers and advisers. As a result the Director is overworked.

3. Costs remain a problem. Our printing operation loses money each year, though the loss is diminishing. We have tried to keep student fees low (about US$11 per course) but may have to raise them.

4. It is remarkable how many textbooks to which we have fitted workbooks go out of print soon after the course is launched! Nor is it always easy to find suitable substitutes, since books for our needs must be midway between heavy theological tomes and "pop".

5. Tutor training is a continuing need. Workshops are held regularly, but we still have too many tutors who have not attended. Much less have we provided adequate in-service training for them. We have found that theological qualifications do not guarantee a good tutor, especially in our programme, which stresses much more imaginative seminars than are usual in extension. We have had cases where the seminar was tacked onto a mid-week prayer meeting for whoever happened to be there, or where student assignments were not returned for months.

6. If training tutors is difficult, recruiting and training course designers is more so. We have had some good writers but too many courses remain unwritten. Again, training for these people is essential; knowledge of the subject matter is not sufficient. Writers must understand the extension concept and the educational aspects of the self-instructional text. We have had sad instances where whole courses, adequate in content, have needed rewriting for educational and methodological reasons. Others, quite good, are being rewritten as we learn from experience or find we need to update them.

The only answer to these problems appears to be to insist on training sessions for all writers and teachers. We would strongly advise others to do this from the outset and to make no exceptions.

At another level, we face these problems:

1. Although most courses have been well received, there have been some centres which, for reasons of churchmanship or on local or personal grounds, have chosen not to enter the programme at all. This may mean considerable loss to people in those parishes who would like to study. In other situations courses have not gone particularly well for a variety of reasons. We probably cannot expect that we will ever gain 100 per cent acceptance, but more work needs to be done.

2. The curriculum, still not all translated into written courses, remains somewhat inadequate. Some years ago an innovative curriculum was designed on the basis of what lay leaders needed to be able to do. It moved beyond the usual course areas into family, com-

munity, and world concerns. Perhaps it was idealistic, and admittedly it did not draw so much as it should have upon the opinions of lay leaders themselves, but it had good potential. Somehow, over the years, this curriculum has been modified until (with some exceptions) it looks fairly like more traditional programmes, which is not necessarily a bad thing.

But some important elements still seem to be lacking. It may be that these will be covered when subsequent courses are written; after all, it is the content, rather than the names of subjects, that counts. We lack, for example, sufficient "open" elements, allowing student choice in the matter and direction of learning. Admittedly this is not easy to structure, but it is essential if we wish to avoid a domesticating approach to learning.

We also appear to have developed, in common with many theological institutions, a curriculum more inward- than outward-looking. Students are rightly prepared for many ministries in the church; this was after all the prime objective. But an effective church leader also needs to be, and to help others be, light and salt in the community, attuned to wider Christian perspectives. Although our courses on the world church and its mission and Christian social ethics have yet to be written, it worries me that to date, after almost a decade, we have had little to say about the Christian family, little about our place in the wider church and the responsibility this brings, and little about pressing social issues such as education, the environment, work and leisure, unemployment, trade unionism, the arms race, or the needs of refugees, the disabled, and other ethnic and disadvantaged groups in our midst. Nor, for that matter, have we said very much about prayer, faith, and the handling of our own doubts, depression and loss, and other concerns of the personal spiritual life.

It is not possible to do everything, and balance in these matters is always difficult to attain. But we must help our students to look inward and then outward, identifying Christian principles, perhaps the hardest task, and applying them in the real world as well as in the church.

Successes

Despite our share of problems, the extension programme overall has been — and we believe will continue to be — a success. Some of our particular achievements, with God's help and that of many keen people, have perhaps been these:

1. New England TEE has pioneered a type of rural leadership training unique in this country and probably markedly different from most programmes of the extension type in other Western countries. We have maintained reasonable standards, but we have not overemphasized academic achievement in a situation which does not call for it. We have added to the usual subjects a number of practical studies in ministry. We have burdened students with fewer hours of study per week than is common in TEE programmes and have taken a flexible and relaxed attitude to the studies. Students have been encouraged to work at their own pace for their own goals rather than ours. Local seasons — school holidays, harvest, shearing, etc. — have been taken into account in scheduling courses. Attention has been given to small as well as large centres, in the true spirit of TEE. And overall, the response to this type of programme has been excellent.

2. We have developed seminars that allow for a good deal more variety and activity in learning than those of some widespread models of extension. Like most, we put great stress on discussion and allow time for testing, questions and a devotional. But activities have been diversified for learning and enrichment. Except on rare occasions lecturing is not used. Great use is made, especially in the ministry subjects, of practical exercises, and all courses include such learning experiences as case studies, role plays, simulation games, planned excursions, drama, music, filmstrips, cassettes and slides. Tutors are trained to exercise creativity and to encourage this in students. Not only do we provide a tutors' handbook of a general kind for the entire programme; we are also working on producing a tutors' guide for each subject, giving specific suggestions for the enrichment of learning in each seminar, as well as information about assignments, grading and so on. This task is not yet complete.

Much of the excitement in learning has come from these activities. I am reminded of a Sunday school teacher who was delighted to learn how to make a gelatine pad for the homespun duplication of exercises for her class. After the TEE seminar she went home and spent some time at her stove, then phoned another student and exclaimed "It works! It works!" In the same centre, a retired headmistress brought a group of children to a seminar and demonstrated the use of spontaneous drama. As the three young men walked fearlessly around in the fiery furnace, and Daniel languished in the lion's den, it seemed that every teacher wanted to try the same ideas next week.

3. We have succeeded, in an inflationary economy, in keeping our costs to a minimum and making good use of voluntary help.

4. The feared débacle of small parishes did not happen, and perhaps TEE can take its place alongside other factors in accounting for this. Certainly, in these difficult times it has helped many country parishioners gain new knowledge and enthusiasm, encouraging them to learn more about their faith, keep their churches functioning, and spread their wings in new forms of ministry. TEE study groups have sometimes led to personal and communal renewal. It has been exciting to see persons not particularly interested in theology, ministry, or the scriptures gradually come alive with new-found enthusiasm.

Europe

International Correspondence Institute
From all nations to all nations

JOHN F. CARTER

The International Correspondence Institute (ICI) is a home study and extension education school with national offices in over one hundred countries. Its purposes include evangelism, Christian growth, and ministerial preparation.

In 1967 Dr George M. Flattery, who had completed much of his own education on the mission field by correspondence, presented to the Division of Foreign Missions of the Assemblies of God a proposal to establish an international school offering study programmes by correspondence and extension. This proposal was accepted, and operations were begun that year in Springfield, Missouri. After several years of planning and fund-raising for the establishment of an international office, ICI was moved to Brussels, Belgium, in 1973 to begin full-scale foreign operation. Presently, the Brussels office is staffed by 20-30 career missionary personnel and 40-60 short-term volunteers who typically serve 1-2 years before returning to the United States. National offices are directed by Assemblies of God missionaries or cooperating national church personnel.

Funding for the programme comes from a variety of sources including denominational support, direct mail fund-raising and sales and tuition revenue. National directors raise funds for their own ministries and all missionary personnel for their personal support.

The Brussels operation is responsible for course development and administration of the international outreach of the school. Printing

• The writer is Dean of the College, International Correspondence Institute, Chaussée de Waterloo 45, 1640 Rhode-Saint-Genese, Brussels, Belgium.

and distribution are handled jointly by Brussels and a branch office in the United States. In a sense, ICI is both a school and a publishing house, although it is the school function which dominates decision-making and is viewed as the primary ministry of ICI. In keeping with this the ICI educational system and accompanying course materials are offered for use to other institutions only through formal educational agreements. This is necessary to protect the academic integrity of the programme.

ICI is accredited in the United States by the Accrediting Commission of the National Home Study Council (NHSC), which is a member of the Council on Post-Secondary Education (COPA). ICI also holds membership in the European Home Study Council (EHSC) and the International Council for Correspondence Education (ICCE). These affiliations have been useful in maintaining an awareness of ongoing developments in the theory and practice of non-traditional forms of education.

The curriculum
Evangelism and Christian education

The Evangelism and Christian Education Division offers correspondence and extension education programmes for general evangelism, Christian growth and lay-worker training.

Yearly, over half a million students are enrolled in ICI evangelism courses. Generally these courses provide instruction on a simple gospel presentation with a view towards conversion. Several of these courses have been translated into approximately 40 languages.

Students are contacted in a variety of ways including mass media advertising, street distribution and referral by other students. Most students complete their study through correspondence, but small group meetings are also common. Recently, we have developed audio cassette versions of our evangelism courses specifically for small-group ministries and use with illiterate people.

At the next level is the Christian life programme, which provides a basic 18-course sequence for new and maturing Christians in six subject areas: Bible, doctrine, ethics, the church, service, and spiritual life. The curriculum is divided into three six-course units, and a certificate is awarded for the completion of each course and unit. This series was completed in the spring of 1981. Table 1 shows the titles in this series.

TABLE 1: THE CHRISTIAN LIFE PROGRAMME

Unit I	*Unit II*	*Unit III*
Your new life	God's design, your choice	How to study the Bible
Your Bible	Study guide: John	What churches do
Your helpful friend	Who Jesus is	Bible ethics
When you pray	Christian worship	Christian workers
We believe	Personal evangelism	The Christian and his community
The church	Marriage and the home	The teaching ministry

The Christian Service Programme offers an 18-course sequence intended to train Christian lay leaders for local church ministries. Unit divisions and subject areas covered are the same as for the Christian Life Programme, but each course covers approximately four times more material, and the entire series is specifically oriented towards preparation for service. Ten of the 18 courses were in print by the end of 1981 with the remainder projected for completion during 1982. Titles in this series are shown in Table 2.

TABLE 2: THE CHRISTIAN SERVICE PROGRAMME

Unit I	*Unit II*	*Unit III*
Christian maturity	Prayer and worship	The responsible Christian
The kingdom, the power and the glory (NT survey)	Tents, temples and palaces (OT survey)	Understanding the Bible
Cornerstones of truth	Alive in Christ	Counsellor, teacher and guide
The Christian church in ministry	Starting new churches	Communicating Christian values
Spiritual gifts	Preaching and teaching	Sharing the good news
Solving life's problems	People, tasks and goals	Abundant living

ICI College

The ICI College projects a four-year Bachelor of Arts degree programme with concentrations in Bible, theology, missions, religious education and church administration. A total of 90 two and three credit-hour courses are included. Approximately 40 of these are currently available.

In addition to the Bachelor of Arts degree awarded after four years or 128 credit hours of study, a student may earn a 64 credit-hour Associate of Arts degree or a 96 credit-hour Advanced Diploma. There is also a series of 14-17 credit-hour certificate programmes for students with more limited or specific educational goals. Students completing requirements for any of the shorter programmes may transfer credits to the BA degree programme.

For students whose previous academic experience has not fully prepared them for degree-level study, ICI is developing a less demanding curriculum called the Christian ministry programme. This programme offers a diploma in Christian ministry following the equivalent of three years of study. This would equate to approximately 48 degree credit-hours.

ICI degree courses include a study guide which leads students through a standard text for the subject. The study guide presents a discussion and elaboration of the subject in a similar way to that given in a classroom lecture. In addition, study questions with feedback lead the student to interact with the material. In most instances our college writers are subject matter specialists at the doctoral level. Writers have come from Egypt, Great Britain, Japan, Holland, India, Indonesia and the United States.

Context and goals

The motto of ICI is "From all nations to all nations". It is intended to capture the fact that ICI's ministries both operate internationally and draw upon international expertise in furthering their fulfilment. Unlike theological extension programmes which operate within a particular national or cultural context, therefore, ICI must approach its educational goals from a more general and perhaps eclectic position. Our central question is not "What is best *here?*" but "What is best *in general?*" While such a strategy sacrifices the ideal for any particular cultural context, it does provide for an efficient allocation of limited expertise towards the goal of benefiting the greatest possible number of individuals. Hence, a foundational assumption for ICI is that it is possible to construct a biblically-based curriculum for intercultural use which provides to a substantial degree the requisite intellectual, spiritual and practical bases for productive Christian living and ministry.

The general objectives of the ICI curriculum are as follows:
— to equip students with basic study, thought, and communication skills;
— to lead students to an understanding of people and nature, including both their own culture and the culture of others;
— to help students know the Christian message, be able to communicate and defend it, and to prepare them for the continuing study of it;
— to lead the students to an understanding of the church and its ministries;
— to train students vocationally for the particular ministries to which they are called;
— to prepare students for leadership;
— to provide students with means for personal spiritual growth and development *(International Correspondence Institute College Catalog, 1981-83).*

These goals along with the general curriculum rationale of ICI were developed following an extensive period of consultation with educators involved in overseas ministry. From information derived from these and other sources a curriculum plan was developed which rested on the following statement of student needs (Flattery, 1979):

— *Content needs:* The Bible is our chief text. Our biblical worldview affects everything else. Other content is included as well. Some of this has to do with basic skills and other disciplines. With regard to other disciplines, we feel it important to integrate into the study a definite biblical perspective.
— *Maturation needs:* Our students have spiritual needs. We feel these needs should be met with the materials. Also included are student needs such as basic skills, awareness of their culture, and so on. Growth in the image of Christ is paramount.
— *Ministry needs:* Every Christian should be involved in ministry or service to the Lord, to the church, and to the world. Thus, the curriculum should include assistance for the various types of ministry. This is true of new Christians as well as for those who are more mature.

It is from these general goals and assumptions that we have developed our approach to theological education. The programmes are designed according to a distance learning (or correspondence) model because educational systems adequate for this form of independent learning can easily be adapted to other kinds of extension or residential education approaches. It is exactly this flexibility which has promoted the growth of ICI's programmes around the world.

Educational philosophy and methods

Already mentioned is the foundational assumption that ICI courses should be intercultural or cross-cultural in nature. Anderson, Walker and Barnard (1975) have described the process whereby this is achieved in the following way:

— Select writers who have a sensitivity to a cross-cultural approach or who are willing to work with others who have. In this respect, the ICI motto, "From all nations to all nations" is implemented by having writers from many nations participate on the curriculum development team in writing the courses. So far writers from 16 nations have shared in the development of the courses. They come from such diverse nations as Japan, Indonesia, Yugoslavia, Tanzania, Brazil, the UK, the USA and Egypt.
— Select and train instructional development specialists who have had extensive cross-cultural experience.
— Use a multicultural instructional development approach. This is done by recognizing and accommodating the course treatment to psychological, ethnic, religious, and motivational factors.

This process has yet to produce a perfect course for cross-cultural use (we remain hopeful) but it does produce a fair approximation for most subject areas. Obviously, our success will tend to vary with the degree to which courses are oriented towards practice. It is easier to devise an intercultural course on soteriology than one on organizing a church school programme. Consequently, when practical areas of ministry are taught, we tend to emphasize general principles and generic models rather than to prescribe specific approaches. Where courses are taught in classroom or seminar settings, of course, there is the opportunity for a teacher to suggest adaptations to the local situation.

Our educational philosophy probably manifests itself most fully in the way we design our instructional materials and the educational system in which they are used. While generally subscribing to the notion that to be effective instruction should be carefully planned and structured towards explicit goals, we recognize that it is also important to provide materials which can be used in a flexible manner. Thus, we have rejected a narrowly conceived "programmed" format in favour of a more eclectic approach which draws heavily from the cognitive movement in education (Wittrock, 1979). Stated instructional goals are as often in the affective, spiritual, and life skill areas as in the cognitive, and we expressly accept that not every worthwhile educational goal can be tested within the narrow confines of what we normally define as a "course". Nevertheless, we believe that it is important to state these as aspirations for the student so we do not lose sight in our course development process of the more general and, perhaps, important outcomes of a theological education.

A second major element of our educational philosophy is a commitment to a mastery approach to the educational process. This means that we are concerned with helping the greatest possible number of students demonstrate mastery of our subject matter and are willing to provide a high degree of instructional support for this goal. The particular strategies used to achieve this include the following:

— *Frequent oportunities for student self-evaluation and practice:* Every ICI study guide contains 2-3 times the number of test-like experiences that would normally be found in a traditional educational approach. These appear in the form of study questions, lesson self-tests, and unit tests. Each is designed to provide meaningful interaction with course material so that students are fully prepared for the summative course evaluation (i.e. the final exam).

— *The opportunity to repeat summative (final) examinations:* Students who fail to pass final exams are allowed to retake them following completion of remedial study activities.

— *Self-pacing of study:* Students can establish their own study and course completion schedule. Our college courses are designed to require an average of 48 study hours per credit unit. In actuality this varies as a function of student ability. But students have up to a year to complete course work according to their own interest and desire. We feel this is an essential kind of flexibility which must be afforded to a student body where over 90 per cent are engaged in active ministerial roles.

— *Concern for readability:* Many of our students have not had the academic preparation normally required for college-level study. Others are studying in a second language. Consequently, we take great pains to restrict the reading ability requirements of our courses. The emphasis is placed on short, active sentences and familiar words. Glossaries accompany each course where new or less frequent terms are used.

— *Concretizing of course content:* Wherever possible concrete examples and illustrations are used. Learning research clearly shows that concrete concepts, principles and information are more easily learned than abstract ones. But much that must be learned in any educational endeavour is abstract rather than concrete — and this is especially true of theological education. Even abstract material, however, is made more learnable when it can be represented in concrete forms such as verbal examples and analogies, and visual representations. To an increasing degree we are attempting to develop sequences of instructional art for our materials. That is, art which is intended to facilitate learning rather than to serve a primarily aesthetic purpose.

As mentioned above, overall administration of the school is handled by the International Office in Brussels. But the ICI national director is responsible for local administration and programme development. All recruitment, enrolment and local study supervision is handled at this level. Only for the college programme does the International Office have a direct role to play with regard to student programmes, and this largely relates to maintaining transcripts and correcting final examinations. Otherwise, it is the national ICI director who fills the role of an on-site "instructor." This role includes grading unit evaluations, setting up seminars, and monitoring and encouraging student progress.

Results

What are the outcomes which measure the success of a programme such as ICI, or of any TEE or TEE-like endeavour for that matter? Certainly there are numerous candidates — from "throughput" statistics, such as number of enrolments and graduates, to subjective indicators, such as student testimonies, relationships with residence schools, acceptance by national church organizations, etc. Moreover, what constitutes the criteria by which any of these measures can be evaluated meaningfully? These are questions which should be answered before engaging in any analysis of results. Lacking that, it is difficult to compare what "is" with what "should be". Nevertheless, having issued the caveat let me proceed to describe the results of the ICI programmes as they have unfolded thus far.

The two ICI programmes which have been in operation for a sufficiently long time to yield meaningful results are the two at the extreme ends of our curriculum: the evangelism and college programmes. It would be premature to report on the Christian life or Christian service programmes since one has only recently been completed and the other is still under development.

The ICI evangelism programme has operated since 1967, when the first course called *The Great Questions of Life* was printed. Since that time over 7,000,000 first lessons of this course and another called *Highlights in the Life of Christ* have been distributed. About half of those receiving a lesson have "enrolled" by returning the lesson and requesting subsequent ones. Conservatively, about 300,000 students have completed the course, and most of these have registered a testimony of conversion.

Generally, missionaries and others who use ICI evangelism courses in correspondence and extension ministries have described the curriculum as being extremely effective. Some ICI national offices report cumulative enrolments numbering several hundred thousand. This has been an especially effective way of inserting a Christian witness into otherwise "closed" situations, such as prisons, remote areas of a country, and countries not open to direct missionary witness. In many places the office is more limited by its ability to service requests for the materials than by a lack of response.

The ICI college enrolled its first students in 1973. Since then over 5,000 have enrolled in one or more courses, and currently new enrolments average approximately 100 per month. Students come from a hundred different countries, but a preponderance are European or African. A major limitation is that, at present, most college materials are available only in English. Nevertheless, the programme is growing at an increasingly rapid rate and could become the primary means for training national pastors for the Assemblies of God in the future. Although ICI materials have been designed expressly for correspondence study, we probably have as many or more students studying in classroom and extension-type programmes as study independently. These variations are generally determined by local needs and circumstances and are under the direction and subject to the initiative of ICI national directors. In Holland and Nigeria ICI students gather periodically for seminars related to courses in which they are enrolled. These are probably the best examples we have of programmes closely following a normal TEE model.

In addition, we have begun to work with residence Bible schools under a cooperative agreement through which ICI courses are taught in the school and credit is recorded by ICI. Students may receive a degree from the cooperating institution, a degree from ICI, or a joint degree. In some situations this is the only way students can earn an accredited theological degree in their country. At the least, it allows residence schools to expand their offerings or compensate for a lack of qualified faculty in various subject areas. Several residence school programmes have been set up using ICI courses exclusively in a learning lab approach. In this situation an instructor is present to give assistance, but otherwise students study independently.

In general, we are pleased with the development of the programme thus far, and confident that it is meeting a manifest need for theological education in many parts of the world. At the same time there is pressure to do more — "faster". Some of this has been satisfied by recent strides in curriculum completion, and though there is much left to do we now have a "critical mass" of curriculum offerings which should allow aggressive programme development at the national and local levels.

The biggest unfinished (indeed, barely started) task for ICI is in translation. A concerted effort is underway to translate the Christian life and Christian service materials into major languages such as Spanish, French and Portuguese. But much of the work of translation for local languages will depend on national directors. Moreover, at the college level each project involves translation of both study guides and textbooks. Needless to say, both the work load and the costs for such an undertaking are astronomical! In fact, in many cases it will make better sense to teach students English than to translate the full college curriculum. Because the other levels of the ICI curriculum do not make use of textbooks, it will be somewhat easier and less costly to complete these translation projects, but still no small task. It remains to be seen how quickly all of this can be accomplished, but a 20-year time period would not be unreasonable.

I believe it would be fair to say that while ICI has accomplished much, it has even more which remains to be accomplished. We trust that with God's help we will be able to continue to make progress in that direction.

REFERENCES

Anderson, N., Walker, L. and Barnard, J., *ICI Study Guide Development,* Brussels, International Correspondence Institute, 1975.

Flattery, G.M., *Curriculum Rationale,* Brussels, International Correspondence Institute, 1979.

International Correspondence Institute College Catalog, 1981-83, Brussels, International Correspondence Institute, 1981.

Wittrock, M.C., The Cognitive Movement in Education, *Educational Researcher,* 1979, 8, 5-11.

Northern Ordination Course (UK)

Alternative training
for Anglican ministries

M. A. H. MELINSKY

The traditional pattern of ordination training for the Church of England and for other English denominations has been the residential theological college. Most Anglican colleges date from the mid-nineteenth century and were built near cathedrals or universities. Before that time little formal ministerial training was thought necessary for a clergyman: a degree from Oxford or Cambridge and the status of a gentleman sufficed. The theological college was a cross between a boarding school and a monastery, but since today half the ordinands for the Church of England are married men, this model is not entirely appropriate.

The recognition that older ordinands had wives and families, for whom an uprooting and transplanting for two years could be damaging, was a principal factor behind the formation 20 years ago of the Southwark Ordination Course to serve the area of London and some of southeast England. In 1970 four dioceses in northwest England (Blackburn, Chester, Liverpool and Manchester) cooperated to form the Northwest Ordination Course, which subsequently expanded into Yorkshire and in 1980 changed its name to the Northern Ordination Course (NOC).

In recent years twelve other courses have come into being, so that it is now possible for people living in most parts of England to train

• Canon M. A. H. Melinsky was Chief Secretary of the Advisory Council for the Church's Ministry of the Church of England for five years before becoming in 1978 the Principal of the Northern Ordination Course, 75 Framingham Road, Brooklands, Sale, Cheshire M33 3RH, UK.

for the ministry without attending a residential college. It is not correct to call these courses "non-residential", because in fact they have periods of residence built into their programmes. The Northern Ordination Course requires residence for nine weekends a year and an eight-day summer school each year for three years, which imparts a strong sense of fellowship to its 60 students. Each one of these courses is different in its constitution and manner of working. What follows is a description of one, the NOC, though the essentials are shared by all.

All the students are recommended by their official selection body. That means that their fees are for the most part paid by the sponsoring denomination. The fees for 1981-82 are £1050 per year. The normal intake is about 20 new students a year, but the demand for places in 1981 was such that it was necessary to ask some students to wait a year. Of the 60 present students seven are women training to be either deaconesses or accredited lay workers, and one man is a Baptist; in 1981-82 we expect to have one Methodist and one United Reformed Church student. The rest are Anglicans. The term "Anglican", however, covers a wide variety of traditions, and the NOC contains the whole range from Anglo-Catholic to Anglo-Baptist, and in that respect it differs from the colleges, most of which are partisan.

The pattern of training is based upon residential periods which take place in Manchester, mostly at the Northern Baptist College, and week-night classes which take place in Liverpool, Manchester and Leeds. Students travel to their nearest centre, and travelling time may be anything up to an hour. The staff travel to the three centres and do the bulk of the teaching themselves because they see the teaching and the pastoral care of the students as closely linked. In that respect the course is different from, say, a university. There a teacher may lecture and then have no pastoral responsibility for what that lecture does to a student's faith. Since our teaching is for ministry, we are vitally concerned about what our teaching does to the faith of our students and what it is likely to do to those for whom our students will become ministerially responsible.

Our staff numbers three full-time (all ordained) and four part-time, including two parish priests, one in the inner-city and one in the country; another, the wife of a parish priest, is herself a Hebrew and Old Testament scholar; and one is a Methodist minister and college lecturer. From time to time the course welcomes distinguished speakers on a wide variety of subjects. The staff travel widely, not least to visit students in their homes and places of work, and in that respect also the course differs from colleges.

NOC trains candidates for both stipendiary and non-stipendiary ministry. It does not subscribe to the popular misapprehension that non-stipendiary ministry is somehow easier and less demanding. On the contrary, to carry out ministry while remaining in secular work and also caring for a family is an extremely demanding business, calling for the highest possible personal qualities and training in no way inferior to that for stipendiaries. Our students divide fairly evenly between these two forms of ministry, with slightly more becoming non-stipendiary. Some of these are teachers, an area where non-stipendiary ministry has a long and honourable history. Sometimes a student will change mid-course — either way. One student who lectured in a polytechnic institute had thought of himself as becoming a parish priest, until his employers made a strong request that he stay on as a teacher there and be a "worker-priest", though not a chaplain. After much thought and discussion, he felt that that was the direction of his vocation, and that is where he is.

From what sort of occupations do our students come? A recent group included a theatrical agent, a psychiatric social worker, a sub-postmaster, a farm worker, a county assistant director of finance in local government, an engineering sales administrator, a university lecturer in sociology, a metallurgist, a welder, a housewife, a structural engineer, and a headmaster. Most students are between 30 and 45 years of age.

Until recently the course owned no property at all. It hires what accommodation it needs and is extremely fortunate with the premises it uses. It has had to buy a staff house for its chaplain, however, and may have to buy another. The money is being found by the nine sponsoring dioceses. The principal lives in a rented house, and the other full-time staff member has chosen to buy his own and receives a housing allowance. The staff are paid according to the Lichfield scale for theological teachers which is laid down by the Advisory Council for the Church's Ministry.

The course actually costs just over one-third of comparable training at a residential college, and at a time of financial stringency this fact has not gone unnoticed. But, finance apart, we would claim that the training offered by this kind of course is theologically and educationally preferable to the traditional sort. In the first place, all our men and women are mature people of proven leadership in the local church community and, after all, the word *presbyteros* does imply some maturity. Many of them also hold positions of considerable responsibility in the secular world. In the second place, when students come to an evening class straight from their daily work and settle down to look carefully at the Bible or doctrine or ethics or worship or pastoral care, the likelihood is greater that sparks will jump between theology and real life. In the third place, there is much to be said for students having to study and learn in the sort of circumstances in which they will have to continue their ministry, without leisured hours in quiet places and the support of a disciplined community.

For the task of ministerial formation the course would put spirituality as its first priority, that is to say, helping each student to deepen his or her awareness of God, with the resources of a long tradition. It does not imply a pattern into which everyone is to be moulded; on the contrary, it is emphasized that no one pattern can fit a wide range of personalities. But each student is helped to find his or her own way. Each student is expected to maintain a reading of spiritual classics alongside the reading for other subjects and is urged to find a "soul-friend" outside the course with whom he can share his deepest insights and problems. Every student takes part in two weekend retreats during the three years, where the day begins and ends with formal acts of worship using both traditional and modern orders of service, and each Sunday morning in residence is given over to a devotional exercise of a wide variety of forms using talks, silence, drama, poetry, music and the visual arts.

Students do not just *attend* the course; they are members of a committed community, and the strength of the community spirit surprises visitors, in view of the fact that the whole course does not meet together very often.

Relationships made during the course are basic material for ministerial growth and formation, and as much openness as possible is encouraged. Staff, for example, do not enjoy a common-room of their own in the college; they walk and sit and talk among the students, or retire to a local hostelry with them for a pint of beer. It has now become a tradition that all new students are visited by second-year students before they start, so that they know at least one familiar face when they first arrive. The course embraces a rich variety of traditions not only within but also outside Anglicanism. During the first year many students are perplexed and dismayed to find what the Church of England actually is, but gradually they discern hidden treasures in others' traditions so that "catholic" students begin to value more highly the role of scripture and preaching in the Christian tradition while "evangelicals" grow in their regard for the support of the sacramental life. Matters of authority concerning Bible and church have a similar diversity of understanding, but students are encouraged to hold on to a threefold cord of scripture, tradition and reason, a combination not always easy to maintain.

The course demands a rigorous standard in academic performance. Its syllabus is fairly traditional: Old Testament, New Testament, church history, doctrine, ethics, worship, and practical pastoral studies, but the programme is so arranged that these are not taken in isolated blocks. They are interwoven so that connections may more readily be made between them. There are no examinations; assessment is continuous. Each student has to write a six-thousand word essay in each major area on a subject of his or her own choice, and these essays go to external assessors, usually senior university academics who are recognized specialists in their fields. There is no basic educational qualification for admission, only the motivation to work, a reasonable intelligence, and ability to write coherent prose.

Growing awareness of the need to improve pastoral skills has led to development in the area of practical pastoral training, and students now have written work to do each year making use of basic sociological and psychological insights. In the first year they have to write a description of what they think their own parish will look like in ten years' time, and why. In the second year they have to write a theological appreciation of their own secular work, an exercise which has proved demanding and in some instances painful. In the third year the students have pastoral placements, lasting six months, in carefully selected parishes other than their own, perhaps of rather different traditions, so that they can share the vision which experienced incumbents have of their task and in a small way help them with some ministerial tasks. At the end of these placements the students have to write an account of their experiences and of what they have learned from them.

The course tries to keep students' married partners in view as far as possible, but this is not easy. There are widely divergent views about the role of a minister's spouse in parish life. Some are still willing to see themselves as the unpaid curate; others are glad to cooperate with their spouses' work as far as other commitments allow (and that often means a job of their own); others intend to lead their own life without any obligations to the parish at all. Two annual "quiet days" are arranged for students' partners and families with an opportunity to discuss in groups what their expectations actually are. Partners are invited to share in a third-year set of lectures on pastoral studies, but there are good reasons for not extending that invitation more widely.

The NOC does not normally include students who are not moving towards ordination, though it has had one or two who have paid their own way. Other courses are different in this respect, notably St Alban's diocese ministerial training scheme, where the first year's training is "generic", and students go to their selection conference (for ordination training) towards the end of that year. It is significant that some members who are not recommended for ordination choose to continue and finish the course, paying for themselves. In a few years' time that diocese will have a large number of educated and aware lay people, and it should not be suffering from the shortage of clergy that is affecting the other dioceses of the Church of England.

International Institute of Theology at a Distance

Continuing theological formation for priests, religious and laity

AGUSTÍN GARCÍA-GASCO Y VICENTE

The Spanish Institute of Theology at a Distance was created as a response to the need for continuing or permanent theological formation for priests, religious and laity in the archdiocese of Madrid-Alcala. It is a response to concerns articulated by the Second Vatican Council and His Holiness Paul VI and the pastoral goals of the Cardinal Archbishop of Madrid, Monsignor Vicente Enrique y Tarancón.

The changing situation of society and the church requires a programme of theological formation through which priests can update the knowledge and skills that they acquired in the seminaries and religious and lay persons can be appropriately trained to undertake various ecclesial ministries that are urgent and necessary.

A new concept of education

The Archdiocese of Madrid is gifted with university centres for theological, pastoral and catechetical studies and other programmes of face-to-face formation related to various ecclesiastical offices in the area. The Institute is built on a new model of theological teaching which does not presume to replace these existing programmes but to coexist with them.

Whereas older educational systems prepared people for relatively static social situations by transmitting to them an accumulation of knowledge, today education must equip people to face new, chang-

• Dr García-Gasco is the General Director of the Instituto Internacional de Teología a Distancia, Plaza de Ramales, 2, 2 izqda, Madrid 13, Spain.

ing situations by encouraging integral, ongoing personal formation. Human life can no longer be divided into a stage of preparation, formation, and acquisition of information and another stage of action, service and maturity. Education must be a continual, permanent process. People need to update their professional formation and prepare to meet the insecurity and relativization of acquired knowledge due to rapid, profound and irreversible social change.

With the creation of its new programme of continuing education the diocese of Madrid joined the movement for the reform of higher education based on the following assumptions:
— theological formation is considered to be a right, and a fundamental Christian obligation rather than a privilege limited to a few;
— the participation of lay people in the tasks of evangelization through the exercise of various ministries requires preparation adequate for these pastoral responsibilities;
— the technical resources of modern society offer the possibility of reducing the cost of higher education and at the same time of extending the education to a large number of people with a guaranteed high level of achievement;
— the new pastoral needs that arise daily in urban and rural dioceses require continuing formation of all who are responsible at all levels and in all sectors of the ministry.

A new model

The Institute of Theology at a Distance is designed to serve adult working people who cannot attend regular classes. It makes use of a variety of methods that do not require the regular physical presence of students and teachers together in one place. Relationships and communication are developed through textbooks and written consultation. Professors are available to receive suggestions and respond to any questions the students may raise. Seminars are provided for further synthesis and evaluation of individual and group learning. Systematic, intentional learning is made possible by using such resources in response to the interests and experiences of the participants.

Courses are prepared and guided primarily through workbooks. Each workbook outlines the programme of study, provides an introduction to the subject area in terms of general goals and major issues, and also gives a specific introduction for each unit with its rationale and specific theoretical and behavioural objective. Each unit is divided into themes or lessons, and each theme includes fundamental concepts as a guide for study and all the necessary information and orientation, followed by exercises to enable the students to discover and measure their understanding of the material. Further written work, which demonstrates the students' ability to use the information and concepts to analyze and solve problems, is sent in to the Institute staff for academic evaluation.

These studies are planned with a spiritual and pastoral dimension in mind. They guide the students to meditate on the meaning of theology in their own lives and to formulate and test their conclusions in their own ministries.

Periodic seminars provide another fundamental component in the formation process. They are intended to help the students to complete and to evaluate their studies through a synthesis of the doctrinal, pastoral and spiritual dimensions. This is carried out through individual work, small groups, and plenary sessions. The gathering of participants from different areas provides mutual enrichment, both intellectual and spiritual. Professors facilitate the process, stimulate dialogue, clarify difficulties that have arisen in individual studies, and offer opportune orientation. Students are invited to a seminar after completing the workbook and exercises in that subject.

Programme of studies

The Institute offers three different programmes:
— plan of theological renewal for priests;
— plan of theological formation for laity and religious;
— courses for parish groups, Christian communities, catechumens, etc.

The latter courses are selected or designed according to the needs of each group. Basic theological courses are offered in the areas of Bible, systematic theology, ethics, philosophy, and church history. Pastoral studies are grouped under the following areas: anthropology and education, pastoral action, catechesis, methodology and group dynamics. Students who complete the required coursework and evaluations may obtain a B.Th. degree or a diploma.

The teaching staff is made up of 20 professors who are theologians and specialists in education and lecturers of the cooperating theological faculties. In addition there are technical advisors and administrators. The entire operation is directed by a general secretariat and six departments in Madrid. In addition there are branch offices now in Venezuela, Colombia and Ecuador.

Results

The first academic course was inaugurated on 15 September 1973. The response was extraordinary throughout the Diocese. Soon letters from other dioceses and countries requested information and brought matriculations. By the end of 1973 there were 500 priests and 320 religious and lay persons enrolled. By the end of 1975 the total enrolment was 3,031 with 1,585 priests and 1,446 others. In 1978 the name was changed to International Institute of Theology at a Distance. In 1981 the enrolment reached 6,700, including 27 students in six countries of Asia, 44 in nine countries of Africa, 289 in eight European countries other than Spain, 15 in the US, and 2,354 in 17 countries of Latin America.

INTERNATIONAL INSTITUTE OF THEOLOGY AT A DISTANCE
Enrolment for 1981

Africa		*America*		*Europe*	
Angola	20	Argentina	49	Belgium	4
Chad	1	Brazil	12	England	4
Congo	4	Chile	27	France	16
Ivory Coast	2	Colombia	1,000	Germany	38
Mozambique	3	Cuba	3	Ireland	6
Sahara	4	Dominican Republic	10	Italy	16
Senegal	1	Ecuador	205	Luxemburg	1
Zaire	8	El Salvador	6	Portugal	204
Zambia	1	Guatemala	12	Spain	3,971
		Honduras	60		
Asia		Mexico	275	*Middle East*	
India	5	Nicaragua	6	Israel	2
Japan	4	Panama	75		
Korea	4	Peru	45		
Philippines	11	Puerto Rico	15		
Thailand	1	United States	15		
		Uruguay	4		
		Venezuela	550		

This development did not come about without problems. The project sought to follow the educational technology of other national and international programmes of distance education, but the research and adaptation were difficult due to the ambitious goal of holistic formation. The purpose was not to train theological intellectuals but to prepare witnessing theologians of the Christian mystery according to Vatican II. On the other hand, distance education was considered in some university circles to be a mediocre substitute for classroom education.

It was evident, however, that distance education had some extraordinary advantages and could be an effective, profound, economical and, for some, unique instrument for the formation of agents of ministry. It is now considered not as a simple substitute for classroom methods but as a complement. The interest expressed by the people of God has demonstrated that distance education can initiate a process of systematic, personalized, permanent theological formation in the local churches. The growing recognition of distance education is manifested by the increasing number of students and also by the use of these courses in classroom institutions.

Priests continue to form the largest group of students, and they take the programme for theological renewal. The majority are between 30 and 45 years of age. Among the religious who take the programme of theological formation, many are engaged in teaching. This course has been adopted by some residential institutes as the system of religious formation for the noviciate and scholasticate, although these students study by correspondence. Lay persons are numerous, though fewer than the other categories mentioned. They represent all social classes, professions and vocations. Many belong to active Christian communities with a profound faith commitment. A few are seeking possible ordination as priests or deacons.

This system of education requires a feedback circuit between staff and students. The institute team is greatly concerned to keep in constant contact with the students in order to observe the learning process, difficulties that arise in the use of the didactic tools, and suggestions for improving the programme. In this way formation acquires a personal dimension, and the students' needs are served more adequately. Our files hold many letters in which the students express their judgment of the Institute, and the expansion of the programme is largely the result of their motivation of others to enroll in the courses as an ideal means of training and renewal for the work of pastoral ministry.

Ecumenical Theology Workshop of Geneva
An experiment
in adult theological education

HENRY MOTTU

Since 1974, a noteworthy ecumenical experiment in adult theological education has been under way. Its participants are grassroots Christians who wish to receive rather full and continuous theological instruction (each cycle lasts for two years) and to take part in a new experiment in community life. Our ultimate aim from the start has been "to give back theology to the people of God", including the actual *working out* of the theology. The effort we ask of participants is clearly quite considerable and, to our great surprise, the more exacting we have been, the more people have applied for admission. Since Easter 1974, about a hundred people, Catholics and Protestants, have responded each year to our invitation and signed up for two years (we are at present at our fourth cycle or "set"). The structures of the project are simple.

— First we have a *teaching structure*. Classes are held once a week and last two hours; they are always conducted jointly by a Catholic and a Protestant teacher. A team of 15 tutors, of whom two are women, is in charge.

— We have also made a point of having a *community structure*. This consists of small informal groups meeting once a month, in charge of a second team of men and women leaders, in which participants are involved in ecclesial experience of the basic community type.

• Henry Mottu is Director of the department for adult training and theological education of the Protestant Church of Geneva. His address is 14 rue Baulacre, 1202 Geneva, Switzerland.

— Finally there is *a structure of personal guidance,* provided by a man or woman counsellor chosen in each case by the participants themselves. We attach great importance to this personal association in a dehumanized society like ours.

The content of the courses (first year: introduction to the Old Testament, then to the New; second year: some turning-points in the history of the church, ethical and ecclesiological problems) is thoroughly discussed by a team of tutors which meets regularly (the teaching is therefore ecumenically integrated). The theological dimension, in the intellectual sense of the word, is far from being the only one. The groups engage in an ecclesial, communal, liturgical life, the wealth of which it is difficult to describe in writing. Finally, interaction between the life and questions of the participants on the one hand and the actual teaching on the other is one of the characteristic features of our project, which was intended to be a *workshop* in the real sense of the word. The men and women theologians do their best to provide people with tools they can then use properly for themselves for their own creations. Our project might be summed up by saying that all our collective effort has been to be faithful to our title itself: "Ecumenical Theology Workshop" (ETW). A workshop, because it is not a matter of doing theology *for* the people of God, but *with* them in a sort of fraternal rivalry; ecumenical, because we think that something *irreversible* has taken place since Vatican II; of theology, because it is the *living God* we are concerned with, not simply group dynamics. So much for theory; everyone knows that when it comes to practice, things are much more complicated.

At this point in my account, three courses are open to me. I might sketch from life a portrait of the ETW with its various characters, some of them very colourful ones, nurses and pensioners, mothers of families and young schoolmasters, Catholic trade unionists and Protestant businessmen. But how could I speak fairly of more than four hundred lives in a few paragraphs? Or else, and this is my solution, I shall speak about the project by casting it into theological problem form: three senses of the word "ecumenical"; the particular context; unresolved questions (the limits of the ETW project).

Three senses of the word "ecumenical"

A first sense of the word "ecumenical" refers to the *interconfessional* dimension of the problem of church unity. The denomination or confession, Catholic or Protestant as the case may be, is a reality that is very difficult to define, since it is an amalgam of a diversity of elements (historical, social, psychological, theological, etc.) which fuse into a mentality, a sensitivity, and a view of *the world.* The "confession" is the view of the world which I inherit and which gives me my particular Christian identity.

Is that heritage a poisoned gift or an opportunity, a destiny to be endured or the kind of anchorage which freedom itself requires? How can freedom ever emerge collectively from an inheritance that has not been freely chosen? For the inherited denomination involves an element of non-freedom, of the unchosen, and therefore of suffering, yet it also means identity, collective roots, and therefore legitimate pride.

In this respect it is not without interest to note the road the ETW has followed. Originating in the crisis of May 1968, our Workshop at the start had a vague reputation of offering something as an alternative to hidebound denominations. I have observed a notable change in this respect for some time now. More and more, in fact, we come up against the hard core represented by the denominations as soon as we tackle the historical question (Catholics attributing a special role to tradition, and Protestants, for obvious reasons, being interested in breaks with tradition) and the ecclesiological problem (for Catholics the church is a *mother,* with a mystical and almost biological attachment, whereas for Protestants the Church is a *school,* with more of an educational tie). In this difficult interplay of sameness and difference, we live in a sort of oscillation, sometimes delighted to find we are so close, marvelling at the wonder of it, the miracle, like the dawn of the world; sometimes, however, we are pained to discover how far we are apart, how different, and we grieve at the rent in the body of Christ. In both cases, however, what we have risked is not revoked; we intend to be and to stay together with our differing Christian identities, with our own roots, in order to enrich one another. "Where there is no unity, there is no grief over its destruction" (L. Zander).

The denominational aspect does not begin to cover all the meanings of ecumenical reality. In a second sense, in fact, "ecumenical" means joint response to the challenges of the present-day world. This is the *trans-confessional* dimension of the world. As Philip Potter likes to say, not without reason, the word "ecumenical" comes from a Greek expression which means "the entire cultivated or inhabited world", as opposed to the desert. There is indisputably something universal, global in Christianity. And it is interesting to note in the history of the word itself this tendency to all-inclusiveness. Whereas in Matthew 24:14 "the whole world" means all the known universe and in Luke 2:1 the same word refers more precisely to the Roman Empire, the Revelation to John already uses the word in a more widely inclusive sense by schematizing the policy of kings or the field of awareness of "this world" in antithesis to the policy of God or the field of awareness of the "world to come" (Rev. 3:10; 12:9; 16:14). So with Basil of Caesarea, it would seem, in the fourth century, the word *oikoumene,* which until then meant the whole of the Roman world and therefore of the known or "cultivated" world, came to mean the whole of the inhabited world, without regard to political frontiers, because everywhere Christian churches are to be found. The church is gradually detaching itself from the empire.

Ecumenical, therefore, here assumes a "missionary" and militant sense, and by that I mean *outward-looking.* People do not meet simply becaue they choose to, but in response to the Lord's command and promise "that they may be one, so that *the world* may believe" (John 17:21). It is by endeavouring to heal the wounds of others that the body of Christ mysteriously heals its own. It has always been under the pressure of so-called "external" events and in response to an urgent human question that ecumenism has taken shape; historically this is fairly evident, for in the present century ecumenism received its first impulse from the World Missionary Council (1910). Without attempting here to list the human problems which we have to cope with at ETW, within the Genevan context, I shall simply mention by way of example: racism in the form of xenophobia, with the whole question of migrant workers; the problem of science and its technological applications; women's liberation, with the growth of awareness of the new role of women in the church and in society; the problem of money, of course, with all its social and political ramifications (just think of Switzerland's all too famous "bank confidentiality"), etc. Although there is a specifically Protestant or Catholic attitude to money or to the accession of women to greater responsibilities, these problems are human, universal problems which have to be tackled jointly. We are well aware that this is much more than simply a question of credibility; it is a matter of life and death, of witness or of counter-witness.

We must be careful here to distinguish the militant sense of the word "ecumenical" from the meaning it bears in Stoic philosophy, where it simply means "cosmopolitan" (citizen of the world) or "universal" *(koinonikon)*. What impels us to act is less what there is "in common" between us, than the urgency of challenges to which only a joint response is possible. In this sense, "ecumenical" means that to be Christian, each local situation must acquire a global awareness, a consciousness of the proximity of what is distant. A Christianity which took no account of the urgency of the long-term or of the proximity of "long relations" would no longer be Christianity but a baptized provincialism, to say the least. "Am I a God at hand, says the Lord, and not a God afar off?" (Jer. 23:23)

There is also a basic ecumenism, an ecumenism that is *lived in a habitation*. This will be our third sense. In fact, if the ETW has aroused such wide interest, isn't it because for many people it has been and is a place where they can at last breathe freely, a refuge for all those who have been called "Christians without a church"? For it is well known that all institutions at the present time tend to irritate our contemporaries like ill-fitting garments. The same crisis is perceptible in Marxism. One could speak in this of *meta-confessional* Christianity, that is to say, a splintered minority Christianity of small groups, a *diaspora* ecumenism in which the reading of the Book and community life are more important than discredited or faded institutions, rather as the Judaism of the synagogue was scattered after the destruction of the Temple and of the Jewish state in AD 70.

It must be recalled in this connection that the world *oikoumene* is the feminine passive participle of the verb *oikeo:* "to inhabit, dwell, reside" (in the intransitive) and "to occupy, to administer" (in the transitive). From the same verb come the words *oikia* or *oikios:* "house", *oikema:* "habitation, construction, workshop" (yes, indeed!) and *paroikia:* "parish", with the idea of "living near" (the stress falling sometimes on the idea of visiting a neighbour, sometimes, as in the New Testament, on that of being a stranger to one's neighbours, whose political rights one does not share; hence temporary residence abroad). From this very rich etymology, therefore, we may infer that "ecumenism" bears a resemblance to the idea of dwelling, and moreover, of that of provisional and fragile abode. In this third sense of the word, ecumenism would not mean only the quest for confessional unity (the dream of a Christianity both reunified and varied), or the struggle for the evangelical utopia (work for the establishment of the kingdom in which justice will dwell), but primarily the fight for the creation of new places, though of course transitory ones, where it is possible to live here and now both that unity and that utopia. Unity then becomes visible as a small-scale experience and parable of the eschatological unity of the people of God. The contemporary expression "ecumenical basic community" would suit very well this third dimension of an ecumenism actually lived here and now.

What is ecumenically at stake in all theological education seems to me to be that of combining these three dimensions of the reality which I have tried to differentiate without separating: the honest but not hyper-sensitive taking into account of our different roots, acute awareness of what is far away and of global problems, the possibility of living in hope in such and such a place.

The particular context

Without any attempt to present a scientific analysis of "needs", I shall now try to indicate a few items which seem to me the most important and perhaps the least obvious in our context.

1. Rootedness and sense of belonging

It seems to me that there is a strange and increasing convergence at the present time between ecumenism in the interconfessional sense and ecumenism in the meta-confessional sense (senses 1 and 3). A strong need is obviously felt for roots, without false shame and sometimes even with a certain sense of pride; at the same time, however, participants feel the need for a wider transconfessional attachment. Rootedness relates to history, tradition, the past, whereas attachment is rather a sociological, human, horizontal choice. So the ETW consists in the fact that difference is not achieved at the expense of solidarity, while solidarity does not blur divergences, which are remembered, studied and questioned, sometimes painfully.

2. The church as microcosm

The whole point of the ETW is missed unless it is seen to meet a very deep human need, namely that of living somewhere in some contact with the extraordinary variety of the human condition. In our local situation denominations to all intents and purposes go by families, a whole sociology with a readily recognizable typology. The Catholics are more militant and firmer believers, but less versed in biblical criticism, often of humbler social origins, while the Protestants are more sophisticated, less committed to their church and tend to be middle-class. Of course, that is a gross oversimplification, but the point I am making is the tribal character of the denominations with us.

Now the ETW has created a fantastic mingling and admixture in which people who knew nothing of one another have become aware of their respective riches. Differences in isolation cannot bring mutual enrichment, but in conjunction they can create a veritable microcosm and consequent happiness. For in a fundamental sense a confessional church is not yet, or no longer, a church; the church is found only where all classes, nations and mentalities rub shoulders. If we re-read Romans 16 in this light, we find that the lists of proper names of those greeted by Paul comprise the whole social spectrum of those days. The church is a microcosm or nothing. It "holds together" the world, as the letter to Diognetus puts it, and reflects it; otherwise it is a mere sect or club.

In regard to this human aspect, I shall cite only one example, that of women in the church. For many of them, the ETW represented a new and welcome access to the world of work; many took up professional work again after attending the ETW. Exacting and intellectually honest teaching without paternalism no doubt attracted them, as well as the community life.

3. Teaching and actual experience

The ETW is a typical attempt at restructuration following on May 1968. The originality of the project, however, is its attempt to combine what our culture finds it very hard not to separate: prescription and actual experience, texts and life, norm and existence. What is often experienced as an agonizing division is put to the test here in a sort of friendly duel, fair but uncompromising. I consider that there is great promise for the future, for the churches would be deluding themselves if they were to envisage the future in terms of group dynamics without any confrontation with reality. Teaching here becomes a harsh reminder of the reality of figures, data, objective truth.

The fact that the combination aimed at is problematic in the ETW, that it is constantly the object of passionate argument, that it is never definitively achieved, seems to me, if anything, a good sign. It is perhaps preferable to leave the double structure of courses and groups in polemic parallel than to dream of an undiscoverable and illusory synthesis.

4. Academic theology and church theology

Everyone knows what we do at the ETW; we do theology, church history, exegesis, etc. But what precisely the ETW is, nobody quite knows. Is it a research institute, a parallel theological faculty, one more academic institution or yet another basic community? It is all of these and none of them. The word "workshop" itself shows that the ETW is institutionally a vague entity, which is its weakness but also its strength. Let us recall here that no university diploma is required or conferred at the end of the course; "the only necessary condition is strong motivation", as our prospectus says. To my mind the simplest way to describe the ETW is to call it a hyphen between academic theology and church theology. We are between two stools, general practitioners among specialists, breaking down partitions and straddling disciplines. Of course we share out the work on the basis of proper qualifications, and sometimes we have recourse to university teachers, but the theology we do is an applied theology. The expression "applied science" is to be preferred to the unfortunate word "popularization". In any case I think that a very interesting development is emerging more or less everywhere. Whereas even recently "practitioners" were supposed to be applying a theory, by simplifying it, nowadays there is greater reciprocal interaction between science and its application. To be a good practitioner, one has to be *inventive*. If not, one is a mere parrot or a mongrel. The participants are not deceived. The oversimplified formula, object - operational instruments - application, must be replaced by a very much more complicated one: object - operational instruments - application - new content. As linguists are very well aware, every speech-act is performative; by using it, I transform the object. The passage through the *Wirkung,* the repercussions, the study of what *has been done* with the object and what *has been made* of it either results in the creation of new meaning or it is nonsense.

Unsolved questions

1. Institutional religion and spontaneous communities

Despite what we have said about a new sense of belonging, I sometimes wonder whether such attachment is real. Is it not merely emotional? Here as elsewhere, hope has great difficulty in crystallizing. There is not any, or not enough, feedback of what is experienced at the base, to the hierarchies, the machinery of the great institutions. To take an example: after the Küng affair we promised ourselves we would publish an "Ecumenical manifesto", but we haven't yet done so. Weariness? This seems to me all the more disquieting because everyone knows that the Catholic hierarchy now has to take account of the actual concrete experience of the people of God and must no longer always assume the right to speak in its name. What is to be done to get the spontaneity of the ETW critically to question the institutional? Another example is the eucharist. Here, too, what happens at the base does not go back up to the summit.

2. Taking long-term relations into account

We still have great difficulty in including in our syllabus the "long relations" which Paul Ricoeur distinguishes from "short relations". This is the whole problem of sense 2 of ecumenical reality. Certainly we have spoken of the class war, of ecology, women's liberation, money, violence, racism, etc. These endeavours, however, have to a large extent left us unsatisfied. How can one avoid generalizations, a paralyzing sense of guilt, slogans? How can we make long and abstract relations vividly present? Is there a theological education for this and how could it be achieved? Even our new communities do not succeed in getting any grip on the long, global stratifications. I am worried about this new ebb towards a *non-societal* sense of community which would no longer tackle the problems of society. There, too, as in regard to ecclesiastical institutions the *Gemeinschaft* would live hermetically sealed off from the *Gesellschaft*. The danger here is to fall back into a new communal pietism, stringent in its theological choices but approximate and romantic in its political ones. We lack deep theological reflection on the subject of politics, power, international affairs.

Theologically we are witnessing in Europe the ebb-tide of the theologies of hope, in consequence of the crises of all-inclusive ideologies. But is their replacement by theologies of the cross, of the law, of suffering, sometimes based on psychoanalysis, sufficient? Is it anything more than the theological echo of the withdrawal of Europe into itself? Be that as it may, these great debates have very direct local consequences, of which theologians ought to be aware. Can Christian *praxis,* too, be dependent on intellectual fashions?

3. The local and the international

This problem is certainly connected with the special circumstances of Geneva as an international city and financial centre. Absorbed as we have been by discussion between the Catholic and Protestant "families", we have left aside to some extent the question of the reception given to "internationals" and in general that of incorporating the WCC programme emphases into our project (cf. the role that the Ecumenical Institute at Bossey might play in this respect). The best thing is to work at this difficult combination (often it is a matter of language and availability) indirectly through actual persons rather than by slogans. We know, of course, that every local situation is internationalized willy-nilly, but to *make this perceptible* is quite another matter. It calls for creative imagination.

At present a very understandable anti-international reaction is emerging, a return to the local, the particular, to regionalism. But it would be very serious if this were to occur at the expense of the universal church. Here Protestants can be helped by Catholics, with their concept of a *body,* at once universal and mystical.

Conclusion

Our project can be said to be a first stage of the realization of an ecumenically integrated theological education. It is not our purpose to put forward a new ecumenical theology but to work out, together with our lay partners, a diversified and plural theology starting from our reciprocal commitments and roots. It is too early to know what this theology will be like; we are on the way. What matters is that something irreversible has taken place; we can no longer back off but only go ahead — if only to avoid disappointing those who have trusted us.

Moreover, as soon as ecumenicity is no longer a vague idea or a mere desire but a concrete though tentative realization in the form of a community, new and profound *solidarities* emerge. Whatever takes place within one confession concerns the other to the highest degree. Tomorrow's ecumenicity will be fashioned from such grassroot solidarity, and the gospel will become once more a source of living water for men and women in a given time and place.

Resources

WAYNE C. WELD

It is hardly possible today for theological educators or for church and mission leaders to ignore theological education by extension. The movement has spread to many countries and been popularized during at least the latter half of its twenty-year existence. We might expect efficient regional coordination by prestigious associations, standardized textbooks widely distributed by powerful publishing houses, and popular periodicals devoted to the promotion and perfection of TEE. In reality we find haphazard cooperation, associations and periodicals that appear and disappear, and several of the best texts and books about TEE out of print. Perhaps such circumstances are fitting for a low-profile movement which seeks to do grassroots theological education. Nevertheless, the frustrations remain and the gaps that may be apparent on the following pages are not due entirely to the ignorance of the author.

Included in the list of resources are associations for which TEE is a major concern, periodicals that focus on TEE, books describing the movement, and articles in some widely available publications. Finally some of the major publishers and distributors of extention texts are listed. An attempt has been made to give some regional representation. To determine the languages used by various institutions consult the *1980 Supplement* of *The World Directory of Theological Education by Extension*.

Dr Wayne C. Weld is Associate Professor of World Missions at North Park Theological Seminary, 5125 N. Spaulding Avenue, Chicago, Illinois 60625.

Associations and supporting agencies concerned with TEE

Accrediting Council for Theological Education in Africa (ACTEA)
Coordinator: Paul Bowers
P.O. Box 20, Igbaja via Ilorin
Kwara State, Nigeria

Sponsored by the Theological Commission of the Association of Evangelicals of Africa and Madagascar, ACTEA is developing criteria for the accreditation of extension programmes as well as other kinds of theological institutions.

Asia Theological Association (ATA)
P.O. Box 1477
Taichung, Taiwan, ROC 400

The ATA promotes and coordinates TEE throughout Asia through its publications and the sponsoring of TEE consultations. It publishes a quarterly bulletin.

Asociación de Seminarios e Instituciones Teológicas (ASIT)
Pablo Deiros, Director
Camacúa 282
1406 Buenos Aires, Argentina

This organization functions in the southern cone of South America. It includes institutions with extension programmes within its membership. For five years it has published a quarterly ASIT Bulletin.

Asociación Latinoamericano de Instituciones de Educación Teológica (ALIET)
Jorge Maldonado, Executive Secretary, Casilla 4993
Guayaquil, Ecuador

ALIET was formed in May 1980 from the merger of ALET and ALISTE. It operates in the central and northern sections of South America, Central America, the Caribbean and Spanish-speaking United States. Of some 400 institutions involved in theological education in the area, 58 are members of ALIET. A bulletin is published.

Associacão Evangélica para Treinamento Teológico por Extensão (AETTE)
Caixa Postal 30.259
01000 São Paulo, SP, Brazil

Formed in 1968, it is the oldest and one of the largest associations of extension programmes with some 40 members in Brazil. It coordinates the production and distribution of extension texts and publishes a bulletin.

Association of Christian Lay Centres in Africa (ACLCA)
P.O. Box 9270
Ibadan, Nigeria

Under the leadership of President Adeolu Adegbola this association has in recent years given increasing attention to TEE and non-formal education for "continuing education of the whole people of God". It is a member of CATI (q.v.).

Association of Evangelicals of Africa and Madagascar (AEAM)
P.O. Box 49332
Nairobi, Kenya

The Theological Commission of AEAM has taken over the work of the former Association of Evangelical Bible Institutes and Colleges in Africa (AEBICAM) which had been involved in the production of programmed texts. It publishes the bulletins *Afroscope* and *Edification*.

Association of Southern African Theological Institutions (ASATI) P.O. Box 31190 Braamfontein, Johannesburg, South Africa

ASATI was instrumental in the creation of the TEE College and includes extension programmes among its members. It is a member of CATI.

Association of Theological Education in South East Asia (ATESEA, formerly ATSSEA) Director: Yeow Choo Lak 4 Mt. Sophia, Singapore

Many member institutions have extension programmes, and the association has for years had a special Commission on Non-Traditional Study.

Association of Theological Institutions of Eastern Africa (ATIEA), P.O. Box 50784 Nairobi, Kenya

ATIEA held major consultations on TEE in 1979 and 1981. It is a member of CATI.

Association of Theological Schools in the US and Canada P.O. Box 130 Vandalia, Ohio 45377, USA

The rapid growth of D. Min. programmes during the past decade led the ATS to discuss criteria for extension and satellite programmes at its 1980 biennial meeting.

Australia and New Zealand Association of Theological Schools (ANZATS) Secretary: I. Douglas Fullerton Queen's College, Parkville Victoria 3052, Australia

Various member institutions have extension programmes, and in 1980 the association's council held a seminar on TEE.

Board of Theological Education of the Senate of Serampore College Director: H. S. Wilson 112/2 Nandidurg Extension Bangalore 560 046, India

The BTE membership includes TAFTEE and many schools that run extension programmes.

Bureau de l'EBEX Concile des Eglises Evangéliques B.P. 2475 Port-au-Prince, Haiti

This association has been coordinating the efforts of eight to ten TEE programmes in Haiti for nearly ten years.

Committee to Assist Ministry Education Overseas (CAMEO) P.O. Box 852 Wheaton, Illinois 60187, USA

CAMEO is a joint committee of the Evangelical Foreign Missions Association and the Interdenominational Foreign Missions Association. It has advanced the cause of TEE through workshops it has sponsored and through occasional publications.

Comité Coordinador de Seminarios Luteranos por Extensión en Hispanoamerica (Co-Extensión)
Coordinator: Victor Pavasars
Apartado Aéreo 1681
Bucaramanga, Santander, Colombia

Initiated in 1972, Co-Extensión provides orientation, training opportunities, promotion, and annual meetings for Lutheran TEE programmes in the Spanish-speaking countries of Latin America. The Coordinator visits them occasionally and publishes a newsletter, *El Extensionista*.

Conference of African Theological Institutions (CATI)
P.O. Box 57609
Nairobi, Kenya

Formally constituted in 1980 by the five sub-regional associations of theological schools and the ACLCA, CATI is a channel for the promotion and contextualization of all forms of theological education in Africa, including TEE.

Eastern African Association of TEE (EAATEE)
Secretary: N. Kiranga Gatimu
P.O. Box 189
Embu, Kenya

EAATEE was initiated at the ATIEA consultation on TEE, 1-4 December 1981.

Native American Theological Association (NATA)
122 West Franklin Avenue
Minneapolis, Minnesota 55404, USA

NATA is a consortium of denominations, seminaries, and training programmes for strengthening Indian ministries through education, research, and advocacy. Since it was formed in 1976, it has given priority to TEE as an integral part of ministerial formation.

Pakistan Committee for Theological Education by Extension (PACTEE)
Box 5042
Lahore, Pakistan

PACTEE promotes TEE throughout Pakistan. It distributes a bimonthly newsletter and an occasional bulletin, *Cup of TEE*.

Philippine Association for Theological Education by Extension (PAFTEE)
P.O. Box 6
Valenzuela, Metro Manila
Philippines

This is one of the most active national associations, at least in terms of publications and workshops. It has 14 member institutions at present and publishes a quarterly bulletin.

Programme on Theological Education (PTE)
World Council of Churches
150 Route de Ferney
1211 Geneva 20, Switzerland
475 Riverside Drive
New York, New York 10115, USA

This is the successor to the Theological Education Fund which made a major contribution to TEE through the funding of consultations, regional associations, production of materials, and training of national leaders. The PTE now publishes the periodical *Ministerial Formation*.

Promotor Mexicano de Escuelas y Seminarios Abiertos (PROMESA)
Secretary: Pablo Pérez
Apartado M-8580
México 1, DF, México

This is a committee for the coordination and promotion of TEE in Mexico.

Teach Yourself Programme of Theological Education (TYPTE)
Secretary: W. D. Coleman
Andhra Christian Theological College, Lower Tank Bund Road
Secunderabad 500 003, India

This is a joint committee formed by theological colleges that run external studies programmes.

The Association for Theological Extension Education (TAFTEE)
P.O. Box 520
Bangalore, India 560 005

In India the various denominations do not have separate TEE programmes but rather cooperate in the single programme known as TAFTEE. The association sponsors workshops, produces materials and publishes the *TAFTEE Times*.

Theological Education by Extension Association of Nigeria (TEEAN)
c/o ECWA, P.O. Box 77
Omu Aran via Ilorin
Kwara State, Nigeria

This association coordinates the activities of some 15 TEE institutions including the production of TEE texts.

Unión de Instituciones Biblicas de Colombia (UNICO)
Apartado Aéreo 7681
Cali, Colombia

Once the parent organization for CATA and CLATT, since 1973 UNICO has been the association of TEE institutions only in Colombia.

West African Association of Theological Institutions (WAATI)
Secretary: Mr. J. N. Kudadjie,
Department for the Study of Religions, U. of Ghana
P.O. Box 66
Legon, Ghana

WAATI maintains an ongoing workshop on alternative modes of ministry and ministerial formation. It is a member of CATI.

Annotated list of books describing TEE

Note: The present address of publishers is indicated rather than that when the book was published.

Asia Theological Association, *The Voice of the Church in Asia*, Section I. Theological Education by Extension. 1974, 175 pp., P.O. Box 1477 Taichung, Taiwan ROC 400.

Section I (pp. 9-73) deals with TEE and is introduced by Patricia Harrison, then ATA TEE Coordinator. There follow chapters by various authors on production of texts; curriculum design for TEE; an evaluation of teaching method, which is somewhat technical; the problem of sharing self-instructional materials, which questions the validity of borrowing culture-specific materials; the description of a centre for TEE study and research compared with other centres; and finally the use of cassettes for Christian education. Application to the Asian situation is reflected in all the articles.

Ralph R. Covell and C. Peter Wagner, *An Extension Seminary Primer*, 1971, William Carey Library, P.O. Box 128 C, Pasadena, California 91104, USA.

The first half of this book serves as a background and rationale for the establishment of the extension movement. The authors deal with the nature of the church and of ministry, Jesus and Paul as teachers, and forms of theological education from earlier times to the "seminaries in the streets" in Chile today. TEE is traced from its birth in Guatemala, through developments in Bolivia and Colombia and the Intertext Project, to the expansion of the movement into Africa and Asia. Principles and practices of TEE are described and criticized. The final section links TEE to the growth of the church.

Abraham Díaz Reyes, *Manual para Monitores y Coordinadores de Centros del Departamento de Educación Teológica por Extensión del Seminario Evangélico Unido*, 2nd ed. 1978, 200 pp., Seminario Evangélico Unido, Apartado 20 079, Mexico 20, D.F.

This manual was written in Spanish to be used in workshops to prepare extension centre leaders and coordinators. It gives a brief history of the extension movement and its theological bases. Description of the work of a local TEE coordinator is followed by instructions for the weekly discussion period and the evaluation of learning. The last quarter of the manual contains materials for the curriculum and administration of TEE under the United Evangelical Seminary.

Vergil Gerber, ed., *Discipling Through TEE: A Fresh Approach to Theological Education in the 1980's*, 1980, 192 pp., Chicago, Moody Press (or order from William Carey Library).

The editor has made available some good materials not readily accessible elsewhere and has included some new contributions. Section I deals with making disciples through the church and home. Section II examines the nature of the church and ways of organizing and training for its growth. Section III presents principles of training which have grown out of biblical models and practical experience. The final section contains case studies of contextualization of theological education in Indonesia and extension chains in Honduras. Articles by Lois McKinney introduce and conclude the book.

D. Leslie Hill, *Designing a Theological Education by Extension Program: A Philippine Case Study*, 1974, William Carey Library, Pasadena.

The Philippine (and to a lesser extent the Baptist) perspective dominates this prescription of TEE but there are lessons for everyone. Within a proposal for designing the structure of a TEE programme is a discussion of "Extension Seminary Resident School Relationships" and "Building Equivalence into Extension Training". While TEE solves some problems it raises others. The second half of the book is "Leader: Extension Center Training Manual", which is programmed.

Fred Holland, *Teaching Through Theological Education by Extension*, 1975, 45 pp., Evangel Publishing House, P.O. Box 28963, Nairobi, Kenya (or order from William Carey Library).

Written for African leaders, this small book introduces the basic concepts and patterns of TEE in rather simple language. Brief chapters deal with programmed instruction, the work of the weekly seminar leader, the conduct of the seminar meeting, and the organization of a TEE programme.

F. Ross Kinsler, *The Extension Movement in Theological Education: A Call to the Renewal of the Ministry*, rev. ed. 1981, 294 pp., William Carey Library, Pasadena.

Kinsler's analysis of the extension movement is perhaps the most theoretical and theological and at the same time contains the greatest number and variety of concrete examples of alternate forms of theological education. The scope and flavour of the book can be captured from some chapter titles: Bases for Change in Theological Education, A Working Definition of Theological Education by Extension, Open Theological Education, TEE: Service or Subversion, Mission by the People, New Approaches to Leadership Development in North America, Theological Education by Extension Comes of Age: Current Developments and Critical Questions, Materials for Workshops on Theological Education by Extension.

Lois McKinney, *Writing for Theological Education by Extension*, 1975, 64 pp., William Carey Library, Pasadena.

In 56 modules this guide provides a training course for writers of programmed instruction for theological education by extension. Reference is made to six other books upon whose content many assignments are based. Nevertheless this booklet contains many valuable learning exercises and insights into the writing of better TEE texts. After the preparation for programming there are sections on planning, writing, editing and testing programmes.

Jorge Maldonado, *Manual de Textos Autodidácticos y Programados Usados en Educación Teológica por Extensión en América Latina,* **1979 (photocopies available from author, Casilla 4993, Guayaquil, Ecuador).**

Catalogues of extension texts are very dated materials. It is very hard for the prospective user to evaluate texts without seeing them and they go out of print very rapidly. Given these limitations, Maldonado has produced the most complete and useful catalogue of TEE texts in Spanish. It lists and describes texts by country and institution indicating size, academic level, and price. It also contains indices of texts by areas of study, and of authors, translators and revisers. The analytic section indicates criteria for evaluating texts and TEE in general.

Kenneth B. Mulholland, *Adventures in Training the Ministry: A Honduran Case Study in TEE,* **1976, 220 pp., Presbyterian and Reformed Press, Nutley, New Jersey (or order from William Carey Library).**

An analysis of the Latin American context for theological education and the various forms of training employed begins this case study. Part II gives a brief history of the extension movement. Part III describes the implementation of TEE in Honduras over a three-year period in the stages of experimentation, consolidation and breakthrough. Part IV expresses concerns regarding church growth, pre-theological education, accreditation, the role of the teacher in TEE, and the relationship between residence and extension programmes.

George Patterson, *Church Planting Through Obedience Oriented Teaching,* **1981, 62 pp., William Carey Library, Pasadena.**

George Patterson, *Obedience-Oriented Education,* **1976, 36 pp., William Carey Library, Pasadena.**

George Patterson, *Practical Steps to Apply Biblical Extension Principles,* **1979, 22 pp., William Carey Library, Pasadena.**

These three booklets, in which there is considerable overlap, describe the innovative methods and philosophy which Patterson has employed to plant and nurture churches in rural Honduras through TEE—discipleship training. Among the topics included: the modification of theological education for semi-literate rural people, the building of extension chains, and the integration of theological disciplines in simple booklets whose teachings must be obeyed and then retaught. The ideas presented are concise, well illustrated, practical and iconoclastic.

W. Frederic Sprunger, *TEE in Japan: A Realistic Vision,* **1981, William Carey Library, Pasadena.**

Is there any relationship between Japanese resistance to TEE and the slow rate of the growth of the church in that country? The author examines the positive relationship between extension and growth in the Mennonite Church in Japan. Building upon past experience in leadership training, TEE offers possibilities of promoting healthy growth.

Ted and Margaret Ward, *Programmed Instruction for Theological Education by Extension*, 1970, CAMEO, P.O. Box 852, Wheaton, Illinois 60187, USA.

This book grew out of a series of workshops which Ted Ward conducted in Latin America. If the self-teaching text is the key to TEE, these texts should be made as effective as possible through the application of principles of programmed instruction. A few observations on the way people learn lead the reader into the writing of behavioural objectives and programme frames. The exercises and learning games are in English, Spanish, Portuguese and French.

Wayne C. Weld, *The World Directory of Theological Education by Extension*, 1973, 374 pp., William Carey Library, Pasadena.

Wayne C. Weld, *1976 Supplement to The World Directory of Theological Education by Extension*, 1976, 61 pp., William Carey Library, Pasadena.

Wayne C. Weld, *1980 Supplement to The World Directory of Theological Education by Extension*, 1980, 45 pp., CAMEO, Wheaton.

The original volume attempts in 70 pages to define the crisis in theological education, describe the development of TEE, and evaluate the movement. The bulk of the book is an alphabetical list of institutions and programmes involved in TEE along with indices that aid in the use of the directory. Other chapters describe supporting agencies or activities affecting TEE, and workshops and consultations relating to TEE. In the supplements the list of institutions has expanded but the information regarding each one is reduced. The 1980 supplement gives names and addresses of over 300 institutions, the number and academic levels of students and the languages used.

Ralph D. Winter, ed., *Theological Education by Extension*, 1969, William Carey Library, Pasadena.

Winter, who has been called the prophet of TEE, brought together in this first book about the movement all the basic early documents and articles. The volume is divided into three books which are generally historical, theoretical and practical. Book I: Milestones in a Movement traces the development of TEE in Guatemala, consultations in Colombia and organizations that gave impetus to the movement, and major extension programmes in Bolivia, Brazil and Colombia. Book II: The CAMEO workshop contains papers presented at a workshop in December, 1968. These papers on ministerial training, the extension seminary, and programmed learning furnished a theoretical base for the promotion of TEE. Book III: An Extension Seminary Manual deals with the overall structure of a programme, the operation of an extension centre and an approach to the curriculum.

Articles about TEE

Ralph Brown, "Extending the Principles of TEE to Muslim Correspondence Students" in *Muslim World Pulse*, September 1975.

Edwin Brainerd, "The 'Myth' of Programmed Texts" in *Evangelical Missions Quarterly*, July 1974.

Ray Buker Sr., "Theological Education by Extension (TEE) Catches Fire in Africa" in *Africa Pulse*, December 1970.

David R. Cochrane, "Theological Education by Extension: What Can It Offer Churches in North America?" in *Theological Education*, Summer 1974.

Harvie M. Conn, "Theological Education and the Search for Excellence" in *Westminster Theological Journal*, Spring 1979.

Patricia Harrison, "Evaluation TEE: A Theological Cinderella?" in *Asia Perspective No. 7*, 1977, Asia Theological Association.

Patricia Harrison, "Survey of Programmed Instruction Materials" in *Emissary*, May 1977.

Patricia Harrison, "Theological Education by Extension: A Progress Report" in *Journal of Christian Education* (Australia), May 1978.

F. Ross Kinsler, "Bases for Change in Theological Education" in *Latin America Pulse*, August 1977.

F. Ross Kinsler, "Mission by the People" in *International Review of Mission*, July 1979.

F. Ross Kinsler, "Open Theological Education" in *Theological Education*, Summer 1974.

F. Ross Kinsler, "Theological Education by Extension: Service or Subversion" in *Missiology*, April 1978.

F. Ross Kinsler, Barbara G. Wheeler, and John C. Fletcher, "Trialogue on Alternatives in Theological Education", Auburn Studies in Education; 1978 (Auburn Seminary, 3041 Broadway, NY, NY 10027).

William J. Kornfield, "The Challenge to Make Extension Education Culturally Relevant" in *Evangelical Missions Quarterly*, January 1976.

Lois McKinney, "Theological Education Overseas: A Church-Centered Approach" in *Emissary*, April 1979.

Lois McKinney and Fred Holland, "World Survey of TEE—1977" in *Emissary*, January 1978. (Reprint from *Extension* November 1977.)

Emilio N. Monti, "Extensión y Educación Permanente" in *Cuadernos de Teología*, Vol. V, No. 2, 1978.

George Patterson, "Let's Multiply Churches" in *Latin America Pulse*, October 1974.

George Patterson, "Multiply Churches Through Extension Chains" in *Church Growth Bulletin*, July 1974.

Richard W. Sales, "Tripping and Training in Botswana: The Positive Values of Ministerial Preparation by Extension" in *Christian Century*, 4-11 February 1976.

Richard W. Sales, "Two or Three And God: Extension Theology Recognizes That the Teacher of the Things of God Is God" in *Christian Century*, 2-9 February 1977.

James B. Sauer, "TEE in Zaire—Mission or Movement?" in *Evangelical Review of Theology*, October 1978.

Peter Savage, "A Bold Move for More Realistic Theological Training" in *Evangelical Missions Quarterly*, Winter 1969.

Chris Sugden, "Teaching Christ as Liberator in Extension Education" in *Evangelical Review of Theology*, April 1980.

TEF Staff, "Theological Education by Extension", Chapter 4 in *Ministry in Context: The Third Mandate Programme of the Theological Education Fund* (1970-77). Bromley, England, New Life Press, 1972.

UNICO, "Alternatives in Theological Education" in *Latin America Pulse*, May 1975.

C. Peter Wagner, "Seminaries Ought To Be Asking Who As Well As How" in *Theological Education*, Summer 1974.

Ted Ward, "Theological Education by Extension" in *Catalyst*, January 1976.

Ted Ward, "Theological Education by Extension: Much More Than a Fad" in *Theological Education*, Summer 1974.

Ted Ward, "Types of TEE" in *Evangelical Missions Quarterly*, April 1977.

Ted Ward and Samuel F. Rowen, "The Significance of the Extension Seminary" in *Evangelical Missions Quarterly*, Fall 1972.

Wayne C. Weld, "Extension Education Seen as Meeting Needs of Churches" in *Evangelical Missions Quarterly*, January 1974.

Wayne C. Weld, "The Current Status of Theological Education by Extension" in *Theological Education*, Summer 1974.

Wayne C. Weld, "Theological Education by Extension" in *Mission Handbook: North American Protestant Ministries Overseas 10th ed.*, MARC, Monrovia, California, 1973.

Frederick K. Wentz, "Take the Seminaries to the Candidates" in *Christian Century*, 5-12 February 1975.

Colin W. Williams, "In Defense of the Academic Seminary" in *Theological Education*, Summer 1974.

Ralph D. Winter, "Will the 'Extension Seminary' Promote Church Growth?" in *Church Growth Bulletin*, January 1969.

Note: *Emissary, Africa Pulse, Latin America Pulse*, and *Muslim World Pulse* are publications of the Evangelical Missions Information Service, Box 794, Wheaton, Illinois 60187, USA. Back issues are available for $1.50 each prepaid.

Periodicals concerned with TEE

AETTE Bulletin
Caixa Postal 30.259
01000 São Paulo, SP, Brazil

This quarterly bulletin has been published in Portuguese since 1968. It contains news of TEE in Brazil, catalogues of materials and articles. Donations welcome.

ALIET Bulletin
Casilla 4993
Guayaquil, Ecuador

This bulletin is the successor to the ALET and ALISTE Bulletins which were concerned with theological education in Latin America.

Cup of TEE
8 F. C. College
Lahore 16, Pakistan

Occasional Bulletin of PACTEE. Distributed to Friends of PACTEE who make a minimum annual contribution of Rs. 25.

Extension
c/o Wayne Weld
5125 N. Spaulding Ave.
Chicago, Illinois 60625, USA

This newsletter with shorter articles was published monthly from November 1972 to December 1977. Back issues are available for $3.00 per year.

Extension Seminary
Apartado 3
San Felipe Reu.
Guatemala, C. A.

This bulletin has been published since 1966 when it was called the *Evangelical Seminary*. It contains longer articles as well as news of the extension movement. It is published in English and Spanish three times a year. For Latin America the rate is US $2.00 per year and for all other countries, US $5.00 per year.

Khanya TEE Newsletter
Department of Training for Ministry
P.O. Box 96, Melmoth
3835 South Africa

Quarterly publication regarding TEE and other alternatives in theological education, primarily in South Africa. Subscription rate is US $3.00 or £1.50 (by airmail US $6.00 or £3.50).

Ministerial Formation
Programme on Theological
Education
475 Riverside Drive
New York, New York 10115, USA

This quarterly newsletter has been published since 1978 by the Programme on Theological Education of the World Council of Churches. It contains some thirty pages of articles, reports and news of developments in theological education, not restricted to extension. Subscription rate: US $10.00 for two years.

PAFTEE Bulletin
P.O. Box 6
Valenzuela, Metro Manila
Philippines

Quarterly bulletin of PAFTEE with news, articles, listing of materials published by PAFTEE members, Annual subscription US $4.25 (airmail postage included).

TAFTEE Times
P.O. Box 520
Bangalore 560 005 India

Quarterly bulletin of TAFTEE containing articles, news, lists of materials.

Theological News
c/o John E. Langlois
Les Emrais
Castel, Guernsey, C.I.
United Kingdom

This quarterly publication of the World Evangelical Fellowship contains articles and news about TEE. As of 1982 it has merged with *Theological Education Today*, which was the successor of *Programming News* (1971) and *Programming* (1973) and was published quarterly since 1976. *Theological News* will be sent free to those who request it but subscription-donations are US $3.00 per year or US $4.00 airmail.

Major publishers and distributors of TEE materials

Centre de Publications Evangéliques
B.P. 8900
Abidjan, Ivory Coast

Evangel Publishing House
P.O. Box 28963
Nairobi, Kenya

TEE College
P.O. Box 23923, Joubert Park
2044 Johannesburg, South Africa

Fambidzano
P.O. Box 127
Fort Victoria, Zimbabwe

Extension Seminary, Oldonyosambu
P.O. Box 1396
Arusha, Tanzania

Botswana Theological Training
Programme
P.O. Box 318
Gaborone, Botswana

Centre for Applied Religion
and Education
P.O. Box 9270
Ibadan, Nigeria

TAFTEE
P.O. Box 520
Bangalore, India 560 005

Union Seminary Extension
Department
P.O. Box 841
Manila, Philippines

PAFTEE
P.O. Box 6
Valenzuela, Metro Manila
Philippines

Asia Theological Association
P.O. Box 1477
Taichung, Taiwan ROC 400

International Correspondence
Institute
Chaussée de Waterloo 45
1640 Rhode-Saint-Genèse, Belgium

Instituto Internacional de Teología
a Distancia
Plaza de Ramales 2, 2 izqda
Madrid 13, Spain

Centre d'Etudes Bibliques
Supérieures
151bîs, avenue de Montolivet
13012 Marseille, France

SemBec
10.211 Basile Routhier
Montreal PQ, Canada H2C 2C5

Seminary Extension Department
460 James Robertson Pkwy
Nashville, Tennessee 37219, USA

Bairnwick School of Theology
University of the South Sewanee
Tennessee 37375, USA

Cook Christian Training School
708 South Lindon Lane
Tempe, Arizona 85281, USA

Casa Bautista de Publicaciones
P.O. Box 4255
El Paso, Texas 79914, USA

Learning Resource Center
West Indies Mission
Box 34 3038
Coral Gables, Florida 33134, USA

Seminario Evangélico Presbiteriano
Apartado 3
San Felipe, Reu., Guatemala, C.A.

CLASE
Apartado 321
Guatemala, C.A.

Instituto Bíblico de Extensión
Apartado 164
La Ceiba, Honduras

PRODIADIS
Latin American Biblical Seminary
Apartado 901
San José, Costa Rica

AETTE
Caixa Postal 30.259
01000 São Paulo, SP, Brazil

SEAN (Americas)
Casilla 561
Viña del Mar, Chile

SEAN (International)
Allen Gardiner House
Pembury Road, Tunbridge Wells
Kent, TN2 3QU, UK